BROOKLYN'S

BABE

The story of Babe Herman

Tot Holmes

Holmes Publishing
Gothenburg, Nebraska

For Ann...

'Dignity does not consist in possessing honors,
but in deserving them' ... Aristotle

Copyright © 1990 by Tot Holmes
All rights reserved
including the right of reproduction
in whole or in part in any form
Published by Holmes Publishing
P.O. Box 11   1321 Avenue D
Gothenburg, Nebraska 69138
         (308) 537-3335
Manufactuered in the United States of America

Cover painting by Phil Hanks,
             represented by
             Charles Schurter
             36 Woodleaf
             Irvine, CA 92714
             (714) 733-8672

CONTENTS

Chapter		Page
	Introduction by Maury Allen	iv
	Introduction by Bob Hunter	vi
	Foreword	vii
1	Minor League Odyssey	1
2	Brooklyn Debut, 1926	19
3	A Forgettable Season, 1927	40
4	Front-Office Feud	56
5	Threshold of Greatness, 1928	63
6	Almost a Batting Title, 1929	81
7	Pennant Race, 1930	99
8	Final Brooklyn Season, 1931	129
9	The Trade, 1932	157
10	Cincinnati, 1932	168
11	On to Chicago, 1933-1934	177
12	Pittsburgh and Cincinnati, 1935-36	192
13	Back to the Minors, 1937-38	205
14	Hollywood Years, 1939-44	210
15	Flatbush Farewell	220
16	Off the Field	230
17	The Numbers	234
	Author's Notes	242
	Photos from Babe Herman's collection	
	Cartoons by Willard Mullin	

INTRODUCTION

Some years back I was writing a book about Casey Stengel. I was visiting with the Old Professor at his Glendale, California home when he suddenly said, "Let's go talk to the Babe."

Stengel was in his early 80s then and I thought, of course, the strain of several interviewing days had finally gotten to him. I knew he had not batted against the Babe in the 1916 Series when Ruth was a lefthanded pitcher for Boston and Stengel was a lefthanded hitter for Brooklyn. It had always angered him in light of his later World Series success. Like everyone else, Stengel clearly was proud of his association, however tenuous, with Babe Ruth.

Casey strode from his chair and I followed. We were soon striding rapidly from Stengel's poolside at 1663 Grandview a few blocks away to a handsome home at 1622 Highland.

Babe Herman, a true hero of mine as a youngster growing up wild about the Dodgers in Brooklyn, greeted us at the door. We went out back and sat in soft, reclining chairs. Ann Herman, a delightful woman, brought out some glasses and a pitcher of iced tea.

In some few moments the old Glendale pals began reminiscing about baseball days of old. Names like Cobb, Johnson, Ruth, Speaker, Gehrig, Vance, Wheat, O'Doul and so many more from the lore of the game spilled easily from their lips.

The noon time visit had now gone long into the evening and Edna Stengel had to come by to rescue us for a previous appointment. For me, it was the beautiful beginning of a warm and wonderful relationship with Brooklyn's Babe.

Tot Holmes has captured clearly, warmly and wonderfully the essence of the man who dominated Brooklyn baseball for those glorious years from 1926 through 1931. I wasn't born then but as a Dodger fanatic I had heard the name of Babe Herman as a youngster so many times from my father.

It was the ultimate irony that I would be sitting in Ebbets Field in a half a dollar bleacher seat on July 8, 1945 when Babe returned to Brooklyn as a pinch hitter. He lined a ball off the right field screen facing Bedford Avenue, hustled to first on aged 42 year old legs and fell down attempting to get back to the bag after a long turn.

It fit the image. Unfortunately, the image has cost Babe a spot in the Hall of Fame. He was not a clown, just an affable man who went along with the press when they wrote of his daffy doings. Realistically, he was a very intelligent man, learned about the game, about life, a student of human nature, a deep thinker, a lover of orchids, a dedicated husband and father.

I got to meet Babe a couple of times for a few moments when he was scouting for the Mets and Yankees as I broke in as a sportswriter in the early 1960s. He was almost too legendary to approach for tales of the old days.

Then, through Casey, I became close to the Babe. We talked on the phone often. We saw each other occasionally in spring training during visits to his son working in Miami. I arranged to have him honored by the Baseball Writers Association of America on the 50th anniversary of his 1930 season when he hit .393 and barely missed out on a .400 average because of an injury.

He and Ann stayed with us on that occasion and we were enveloped by their warmth and wisdom He visited again for the last time few years later when he was named to the Brooklyn Dodger Baseball Hall of Fame.

As he stood on the platform outside Prospect Park, just a short outfield throw away from where Ebbets Field once stood, he told more recent inductees and sportswriters that he doubted if he would be remembered after more than 50 years removed form his Brooklyn playing days. Then Marty Adler, the Hall of Fame president, called off his name and the applause began to grow among the crowd. They called out his name, "Babe, Babe, Babe," and roared as it he had just hit another lefthanded shot over that famed right field wall 297 feet from home plate.

He strode slowly to the microphone. Tears welled up in his eyes. He bent his head down and drank in the moment. He was remembered. With the help of Tot Holmes and Brooklyn's Babe, he will always be remembered.

Maury Allen
New York, N.Y.

INTRODUCTION

The story of "Brooklyn's Babe" needs no introduction.

"Brooklyn's Babe" was something that just happened. Never could it have been planned or choreographed. It never would have been believed. Even documented, as it is in the following pages by Tot Holmes, as wrapped up in baseball and the Brooklyn Dodgers as was the Babe himself, this is an amazing story of one of the game's most renowned and beautiful buffoons, a skilled player who was "dumb as a fox."

I have known "Brooklyn's Babe" for almost half a century, or since he was an outstanding athlete at Glendale High School.

I have been to his home, met his family, and even covered him when he was playing with the Hollywood Stars, finishing up his storied career in the old Pacific Coast League.

He received $5,000 for a season's pay, but only after a lengthy salary hassle with its owner Bob Cobb, and after he had tapped out his expensive cigar ashes and rested his feet on the owner's immaculately polished desk, telling him he "could take it or leave it."

Herman, the "clown" who doubled into a triple play (which actually scored the winning run), was a director of a successful Glendale bank. He was a wealthy turkey farmer. He was a good father whose children became splendid musicians.

The "Brooklyn's Babe" is a rare story, faithfully told here, while interspersing many, many anecdotes that reflect the true Floyd Caves Herman, whose only regret, along with that of many of his admirers, is that he did not live to see his statue in the Hall of Fame.

Tot Holmes' laborious research, as well as his long knowledge of the game and Brooklyn lore, separates the fact from the fiction that followed Herman, much as it has the Yogi Berras, Joe DiMaggios, and Dazzy Vances.

I enjoyed the rough draft so much, I can't wait to get hold of the book. The author, indeed, has completed a work that will be on baseball lovers' book shelves long after "Brooklyn's Babe" is in his final resting place—Cooperstown's Hall of Fame.

Bob Hunter
Los Angeles

FOREWORD

On a steamy August afternoon in 1926, the Brooklyn Robins, named for their manager Wilbert Robinson, were playing the Boston Braves in the first game of a double-header at Ebbets Field in Brooklyn.

With the score tied, the bases loaded and one out, rookie Floyd 'Babe' Herman came to the plate, setting in motion an incredible sequence of events that have stitched themselves into the very fabric of not only Brooklyn baseball history, but the history of major league baseball itself.

This unique happening, with considerable embellishing from the many newspapers who had representatives covering the contest, branded Herman as the leader of what they called the "Daffy Dodgers," a freewheeling group of players who marched to the beat of a wild but fun-loving drummer.

The story has been twisted and bent to the whims of the teller over the years, making an improbable happening even more exotic as each added his own nuance to the events. And the original 5,000 or so in attendance that day swelled to a half-million Dodger fans who later claimed they were at the park on that wondrous afternoon.

The basic facts are clear. With the bases loaded, Herman lined the ball off the right field wall to score Hank DeBerry from third with what would turn out to be the winning run. Running from second base Dazzy Vance rounded third, then for some inexplicable reason, retraced his steps and lumbered back. Chick Fewster, thinking he could score from first on the smash, roared on toward third base.

Herman, finding he had a cinch double, slid easily into the bag at second then heard the second baseman shout, "Throw it home." Herman thought it must be Fewster heading for the plate and when he saw a runner between third and home in an apparent rundown, he scrambled to his feet and raced toward third base with his head down.

When Babe slid into the bag he looked up and saw an odd congregation of runners and infielders. Fewster, who arrived at third only to find Vance already standing on the bag, had stopped short of the base to try to sort out the perplexing situation. As Herman slid in, Fewster jumped over Babe to avoid his spikes.

That left Vance standing on top of third base, Herman on the ground with one foot on the bag and Fewster standing a few steps away with a puzzled look on his face.

The umpire said, "Herman, you're out for passing the runner." Babe got up, dusted himself off and walked back to the dugout and Fewster headed toward second base to get his glove. The Braves second baseman yelled for the ball, and tagged Fewster in short right field for the third out.

The papers noted the play as 'unusual' but nothing was said about it in the Brooklyn dugout when the promising inning ended so abruptly. But the next day one paper blazed the headline,

HERMAN TRIPLES INTO TRIPLE PLAY

Babe questioned the writer the next afternoon, pointing out there was one out when the whole thing started. "How could I have hit into a triple play with one out?" He asked. Embarrassed, the newsman could only shrug.

The story grew from that point. Manager Wilbert Robinson was supposed to have said, "Leave them alone. It's the first time this season they have gotten together on anything."

Third base coach Otto Miller, who wasn't even on duty during the play, would incorporate the story into his after-dinner repertoire, "I am the only third base coach to ever put three men on third base at the same time," he would boast.

Obviously the major portion of blame for the unique gridlock should be placed at the large feet of Dazzy Vance, who for reasons unknown even to him, decided not to score from second on the double. Later Vance apologized to Herman, saying, "It wasn't your fault, it was mine."

That single play, occurring in Herman's rookie season, tagged Babe as a clown and from that moment, other newsmen, for there were more than a dozen in all that regularly covered the Brooklyn club during that period of history, vied with each other in a 'Can You Top This' atmosphere to concoct the perfect Herman joke. Certainly it was much more appealing that writing about a Brooklyn club that seemed to be permanently stalled in sixth place.

Others got into the act, too. Trainer Andy Lotshaw of the Chicago Cubs used this on the banquet circuit:

"Are you going to buy your children an encyclopedia?" He asked Babe.

"No," Herman replied, "they can walk to school just like I did."

Many of the other stories, authors now unknown, have survived, including:

Showing off his son, Bobby, at Ebbets Field one afternoon, Babe asked him, "What is seven and three?" and the youngster said, "eight." Babe beamed and said, "He only missed it by one!"

Or:

Arriving for dinner at a plush cafe in a spectacular white linen suit, a pretty young lady remarked to Babe, "My, you look cool."

Herman blushed and returned the compliment, saying "You don't look so hot yourself!"

Or:

Two players were sitting close to Herman in a hotel lobby as a man walked by and one said, "You know, he used to be rich but he lost all his money in the war."

Babe spoke up and said, "Why, did he bet on the Kaiser?"

And this classic is still being reported: One afternoon in St. Louis Babe had just lit a cigar when he was called to the phone. He thought the cigar was out and stuck it in his breast pocket. After the phone call, he returned to the hotel porch where a number of newsmen were sitting.

Pulling the cigar out of his pocket and noticing there was a live coal on the end of it, he declined a light and started puffing away.

The newsmen shook their heads in wonder at a player who would carry a lighted cigar in his pocket and three different stories leaped from the true incident, each adding something to the tale and each happening in three different cities.

The "Three Men on Third Story' spawned a delightful string of tales that swirled around the Brooklyn franchise until the day they left for California.

One classic has a taxi driver stopping outside Ebbets Field and shouting up at one of the customers in the stands, "How are we doing?"

"We have three men on base," the bleacherite called.

"Which base?" was the driver's question.

Years later John Lardner wrote, "Floyd Caves Herman, known as Babe, did not always catch fly balls on the top of his head, but he could in a pinch. He never tripled into a triple play, but he once doubled into a double play which is almost as good."

Jim Murray noted years later that someone should have written, "Herman then doubled to load the base."

The stories were clever, and Babe laughed with each of them as they unfolded. He was asked at one point why he would put up with the obvious fabrications and he just smiled and said, "I don't care what they write about me. They have to make a living too."

Some of the stories were as biting as they were clever.

"It is said," one writer commented in his column, "that Babe Herman while playing first base for Brooklyn, picked up a ground ball and threw it into the left field stands in Pittsburgh. That may not be truthful. It might have been in St. Louis."

Many of the stories evolved from Herman's quick wit. When ordering a sardine sandwich one afternoon, he was asked by the waitress if he wanted the domestic or imported sardines.

"What is the difference?" he asked.

"The imported ones are 50 cents more."

"I'll take the domestic," he said. "Darned if I'm going to pay passage money to America for some lousy sardines."

A funny comeback if authored by most players, but coming from Herman it was received with rolling eyes, a knowing look and a slight nod of the head.

A little man in Germany once learned that lies, when told often enough, become truths. Baseball stories, told often enough become myths. And the myth of Babe Herman is as interwoven into the folklore of baseball as are the stitches of the official ball itself.

Floyd Caves "Babe" Herman was not a clown. He was not a buffoon. He was not a incorrigible fielder. He was never hit on the head by a fly ball.

Herman was, however, undoubtedly one of the most remarkable

hitters ever to wear a Brooklyn uniform, or any uniform for that matter. When young Ted Williams was dismantling the American Association in 1938, John Kiernan, in a New York paper, paid Williams the ultimate compliment when he wrote, "He looks like a young Babe Herman when he swings."

Rogers Hornsby said he was the hardest hitter in the National League. John McGraw called him one of the greatest natural hitters he had ever seen. Al Lopez, when comparing the great hitters of his time, said that Herman was the real stylist of them all. All are Hall of Famers and their opinions were voiced when Herman was still flattening baseballs around the National League. He was considered by some as better than Mel Ott at the same time in their careers.

During the 1930 season he set seven Brooklyn single season records, including home runs (35), runs batted in (130), average (.393), slugging percentage (.678), hits (241), runs scored (143), extra base hits (94), and total bases (416). And incredibly, after an assault on those marks by the likes of Dolph Camilli, Dixie Walker, Duke Snider, Gil Hodges, Jackie Robinson and Roy Campanella, and by a talented crop of Los Angeles Dodgers, he still holds six of the eight. Snider broke his home run record and Campanella his RBI record—but 26 years later.

A SABR analyst recently looked at Herman's 143 runs scored in 1930 and asked, "If he was so bad on the bases, how could he score that many runs?" Lou Brock, Vince Coleman, Maury Wills, and Max Carey, all acknowledged as exceptional baserunners, never scored 143 runs in a single season. Ty Cobb (147) and Rickey Henderson (146) only just surpassed the mark.

He led in runs-batted-in each of the major league teams he played with during eleven full seasons, missing only once. He is the only player to hit for the cycle (single, double, triple and home run in one game) three times in the major leagues, adding another pair of cycles during exhibition and minor league play. He twice earned All-American honors, at first base in 1926 and in right field in 1929, each time being selected by vote of National League baseball writers.

But the conclusion by many, and obviously by the Hall of Fame Veterans Committee, seems to be—great hitter, terrible fielder, impossible baserunner.

Yet he finished his 13-year major league career with a .971 fielding average, a dozen points ahead of Ty Cobb's mark. He was forced to learn the technique of outfielding in the major leagues after seven minor league seasons at first base and managers, players and writers of his era admitted that he became not just an adequate fielder, but often a brilliant one. He possessed a remarkably strong throwing arm, recording 42 assists over the 1931 and 1932 seasons, each time finishing second in the National League.

Comparing Herman's .971 fielding average with Hall of Fame outfielders of his era you must include contemporaries Heinie Manush

(.979), Paul Waner (.976), Mel Ott (.974), Kiki Cuyler (.972), Edd Roush (.972), Tris Speaker (.970), Babe Ruth (.968), Max Carey (.966), Zach Wheat (.966), Sam Rice (.965), Hack Wilson (.962), Chuck Klein (.962), Ty Cobb (.961), and Goose Goslin (.960).

Yet each of his errors seemed to come at the most inopportune time and often seemed to cost not only a run but the game.

In an interview, Pie Traynor, Paul Waner and Lloyd Waner told the world that he was a good baserunner, and to prove their point he finished second in the National League in stolen bases on two occasions, but few seemed to notice.

Insurance actuary experts agree that some persons are 'accident prone,' having an uncanny facility for getting caught in the middle of things much more often than the average citizen. They resemble the Al Capp cartoon character who had a small, black rain-cloud hovering over his head at all times.

Babe Herman is obviously the prototype.

Strange things seemed to happen to him on a regular basis. The three-men-on-third incident was only the start. Two teammates hit homers and passed him on the bases in the same season, thus nullifying their long drives. He hit .381 and .393 in successive season, yet he finished in the runner-up spot in the league each time—and to compound things, to a different player each season.

He hit the first home run in a major league night game but earlier in the same season, during a bizarre mob scene in Cincinnati, a woman came out of the stands, took Herman's bat from his hands and went to the plate. She tapped out to Cardinal pitcher, Paul Dean, while umpires and stadium guards watched in stunned silence.

Herman's lifetime batting average of .324 should have long ago earned him a niche beside his old friend Casey Stengel in the Hall of Fame. Herman badly wanted that honor during his final years and was obviously disappointed each time his name was not called by the Veterans Committee. Many think that personal animosities may have kept him out of the select circle.

Be that as it may, join us as we attempt to untangle the myths that still hover about the memory of this unique, gentle man and travel with him through one of the most remarkable baseball odysseys in the history of the game.

Willard Mullin echoed the feelings of Dodger fans everywhere when Babe Herman returned to the Dodgers in 1945 afater an absence of 14 years.

Chapter 1

Floyd Caves Herman was born on June 26, 1903 in Buffalo, New York. His mother, whose maiden name was Caves, was terrified of lightning and thunder, and when she read a newspaper article that said California had neither, she asked her husband to move the family west.

Charles and Rosa Herman moved to Los Angeles in 1905. In 1917, along with sons Elmer, Floyd and Stanley and daughters Claire and Cora, they moved to Glendale where Charles, a building contractor, built three homes in the city that nestled up against the Verdugo Mountains. He moved his family into one of them.

The youngster they called 'Lefty' was an exceptional athlete, competing in football, basketball, track and baseball at Glendale Union High School. He earned 12 letters, three each in football, basketball, baseball and track. He played both offense and defense during the football season and as the team's punter he averaged 52-years a kick.

In a triangular track meet with South Pasadena and Franklin High, Herman, as captain of the team, entered 12 events and won 10 of them, including the 100, 220 and 440. He finished second and third in the two events he didn't win.

'Lefty' had only one hit during his freshman baseball season but it was a grand slam homer that won a game. And despite being left-handed he played third base, moving to first base as a senior.

His sophomore season of 1920 saw him hit an even .800 in league action and the team played in the CFS Championships at San Diego.

Herman hit a ball over the distant left field fence and went into his home run trot. The fielder ran around the fence, grabbed the ball and threw it in, forcing him to speed up his leisurely pace to beat the relay home.

Glendale lost 2-1, when three errors in the ninth cost Herman's team a chance to play in the title game.

He was a 10 second 100-yard dash man and set an AAU 'record' in the 50-yard dash during one meet, but officials were skeptical and when they later measured the track they found it was five yards short.

Herman played guard in basketball his first season. "Only ten turned out for the team, so the coach went out and drafted a big fat guy and put him at the other guard," Herman said with a laugh.

In the spring of 1923, still only 19 after his second season of professional baseball, he was working out on the Glendale track in preparation for the baseball season. He was talking to a friend and said "If I worked hard the final 20 yards, I could beat Frank Wycoff in the 100." Wycoff would later go on to be an Olympic sprinter and earn the billing of "The Fastest Man in the World." He was the first to run a 9.4 100 yard dash while attending USC.

Wycoff walked by at that same time and said, "What are you popping off for? I can spot you 20 yards and beat you."

"You can like hell."

Herman, still in his baseball uniform, stripped down to a pair of running shorts and his baseball spikes. The coach came by and asked what was happening and Herman told him that the kid wanted to spot him 20 yards.

"Oh, he hasn't a chance. Run him even, Lefty."

Babe beat him out of the blocks and won by two yards. On the way back to the starting line, Herman smiled at Wycoff and said "Go get a reputation before you pick on me again."

In 1924 Wycoff ran in the Olympic games at Paris, competing in the 100 and earning a gold medal as a member of a relay team. He also competed in Olympic games in Athens (1928) and Los Angeles (1932).

Floyd Herman's long and sometimes torturous road to Brooklyn started innocently enough on beautiful Catalina Island. Two long home runs in a semi-pro game drew unexpected publicity and cost him his final year of high school eligibility

Rules at the time allowed semi-pro play before the high school league schedule started but Glendale had already played an official game when Herman was invited to play in the Elks All-Star game on Catalina against the Catalina Cubs. The park was located deep in a canyon beside the golf course and the team dressed at the St. Catherine Hotel.

During the game Herman smashed a pair of gigantic home runs off a pitcher by the name of "Squirrel" Darcy. One of the shots cleared the right field wall and a row of tents set up behind it.

Brick Laws, later president of the Oakland Oaks in the Pacific Coast League, was student manager Babe's junior year and has often described a Herman home run that cleared the outfielders, the running track, the fence and finally hit against the Elks Club across Colorado Boulevard.

Back at Glendale, Herman smacked a long shot in batting practice. Lehman Crandall, a former Glendale player and one of the pitchers in the doubleheader on Catalina, said, "If you think that was a long hit, you should have seen a couple Lefty hit last Sunday."

Calling the team together, the Glendale coach said, "Anyone who played in the Elks game on Catalina Sunday is declared ineligible. Did any of you play there?"

Babe raised his hand, realizing the coach knew he had played, and said, "I did, so I guess I'm out the rest of the season."

Despite being ruled ineligible for his senior baseball season, Babe still wanted to play football at California where most of the good Glendale players seemed to wind up. He had already received scholarship offers from Dartmouth and Stanford, but was at the Spring Street gym looking for Charley Erb who he thought might help him get into Berkeley. Erb was the captain of the University of California football team.

After watching the fighters for a time he went upstairs to the sporting goods store and met Joe Rafferty.

"Lefty, do you want to play baseball?" Rafferty asked. "I can get you $175 a month to play in Edmonton if you want to." Edmonton was in the Class 'B' Western Canada League.

Herman thought about the long summer ahead of him with little to do and quickly accepted the offer for more money than he thought possible. However, his father didn't think much of either the offer or the move.

"Stay home and be a contractor like me and you'll have something some day," he told his son. "You don't get paid for playing in this world."

"I'm going to play anyway," Herman told his father.

"You'll be writing for money to come home on."

"I'll come home in a boxcar first."

The 17-year-old signed the contract and was sent to near Crockett, California, to train with the other minor league players. Then they took a boat to Victoria, British Columbia. A 19-year-old youngster from Tuscumbia, Alabama, Heinie Manush, who had been playing Sunday baseball in Ontario, California, signed at the same time. The understanding was that after manager Gus Gleichman got over his injury, one of the two kids would be released.

Former Giant Fred Snodgrass, a brother-in-law of Gleichman's, was helping with the team. Gus asked him, "Which one of them should I release?"

"Don't release either one of them," Snodgrass told him. "I've never seen a pair that young hit like they do."

So Gleichman kept them both, putting Herman at first and Manush in the outfield. When Gleichman's injury had healed, he took over first base, but the fans were on him immediately.

"Get off the bag you old fool!" they shouted. "Let that kid play."

Moments later Gleichman booted a ground ball and the crowd again hooted at him. Returning to the dugout, the red-faced manager told Herman, "You go back in at first base. And forget about pitching tomorrow, I'll start the game."

In mid-season, Herman crushed a ball that cleared the distant right-field scoreboard in Edmonton Park. The event caused such a stir it brought out city officials and photographers the next day to admire a feat that had never before been accomplished.

He finished the season with a .330 average and led the league in hits with 135 and triples with 18. He was second in the league with 24 doubles and third in home runs with seven. He also led the league by striking out 79 times.

Frank Judd was the league's leading hitter with a .335 average, although he only had 343 at bats in 100 games. Manush hit .321 and had nine home runs.

Manush and Herman played a game for Fernie against White Spruce Camp to earn expenses for their trip home. They got $350.00 extra. A match game was also arranged with rival Calgary, who had paid $500 for a pitcher to work against Edmonton. Herman and Manush agreed to play, but asked for their money before the game.

Manush was knocked down his first time at bat and when he got up he called to the pitcher, "Are you throwing at me?"

"You damn right I am," was the reply.

Manush turned to Herman in the on-deck circle and said, "OK, Lefty, let's go to work." The two got seven extra base hits between them and Edmonton won easily. The promoters of the game lost big money betting on it and tried to charge the players for the bottles of beer they had sent down to the bench during the game.

"Nuts, to you, we didn't order it," they said as they trooped off the field with the satisfying victory.

Edmonton had a working agreement with Detroit and both Herman and Manush were transferred to the Tiger reserve list for 1922.

THE OLD PEPPER GAME—Detroit spring training was held in Augusta in 1922 and early workouts included the traditonal pepper game. Above George Cutshaw, Lou Blue, Johnny Mann and Babe 'Lefty' Herman toss the ball around in front of the vacant grandstands.

Detroit trained in Cobbs' home town, Augusta, Georgia, and Cobb had rented two large old mansions for the team to stay in, since the downtown hotel they were to use had been destroyed by fire.

A new club house had been built at the park and Cobb was determined to provide a good training table for his players. He also had scheduled only four weeks to get the club in condition. An exhibition tour of just 14 days had been set up, one of the shortest training periods in the history of baseball.

Cobb felt the shorter period of time he spent in training, the better he played. He had hit .420 in 1911 after arriving in camp only four days before the opener.

Cobb also felt that more pitchers go stale if over-trained than because of lack of work, so he vowed that none of them would go nine innings before opening day of the 1922 American League season.

Sixteen rookies were included in the Tiger camp along with Herman and Manush. Among them were a number of future major leaguers, including pitcher Sylvester Johnson; third baseman Fred Haney; second baseman George Cutshaw and outfielder Robert Fothergill.

When Herman got off the train in Atlanta, a black man asked him if he was Ty Cobb. Herman said, "Are you kidding me?"

"No, sir," he said. "My boss is over there in that big black car and asked me to find Ty Cobb for him."

Cobb got off the train and Herman said that the man in the car wanted to see him. "Oh, yes, that is Mr. Woodward," Cobb said. "Tell them to put my trunk in my room."

Later Cobb came into the clubhouse and told the team, "Fellows, there is a new drink developed here in Atlanta. It's been tried for a year and it is going to go. The name is Coca-Cola and it's selling for $1.00 a share."

Herman had $60.00 from the expense money given him earlier and had just received another $100. "I am going to buy $100 worth of that stock," he said to Howard Ehmke.

"I wouldn't buy anything that S.O.B. recommended," Ehmke told him. "He wouldn't help out his mother." Babe reconsidered the stock purchase, reluctantly deciding to follow Ehmke's advice. Herman later estimated that the stock would be worth as much as $5 million at current prices. A number of other players bought $500 or $1000 worth and when it got to $3500 they sold it. Cobb was the only one to hold on to the stock and he made millions.

Coach Dan Howley called Herman over during one of the early practices and asked, "What's your nickname, kid?"

"They called me Lefty at home."

"No, that won't do."

"Well, that's what they called me in school."

"Didn't they call you Tiny or Babe or something?"

"There was a woman fan up in Canada who called me Babe now and then."

"OK," Howley said, "From now on you're my Babe."

Detroit played a series of games with their Rochester farm club, and manager George Stallings was out to beat the Tigers, but more directly Cobb.

Herman was using a huge, "Dad Meeks" model 54-ounce bat and hit often and hard as long as they threw him fastballs. But during an intrasquad game the pitcher threw him a change. He spun around so hard he nearly fell down and from that moment on the big bat was the joke of the camp.

He and Manush had both used the bat during the 1921 season in Canada and it was nailed and taped to hold it together.

Harry Heilmann, who had led the American League with a .394 average the year before, came to Babe and said, "You know, Babe Ruth uses a bat that is 44-48 ounces. I know, because I have used one of his bats. I use a 42 ounce bat and I'm bigger and stronger than you are. So why do you think you can swing a 54 ounce bat? Take one of mine and try it."

Babe did, but quickly broke six of them. Then first baseman Lu Blue told him, "Mine are the same as Heilmann's, but I can't hit with a bat with my name on it. Use some of mine, I don't need them."

Babe tried Blue's bat, with limited success, but then he found a Jimmy Austin bat that weighed 38 ounces and was the same configuration as his 54 ounce bludgeon.

Herman took the Austin bat to Omaha with him and hit .416. Later he ordered some for himself in the same style. Officials at the Louisville Slugger Company said later that Herman ordered more bats than any other player in the major leagues, not because he broke so many but because he gave so many of them away.

He also would let the pitchers use his bats and every day they would break one of them. So he kept a few out for practice, one for left-handed pitchers and one for right-handed pitchers. He used different bats during batting practice, constantly searching for the perfect stick and when he found one, he would put it away for games.

He may have learned that from Ty Cobb who would check each dozen bats he received from the factory and keep only two or three, putting the others in the bat rack for anyone else to use.

"A good bat is one that won't sting your hands. I had a certain

3/4 grain that I liked," Herman said. "A guy at the bat factory showed me that the black grain in the bat is the soft part and the lighter part between is hard. You want bats with more hard wood to hit well."

Babe switched to a Bobby Doerr model, about 33-35 ounces, while playing later in the Pacific Coast League. He used one of them for five years.

The Detroit regulars disliked the tour with the minor league club from Rochester, hesitant to take chances on the rocky minor league fields they played on each day. Herman played in many of the intrasquad games, batting between Cobb and Harry Heilmann. He also pinch-hit at times and on March 25, 1922, Cobb left the game in the ninth with the team trailing by three runs. Herman hit for him and singled to knock in a run as Detroit rallied to tie, then went on to win in the 10th inning.

After a long home run he returned to the bench and Cobb grabbed him and said, "Don't you ever swing any harder than that. That ball would have gone out of any ballpark in the major leagues. I want you to try to hit the pitcher right in the forehead with a line drive. Let the ball go where it wants to, just aim it at the pitcher."

Cobb also told him, "Don't ever try to copy Ruth. He perfected that big swing and doesn't worry about his strikeouts. Anyone else would have trouble even hitting the ball with that swing and would be back in the minors in no time."

Ruth was pitched inside a great deal, because no pitcher wanted him hitting the ball through the box at him. Babe would fall away and sort of inside-out his swing so he would not pull it foul. Herman studied Ruth's swing to see why his shots down the line would pull foul and Ruth's wouldn't. He found it was Ruth's hand action that kept the ball fair.

Cobb apparently took a liking to the big, blond kid and one day when Herman was arguing with another rookie, Cobb came by and said, "Fight the other team, not your own."

They became friends later in life and Cobb told him, "If I had it all to do over, I'd do the same things, except one."

"What's that?" Babe asked him.

"I ought to have 10 million friends, but I made enemies out of most of them," Cobb confessed.

When the team broke camp, Cobb called him in his office and told him, "I can use you, but you're so young I hate to keep you on the bench. Lu Blue will play first for us this year so we'll send you out where you can get some experience."

He was sent to Omaha and H. C. Walker wrote in The Sporting

News, "Babe Herman has shown he can play first base and can hit, although Lu Blue will play for Detroit. Babe is too valuable for Detroit to lose title to. The kid will be back in a year or so and will be a star."

Herman was sent to Omaha but the manager used John Snedecor to play first base and Babe was exiled to the manager's doghouse early in the season. In an exhibition game he was arguing with the first base umpire about a bad call he felt had made earlier when a throw went through him at first and into right field, allowing two runs to score. Owner-manager Barney Burch said Babe's work at first "did not please him."

Mike Finn and Barney Burch were in partnership in Omaha, Finn in the office and Burch on the field. Finn dropped dead at a game and Burch also became general manager.

His first move was to make Snedecor playing manager and since Cobb had demanded that Herman play first base only, Snedecor would start, with Babe coming off the bench when needed and finish at the bag. On a few occasions, Babe was asked to play right field so he could get some playing time.

Herman opened the season in right field, the first time he had played the outfield in professional baseball, and singled twice in two trips. He pinch hit twice in the next six days before getting a second start. He smacked a homer, then found himself back pinch-hitting the next day again and he belted a three-run double to win a game.

He stayed glued to the bench until Snedecor was injured, and when finally given a chance banged out 11 hits in 21 trips to the plate in the next five games, with two doubles, two triples and a homer good for four runs batted in. But then Snedecor healed, and Herman was back on the bench.

During the second game of a double-header on May 14, he watched as Omaha made four putouts in the second inning, an event that went unnoticed at the time. The mixup may have been the final straw, but in any event he was hitting an even .400 when he called owner Frank Navin in Detroit and asked if he could be sent where he could play regularly. Navin sent him to Reading in the International League to replace first baseman Otto Palman who had yellow jaundice.

He hit in six of eight games for Reading, but International League pitching was much tougher and he could only manage a .267 average.

When Palman recovered, Herman, who was on loan, was sent back to Detroit for reassignment. Earlier, Cobb's partner had wanted Herman to play in Augusta, but Cobb said he was too good to play there. The partner offered Babe $300 to play and $350 extra from his cotton gin business. But after being returned to Detroit, the offer was cut to just

$300.

Herman told him, "I'm not going below the Mason-Dixon line this year because at the end of the season I may not have enough money to get home. I have enough money to get home now."

Cobb contacted Burch and he said he would be glad to have Babe back on the team in Omaha.

He was used in left field briefly and had three errors in the first five games but on June 16 he was put in right field due to an injury and finally was given some playing time.

The Omaha World Herald correspondent wrote: "Travel seems to have dimmed his batting eye, and probably spoiled the youngster who might have developed well had he been given steady treatment somewhere."

The sympathetic comment was just a bit premature.

Starting the 16th of June, he hit in 19 straight games and the Omaha club won fourteen straight, moving from a record of 27-29 to 42-34 during Herman's batting surge.

He was even scheduled to pitch a game and had warmed up when one of the outfielders stepped on a ball an turned his ankle, making it necessary to return him to the outfield. The Omaha team scored eight runs in the first inning that day, which would have almost assured Babe a victory. Herman had pitched against professionals in California and had a good fastball and an overhand curve that in those days was called a 'drop', but he never got to use them in an official game.

On the Fourth of July, Babe's father came to watch him play for the first and last time in Herman's professional career and he put on quite a display to honor the occasion. His father had been visiting relatives in Buffalo, N.Y. and stopped in Omaha on his way home to California.

In the first game he boomed a grand-slam homer against Denver and lined three doubles and a single in the second contest.

After the game he and his father went to dinner together at the hotel and Mr. Herman bought the night 'Pink Sheet' edition of the paper before they went to the dining room.

"What do you think about the game?" Babe asked. "I did pretty well, didn't I?"

His father folded the paper back on the sports page and pointing, said, "Huh, it isn't even your picture." The paper had Herman's name all over the sports page but had used the photo of George Grantham on the story.

The elder Herman never said much about his son's baseball playing. When Babe held out for more money, he would only say, "All that

OPENING DAY—The 1923 Opening Day lineup for the Atlanta Crackers at Nashville, included (from; left) Johnny Ring second base, Joe Guyon center field, Ken Killinger third base, Babe Herman first base, Mike Burke right field, Sam Langford left field, Ed Moore shortstop, Otto Miller catcher, and pitcher Oscar Tuero.

money for playing baseball and he wants more." The elderly Herman made $5.00 a day as a contractor and might only make $200 on an entire job.

Babe's mother saw him play in Orange, California when the left and center field areas ran directly into orange groves. A hard thrower was pitching and Babe hit a ball into the grove in left field, circling the bases easily for a home run. After the game his mother asked, "Why didn't you run around twice and get two home runs?"

Herman and Manush were socking the ball with regularity and years later a writer came up with a story about Manush being walked to load the bases only to have Herman unload them with a long shot over the wall.

"Imagine that," Herman was supposed to have said as Manush shook his hand as he crossed the plate, "walking a .380 hitter to get at me." Another entertaining story, but later both denied that it had been said. Manush and Herman were very close, having roomed together for two years.

Herman was hitting .436 at the end of July after banging out 52 hits in 110 trips through the month for a .473 average.

The Missouri Valley semi-pro tournament was taking place in Council Bluffs, across the Missouri River from Omaha, and manager Harry Baumgartner of Corning, Iowa contacted Herman to see if he would play for him. Babe agreed to play in the finals for $350, a month's salary for the young ballplayer. Babe told him that Manush would like to play, too, but Baumgartner said, "Gee, I'd like to have him but I can't pay him that much."

Following their scheduled game Sunday afternoon against Sioux City, a long, black car pulled up in front of the Omaha dressing room and Herman and Manush ducked into it for the ride across the bridge, turning their uniforms inside out in the limousine.

Herman played under the name of "Carey" and Manush as "Farrell." The two belted the ball hard enough to earn Corning a win in the finals, with Herman slugging a homer, but loud protests were heard and some thought that Commissioner Landis should investigate the contest.

Shortly after that game Herman was released to return home due to the illness of his mother. Herman and Manush were both claimed by Detroit on options at the end of the season.

Herman hit a blistering .416 during the season, banging 129 hits in 92 games and adding 34 doubles, 7 triples and 9 home runs. Manush hit .376 with 20 homers in 167 games.

The two remarkable young hitters parted company at that point, with Manush going on to play in Detroit, St. Louis, Washington, Boston and finally in Brooklyn, but well after Herman had been traded.

Heinie won the American League batting crown in 1926 with a .378 average and ended his major league career with Pittsburgh, finishing with a lifetime mark of .331. In 1933 he hit in 33 straight games for the Senators. He later managed in the minor leagues and scouted or coached for Boston, Pittsburgh and Washington. He was elected to the Hall of Fame in 1964.

Herman had not been paid for the final month in Omaha and repeated letters to Detroit seemed to be little help. Finally, on the advice of an older player, he wrote a final time to Detroit and said, "Somebody owes me some money and if I don't get it, I'm going to ask Judge Landis about it."

He should have never mentioned Landis. The move put a black mark behind his name on the Detroit roster and eventually cut him out of the organization.

Detroit owner Frank Navin quickly wrote back and told Herman, "I'll pay you but you'll be the loser in the long run."

On October 30, 1922, Navin traded pitchers Carl Holling and Howard Ehmke, infielder Danny Clark and Babe Herman, along with $25,000 to the Boston Red Sox for second baseman Del Pratt and pitcher Rip Collins.

Herman went to spring training in 1923 with the Red Sox in Hot Springs, Arkansas. Frank Chance was the manager of the Sox and was delighted with the youngster's hitting ability. Following spring training asked if Herman would like to go north with the team.

"Do you want to sit on the bench?" he asked. "You'll get to play a little."

"I don't want to sit on the bench for a last-place team. I'd rather be out playing someplace," Herman replied.

"I'm glad to hear that," said Chance. "I'll send you to a good club."

Herman was shifted to Atlanta and he took the place by storm, clubbing doubles and triples to every corner of the park. He showed exceptional power early in the season and for a short time the Atlanta paper ran a 'Ruth Meter' and a 'Herman Meter' in the paper, with Herman leading in the race. But Ruth hit four in two games in St. Louis and moved into the lead for good. Herman felt he could have hit as many as 50 homers if he had remained in Ponce de Leon Park in Atlanta. Only he and Ruth ever hit the ball over the top of the hill behind the right field wall, but the actual fence was easy to reach for Babe. After going hitless in the opener, he connected in six straight games and his nine safties included four doubles, a triple and three homers.

The youngster got into an argument with manager Otto Miller, veteran catcher who had been recently released by the Brooklyn Robins. Herman took a wide throw on the foul side of the first base bag to keep the ball from going over his head and when he returned to the dugout, Miller said, "Take the ball right. Don't you have any guts?"

Herman bristled up quickly and nose-to-nose said, "You don't think I have any guts? Take that monkey suit off and get up."

Miller refused to get up, but told owner Jack Corbett to get rid of the young player. Corbett was reluctant to rid himself of such a solid hitter and delayed the decision.

The tension between the 19-year-old Herman and the 33-year-old Miller was apparent to everyone and it seemed to affect Babe's attitude and play. An Atlanta writer noted: "Herman's poor fielding, coupled with his indifferent play, got him in bad with the fans. He was then moved to the outfield. He is still one of the most dangerous hitters in the league and if he could be taught to let the bad pitches go by, he would be one of the batting wonders of the decade."

The Crackers were on the road in Birmingham and Herman broke up three straight contests in the late innings. "On the final day I hit one a ton," Herman said. "A gale was blowing in from right field and the ball blew back onto the field and the right fielder caught it up against the wall. I never hit a ball harder in my life and if it would have gone out, we'd have won that game, too."

Returning to Atlanta, Miller told Corbett, "He breaks up every game we play, but I still want to get rid of him."

Corbett went to Herman and said, "Miller wants to get rid of you. He said your play is indifferent."

Babe told him, "I've won the last six games for you."

"I know, I've been reading the paper, but he wants to get rid of you anyway," Corbett told him.

"OK, so let him," Herman replied angrily and he was 'loaned' to Memphis, hitting .340. Atlanta was in fourth place at the time, four games over .500. Memphis was sixth, six games under .500.

The Memphis paper welcomed the youngster and his big bat. The local sports editor, unaware of the personality conflict that motivated the move, noted, "Babe Herman, the Chickasaws' new first baseman, has learned a lesson from his experience in Atlanta that will very likely serve him well in the remainder of his baseball career.

"Herman, who is a terrific hitter and who can also field around the first sack with any doorman in the league, was the idol of the population in Atlanta the first part of the year, but he got in bad with the fans because of alleged indifference and his disinclination to hustle.

"But the change of scenery will help him out wonderfully. He says he is glad to play in Memphis and says he intends giving manager Johnny Dobbs all he has the rest of the year and that if he comes back to Memphis next spring he'll start right off the bat to help with a winner.

"Herman is a young ball player and he has a lot to learn. But he is an apt pupil and his experience in Atlanta, when he heard the cheers of the fans turn to jeers, is going to prove valuable to him."

Herman continued to belt the ball for the Chicks and took particular pleasure banging Atlanta pitchers, hitting in 12 of the 13 games played against the Crackers. Babe also took pleasure in the fact that Memphis finished the season 76-70 in third place and Atlanta finished 78-73 in fourth.

Babe hit in 16 straight game for Memphis and had a stretch of eight straight games in which he collected extra base hits.

Kiki Cuyler was selected the "Most Valuable Player" in the Southern League and hit .340. Herman hit .339 and was second in the league with 13 home runs and an even 100 runs batted in.

Herman's entanglement with an official scorer's brother who was a league umpire cost him dearly in the final games of the season. The scorer ruled error a number of hard-hit balls in a final doubleheader, costing him important points on his average and a possible batting title.

The New York Yankees had a working agreement with the Atlanta team in 1922 and thus had first choice of any player on the roster. They selected Herman, much to the chagrin of the Boston club.

General manager Bob Quinn quickly called Corbett, telling him that Herman belonged to Boston, not Atlanta.

Quinn threatened to bring Landis to Atlanta to stop the deal and Corbett had to call the Yankees and tell them the deal was nullified. Yankee owner Ed Barrow said he understood. New York also had signed a college kid by the name of Lou Gehrig who would eventually fill the anticipated vacancy at first base.

For a second-straight season, the Red Sox illegally covered Herman up by sending him to San Antonio in the Texas League. He seemed to be a favorite of Boston manager Frank Chance, and he was promised the Boston first base position but Chance died after the 1923 season. He was used little by new Boston manager Lee Fohl during spring training at San Antonio. Herman was with the Boston club the first week of the American League season but Fohl preferred Joe Harris at first base and Babe didn't get into a single game.

Herman, now 20 years old, was coveted by Wade 'Red' Killefer of Seattle who was unable to play after being hit in the head by a pitch and wanted to purchase Herman for use at first base. However, the Sox didn't want to lose Babe's explosive bat and turned his offer down.

Bob Coleman was the manager at San Antonio and he used Herman exclusively at first base. During the first 21 games of the schedule, Babe hit .349 and had 21 runs batted in. He had made only one error and had a .946 fielding average.

Then some old friends of Babe stopped by. They played for Dallas, also in the Texas league and said: "Babe, we could beat Fort Worth if you were playing first base for us."

The more they talked, the more they were convinced that they could stop the perennial league winners if Herman would only ask to be switched to their team.

Babe finally agreed and asked Coleman if the transfer could be made.

"Certainly a transfer could be made," Coleman said, and to show the youngster who was in charge promptly moved Herman to the Little Rock team in the Southern League.

However, Coleman announced that Herman was going to Little Rock "because he doesn't fit in on our ball club. He thinks he's a big leaguer and he sneers at this league. If he gets a couple of hits, he wouldn't worry about anything else; that's the attitude he's been taking. The fellows are down on Babe. Yes, he's a good hitter and a good fielder when he wants to be, but he doesn't seem to want to be in San Antonio. I threatened to take his money in fines a dozen times but I never did."

Babe hit well for Little Rock, banging a double and a homer in the first game and collecting a double, triple and a homer two games later.

He was hitting .378 on June 12, and while playing in Mobile, Al Devormer stepped on his foot at first base and cut him badly. Devormer became delirious and went into the hospital the next day with typhoid fever, and didn't realize, until a conversation with Herman five years later, that he had even stepped on him.

Herman's lacerated ankle would not heal and on top of that he had contracted a case of malaria. Limping badly, Babe came back two days later and made a pair of errors. He booted three more in the next five games as the ankle continued to bother him. The team dropped into last place and Herman's hitting tailed off.

He finally went to manager Kid Eberfield and said, "Let me go into the hospital to treat this malaria and so that my ankle can heal and I'll be OK in a few days."

The manager told him to play or he wouldn't get paid. The local papers had been on Eberfield, saying either the team or Kid had given up and were not fighters. It was rumored the club would be sold at the end of the season and moved to another city.

Babe considered his ultimatum and said, "Today's a day off and I ought to get paid for that, so pay me for today and yesterday and I'll go home."

The club paid him and put him on the Little Rock reserve list, reporting he retired because of "bad health." Herman returned to Glendale to recuperate.

He finished with a .318 average at Little Rock, second-highest on the club, and with only 18 strikeouts in 239 at bats.

During the winter meetings, Wade Killefer finally got his man, buying Herman from Little Rock for Seattle in the Pacific Coast League. The club trained at Santa Maria, just up the Pacific Coast Highway from Los Angeles.

Seattle had also purchased Ace Elliott from the Cubs, who had broken his leg during spring training in 1924, and it was assumed he would fill the first base position. Killefer penciled Elliott in at first and Herman in an outfield slot. In the first exhibition game, Babe played right field and doubled against the Pirates in Paso Robles.

He opened the 1925 season with a 3-for-3 game at San Francisco and then homered in the next contest. Just over a week into the season, Elliott covered home on a wild pitch and the runner crashed into him, again breaking his leg.

Babe went back to first base and was slashing the ball all over the field. In May Herman had seven hits in two games against Salt Lake City, including three doubles and two homers. In June he banged out four hits in seven trips, including three triples and a homer, against San Francisco and in July he had six hits in ten trips, with three doubles, against Los Angeles at Seattle. He was 9-for-14 against Salt Lake again later in the month and during one of these torrid streaks Brooklyn scout Spencer Abbott wandered by. His eyes popped at the young man's sweet and powerful swing.

Years later the Brooklyn scout said, "I had gone to Seattle to check out a different player and saw Herman get 11 hits in three games—each one a line drive. I make a deal for him on the spot." Abbott also raved about Herman's work around first base. He cost the club $15,000.

Abbott reported to Robinson, "I don't know if he can field, but when I see a kid go up there and bust three or four hits every day, I've got to go with him." He purchased Herman for the Robins with delivery set for 1926.

A leg injury slowed Babe as he moved into the month of September hitting .336. He finished at .316 with 115 runs scored, 206 hits, 52 doubles, 13 triples, 15 homers, 22 stolen bases, 131 hits and a spot on the Pacific Coast League All-Star team along with Lloyd Waner, Charlie Root and Lefty O'Doul.

Killefer said, "Taking everything into account, Babe Herman is the best first baseman in the Pacific Coast League."

The Brooklyn Robins had finished only a game and one-half out of first place in 1924, then finished just a half-game out of the cellar in 1925.

On the way to the World Series in the fall of 1925, Wilbert Robinson told reporters, "I'll have a story for you fellows in the morning. Spencer Abbott is meeting me in Pittsburgh, and from what he told me on the phone the other day, I think he has bought Paul Waner for us."

But the next morning it was discovered that Pirate owner Barney Dreyfus had put in a quicker and more emphatic call and had purchased Waner for the Pirates.

Abbott, meeting the train in Pittsburgh, commiserated, "A tough break, Robbie but I bought you another youngster who is a better hitter than Waner. A big fellow out of Seattle named Babe Herman."

Herman had been discovered earlier by Bill Lange, uncle of George Kelly and Pacific Coast agent for John McGraw and the New York Giants. He sent word that Herman was the best looking prospect in the Pacific Coast League, including Waner.

However, the Giants had Kelly at first and a young Bill Terry waiting in the wings so they passed on Herman. One can only speculate how his career would have benefited by playing 77 games in the Polo Grounds with its 250-foot foul lines.

Chapter 2

Herman was not happy with the contract that arrived in the spring of 1926 from Brooklyn. "I wanted to play in the major leagues," he said, "but I didn't want to take a cut in pay to do it." He was offered $5,000 to play for the Robins, but had been making $7,000 in Seattle.

At about that time, a typical Brooklyn rhubarb was taking place as manager Wilbert Robinson was attempting to trade for Minneapolis shortstop Johnny Butler. He sent pitchers Dick Loftus and Bill Hubbell to Minnesota manager Mike Kelly, but he had received a better offer and sent them back.

Robinson was furious and threatened to call Commissioner Landis. Kelly then said he had bought the two pitchers and had agreed to included them in a trade if the Robins made a deal for Butler. Finally the Robins traded the pair, along with Cotton Tierney, Charles Corgan, Horace Ford, and John Hollingsworth, plus Babe Herman sent on option, for Butler. Only Ford signed with Minneapolis, all the others held out for raises.

Babe received a call from the Minneapolis owner who said, "I'll pay you $1000 a month until Ted Jourdan gets well." Herman agreed, and reported for training in San Antonio.

Butler had been touted as the player who would finally solve the Brooklyn shortstop problem. But his arrival in Clearwater, Florida where the Robins trained was again, typically Brooklyn.

When his train pulled in, a number of players and fans were on hand to greet this exceptional player. The train stopped and everyone waited, and waited—and waited.

Finally a window in the train opened and out came a stretcher with Butler on it. His ulcers had overcome him. Butler would not help Brooklyn much. He hit only .269 in 1926, .238 in 1927 and was traded.

The club that Herman joined was a delightful mix of characters, night prowlers and free spirits. Couple that with the large press corps that covered them, trying (and usually succeeding) to outdo each other with fanciful stories, some true—some not, and you have the unique mix of what one paper called "The Daffiness Boys."

In all probability the club had no more characters than any other club, although strange and wondrous things always seemed to be happening to any team that inhabited Ebbets Field. But the combination of an unusual number of exceptional writers and wondrous subject material made sure each unusual occurrence was given full coverage. That made for hilarious (if sometimes creative) stories, entertaining reading and increased newspaper sales.

Within the club was a group that called themselves the 'Big Four.' There is no indication that Robinson knew about them, but they were certainly known around the league and were a source of great delight for the baseball writers covering the club.

The four were pitchers, thus constant candidates for an 'oh-for-4' day at the plate. Dazzy Vance gave the club its name and Tom Meany, covering the team for the Brooklyn Times, coined their motto, "One for all and four for oh."

One of the members, Jesse Petty, was fined for staying out well after the club's curfew. This (getting caught) was in direct violation of the rules of the Big Four and Petty got a notification to that effect in his mailbox while the team was on the road.

He was asked to report to the membership committee who would judge the gravity of his offense. He was asked to defend himself in writing.

Petty enlisted a pair of writers to frame his defense. They worked out an elaborate reply and neatly typed it on one of their machines.

The next day the Big Four put another note in Jesse's box, stating that they knew he did not write the note himself, since he hadn't been carrying a typewriter along on the trip, and that he had compounded his offense by going outside the club for help.

He threw himself on the mercy of the court and copied, in longhand, another letter composed by the writers.

Called in to face the music, Vance said, "It is the wish of the committee that you should read your defense out loud."

Petty gave it a try, stumbling over the big words the writers had composed for him. The committee was silent for a moment, then Vance said, "We have great wisdom and know that you did not write that statement yourself. Answer one question for us:

"What does ignominious mean?"

Petty fumbled for a moment, then stammered "It means I was cold sober."

Without a smile, Vance said, "It is the judgement of the council that Jesse Lee Petty be stricken from the records of the Big Four and the following notation be attached, Tried—and found wanting."

Another time Robinson decided to form a 'bonehead club' and fine a player each time he made a mistake, putting the money in a fund, and intending to cut it up at the end of the year. "Hell, we'll have more than a World Series share the way this club plays," he said.

But that same afternoon, Robinson told Ernie Lombardi he would catch, then wrote Al Lopez's name on the lineup card. Lombardi singled in the first but Cardinal manager Gabby Street protested, the hit was nullified, and Lopez was put into the game.

Lombardi was barred from 'returning' to the lineup and the club was fined $25 by the league for failing to announce a substitution.

The next day a Brooklyn paper said: "The Manager of the Dodgers formed a Bonehead Club before yesterday's game and promptly elected himself a charter member."

Herman was certainly not daffy, but the six-foot, four-inch youngster who had made a near-complete tour of the minor leagues, possessed certain qualities that made it easy to include him in the general hilarity that pervaded the club.

And, except when the Robins infrequently surprised the league with a serious pennant threat, newsmen found it easier and much more enjoyable to write about the strange things that happened to the team on the bases and in the field, instead of reporting the numerous losses that a perennial sixth-place team is heir to.

Include a fanatical group of baseball fans that supported the Brooklyn team religiously, and a second group that came to watch and ride the players when they booted the ball or forgot how many outs there were; you have a special mix that has never been duplicated.

The 1926 Dodgers were again a makeshift club. They had nearly won the 1924 pennant, losing by a few percentage points, but then they lapsed back into sixth place in 1925. Robinson was again rebuilding with what talent he could salvage and the few youngsters discovered by the only full time scout the club owned, Larry Sutton.

Zach Wheat anchored an average outfield, although it was probably the best part of the club, and played left. He held most of the Brooklyn offensive records and would later be elected to the Hall of Fame. Journeymen Dick Cox and Eddie Brown joined him in the garden.

Jimmy Johnston had finished a long and productive career at third base in 1925 and he was replaced by a variety of hopefuls, including 33-year-old Bill Marriott who eventually got most of the playing time. Chick Fewster was at second and Butler worked most of the infield spots before settling for the most part at short. Jake Fournier was a fixture at first and Mickey O'Neil, Charlie Hargreaves and Hank DeBerry shared the catching spots.

Dazzy Vance was the ace of the staff, having won 22 in 1925. Jesse Petty, Burleigh Grimes, Doug McWeeney, Jesse Barnes and Bob McGraw manned the other starting slots. None of them, even the great Vance, would win more than they lost in 1926.

The Robins had come north in 1926, playing against the Yankees and had lost all 12 exhibition games, the New York team slugging the ball for a near .400 average. Brooklyn had been picked to finish sixth again. Robinson was trying to work outfielder Gus Felix into a backup position at first behind veteran Jake Fournier.

Fournier, obtained from St. Louis in 1923 at the age of 30, had hit .351, .334 and .350 since coming to Brooklyn, leading the league in home runs in 1924 with 27. He was as close to a star as the club had, save the ageing Wheat, and with the club's obvious problems, Robinson wasn't looking too hard for a first baseman in the spring of 1926.

The Robins had left Clearwater, Florida, that spring with the thought that they would find a different training base in 1927. Poor facilities and poor attendance were part of the problem. An angry Thomas Rice wrote in the Brooklyn Eagle:

"Brooklyn put this jerkwater on the map, started and boosted its real estate boom, but the total receipts in spring training exhibition games was only $800 this year, compared to $900 in 1925."

The boom was real enough and Brooklyn players Jake Fournier and Milt Stock told friends that they had made $75,000 on one deal earlier in the year.

Babe trained in Texas with the Minneapolis club but when they decided to go with their veteran first baseman after he healed, Herman was no longer needed there so he took a train from Indianapolis, where the team was playing and signed with Brooklyn.

On opening day in the Polo Grounds he was on the bench as Jess Petty shutout the Giants 3-0 on one hit.

Brooklyn Eagle reporter Tommy Holmes, noting Herman's travels through the minor leagues, wrote: "At 22 he has been connected with every league of importance save possibly Epworth and the Anti-Saloon." And after Herman had captured the hearts of the Brooklyn fans, he wrote: "The promiscuous way in which he was shipped from one corner of the world to the other would be enough to discourage an ordinary human being. On the contrary, it has fitted Herman with the nerve of a landlord. You couldn't rattle this big, blond kid if you lit a cannon cracker behind him. A gent with that kind of temperament is an asset to any club."

The first to greet Herman when he arrived was Otto Miller, his old nemesis from Atlanta, who said, "Hello, Babe."

"Hello, Otto. Surprised to see me?" Herman replied.

As he walked on, Robbie turned to Miller and asked, "How do you know him?"

"I had him in Atlanta in 1923. Take my advice, Robbie, and don't ride him, no matter what he does."

Robbie snapped, "What's so important about him that I can't ride him?"

"He's sensitive," Miller said. "And pretty hard-headed, too. But he can

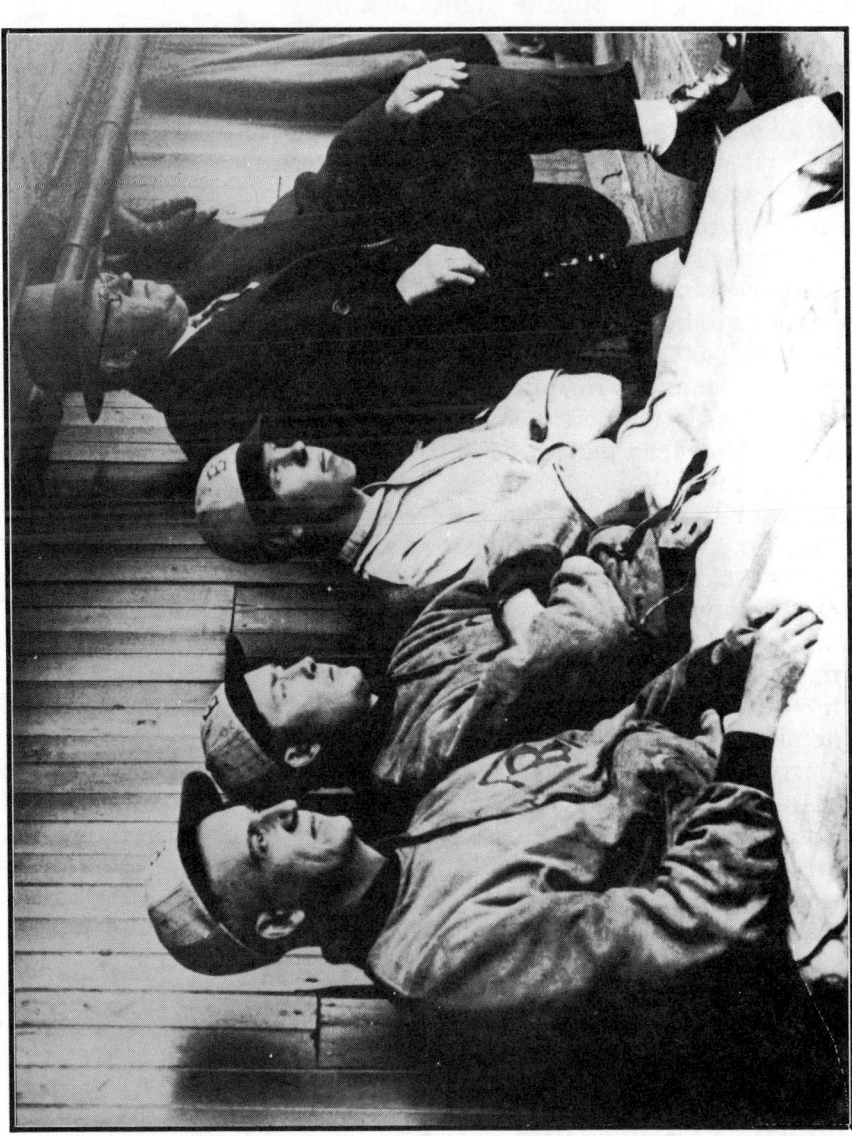

WATCHING THE ACTION— From the Brooklyn dugout, were Jesse Petty, Jesse Barnes, Babe Herman and manager Wilbert Robinson. The photo was probably taken in 1927.

hit that ball. He and I got into it when I tried to tell him something about playing first base. A couple weeks later we sold him to Memphis for $350."

"Hell," Robbie said. "I paid $15,000 for him."

"Well," Miller said, "He's got more sense than he had three years ago, but take my tip and don't ride him."

By then a smiling Robbie was watching Herman slash line drive to all corners of the park during batting practice. "I won't ride him," he murmured.

Babe made his first appearance in a Brooklyn uniform on April 14 when he walked for shortstop Rabbit Maranville, just obtained on waivers from Boston, but the Giants won 9-5.

He pinch-hit again on April 16th and grounded to Frank Frisch at second. He hit for pitcher Doug McWeeney on the 22nd and grounded into a force play.

Meanwhile, Fournier was stinging the ball. He hit in 10th straight games and won one from the Giants in Brooklyn with a home run. Robinson was thinking about trading Herman back to Seattle for third baseman Frank Brazill, and Seattle was anxious to get him back.

On April 28th, Babe earned his first major league hit when he doubled to left in a pinch-hitting role as the Robins rallied for three runs in the ninth to beat the Braves in Boston.

Trailing 3-2, Dick Cox walked and Herman was called to bat for third baseman Bill Mariott. He quickly slugged a double to left. Wheat walked to load the bases and Fournier singled off the second baseman's glove to score two. Gus Felix plated the final run with a single.

The Brooklyn fans discovered, to their surprise and delight, the Robins were in first place with a 9-5 record as April ended.

The Brooklyn club was still first on May 4th after beating the Braves in Ebbets Field. Two days earlier 30,000 were admitted to the park and almost as many were locked out. But that day Fournier, hitting over .370, slid hard back into second base on a pickoff play and injured his ankle. Herman replaced him and with the Robins trailing by a run in the ninth, Zach Wheat singled, Herman doubled, Gus Felix walked and after a force at the plate, Mickey O'Neil singled Herman across for the win.

Garry Schumacher, writing in the Evening Journal, noted, "Babe Herman, the lanky Coast Leaguer, should prove to be an acceptable substitute for a few days. 'Babe' is a fancy but somewhat erratic fielder but he can belt 'em. Still he is hardly in Fournier's class as a hitter, and Jack will be welcomed back with open arms when he is ready."

Babe started his first game on May 6th in St. Louis and doubled in the sixth inning. He was out moments later when he tried to score from second on a ground ball, exhibiting an aggressive style that was later would be mistaken for dumb base running. Tommy Holmes, writing in the Brooklyn Eagle, said: "It was a good play even if it didn't work." Herman crashed into Cardinal catcher Bob O'Farrell at the plate and

O'Farrell's knee slammed into Babe's ribs, causing him extreme pain.

Richard Vidmer in the New York Times noted, "Babe Herman was at first in place of Fournier and looked as graceful as Hal Chase on thrown balls. His ability to stretch makes him a good target at which to throw."

He got his first error on a ground ball the next day. With a runner on second, Babe scooped the ball up and threw to Butler at third, who decoyed the runner as if there were no play, then grabbed at the ball and attempting to make the tag, dropped it. The error was charged to Herman. Later that night in their room, Butler told him, "I catch that ball every time, but I didn't today."

The Robins took the next three games from the Cardinals and were enjoying an unusual first-place position. After losing the opener, Herman had an RBI in a 7-1 victory and then on May 8th he hit his first major league homer.

Herman singled and scored the first Robin run in the second inning, but the Cardinals fashioned a 3-1 lead going into the sixth. Brooklyn scored a pair to tie the game at three each.

In the seventh inning, Fewster lived on Bell's error and Wheat bunted him to second. Herman lined a ball down the right field line that went foul by inches. Then Babe blasted an Arthur Reinhart pitch into the right field pavilion seats to win the game. Tommy Holmes noted, "Fournier never hit one harder."

Babe's ribs were still extremely sore from the collision with O'Farrell and on an open date, he had them checked. He was taped by the doctor and could hardly breathe. Weeks later, an X-ray determined that the ribs had indeed been broken.

With his ribs wrapped tightly, he continued to play and after the next game at Pittsburgh, Brooklyn writers waxed poetic, proclaiming that Herman was a better fielding first baseman than Fournier.

Tommy Holmes noted in the Brooklyn Eagle: "Herman promises to be a great player when he grows up. He is a dangerous hitter, not a good one. He is one of those all-or-nothing swingers. He can be made to look bad on almost any kind of pitched ball. But he also may step in there at any moment, swing at any kind of pitch, and break up the game. He takes his cut, and if the ball is where he's swinging, it's a two base hit or better."

And Thomas Rice said in The Sporting News: "When Fournier returns, Babe should be placed in the outfield. Herman might go wrong defensively, but his offense far outclasses the other five outfielders. Herman is no flash in the pan. He has made a tremendous impression on the fans with his work around first base and his heavy wallops.

"Herman is shaping up as the best minor leaguer to break into the big show this year. His fielding at first base is beautiful, he is fast and he is hitting consistently and powerfully. Moreover, he is hitting to left, center and right in almost equal proportions, whether facing left or right handers.

"In his first 33 games he has 39 hits. He has hit .377 against right handers and .355 against left handers. Fifteen of his hits have been to right field, 12 to center and 14 to left field.

"His hitting has thrown his fielding into a shadow, but observers at Ebbets Field are beginning to realize he is one of the best fielding first basemen in baseball. He does not seem to be particularly sure of pop flies, but in all respects he is an ideal man for the job. He can stretch as far for a thrown ball as George Kelly and, being left handed, can make plays on bunts down the first base line that Kelly could never make."

Babe won over the Brooklyn fans early. On his first trip to the plate in Ebbets Field an undercurrent of applause went through the stands. Crowds took to him instantly and he would respond with a pleasant smile. They knew he could give them a thrill any minute and break up a game with one swing.

Herman slugged his fourth consecutive hit against the Pirates on May 15th, knocking in the leading run in the seventh only to have rain wash the hit away as well as the Robin margin. Three days later he again banged out four straight hits, only to have rain erase the final double that put the potential winning run at third base.

Tommy Holmes wrote: "Ex-coast league players say Babe isn't taking a natural cut, that he is handicapped by the collision with O'Farrell. If this is so, it's a good thing for m'sieu Jack Fournier that he will probably be back before Herman begins to feel natural."

Herman hit in eleven straight games and 15-of-16 as the Robins stayed at or near the top of the National League standings.

Fournier returned on May 25 and Herman moved to right field, in the Polo Grounds, throwing out the speedy Ross Youngs of New York at the plate and nipping another Giant at third base in his outfield debut. On his first trip to the plate, with runners on first and third, he swung and missed a Jack Scott pitch by almost a foot. The second pitch he crushed off the back of the upper deck in left field—but foul. On the third pitch he hit a smash off George Kelly's glove at first base that was so hot it deflected into foul territory for a double and earned him two runs batted in.

Herman told Robinson he had trouble gauging flies but would try the outfield if that was what he wanted. Robbie told reporters he was astounded at Herman's frank self-assessment.

In late May he delighted a large Ebbets Field crowd by stretching a Texas League single into a double. He then scored from second on an infield tap and received a great ovation from the leagues' most knowledgeable fans.

But the New York writers were wondering about his switch to the outfield. One said, "The socking of the blond rookie has earned him a permanent berth with the Brooklyn Robins, but some doubt exists as to the exact location of the berth he had earned. He isn't a particularly versatile fielder. First is his position, and he's a good first baseman. He is too valuable to leave on the bench and is playing the outfield only to allow Fournier's bat to stay in the lineup."

The Sporting News reported: "What to do with Herman is a problem. He is not an outfielder. Nobody knows better than Herman he has not the physical eye to judge fly balls. He has baseball instinct that has improved with experience, but he is not now an outfielder. While Fournier was out with an injury, Herman was playing at first base where he feels comfortable. It is sweet agony for Robinson to have two top flight first basemen, but men who are not so good in another bent."

Herman and Fournier both homered in early June as the Robins stopped the Giants 10-1. Herman was second in the National League with a .361 average.

Playing in Ebbets Field, Babe banged a ball down the right field line and it bounced around in the bullpen. He pulled up at second when the third base coach gave him the stop sign but glancing back he could see they were still looking for the ball under the player's bench.

He dashed on to third and was again given the stop sign. As he looked back into right field, he could see the outfielder was just getting the ball back to the infield, costing Herman a certain inside-the-park home run.

Joe Kelly, a teammate of Robinson's on the old Oriole team, was coaching third and while the crowd booed wildly, Babe said, "What in the world is going on? Why'd you stop me at second when the fielder is still looking for the ball?"

Kelly put his hand on Herman's shoulder and said, "Babe, without my glasses I can't even see who's pitching, and I won't wear my glasses on the field."

When Babe asked him why not, he straightened himself up and said, "Pride." It was not long after that Kelly was replaced as third base coach by Otto Miller.

On June 6th, Babe doubled twice and threw Earl Smith out at the plate on a double off the right field wall in Ebbets Field. The perfect throw kept Paul Waner at third base, preserving Grimes' 3-0 victory. And he demonstrated a talent that would drive outfielder's wild as they tried to position themselves for his slashing hits. On successive pitches, he boomed a long shot over the right field wall that just curved foul, then cracked one off the left field wall for a triple.

One writer accused him of being a place hitter.

"Place hitter? What is that?" he said. "I'm a slugger. I place about three hits a year. I just take a cut and let the ball go where it will. When I start my swing, I don't know or particularly care where the ball goes unless I'm trying to hit behind the runner.

"I don't mean I cut blindly. I aim to hit each ball I swing at with my bat on a level plane. I swing at every pitch the same way, with no effort to 'pull' or 'push' it to any particular field. The way the ball is pitched to me determines where the ball will go if I hit it.

"Before I start my cut, I have no preconceived idea of where I'll hit it. But when I miss a swing, I know where the ball would have gone if I had connected."

Back at first base later in the week, Herman threw three runners out at second base on attempted sacrifice bunts. After another great performance later in the game, he drew this rave: "Herman made two flashy plays in the sixth. Blades of the Cardinals was picked off by Vance, but it took an exceptional tag to make the play. Then Herman became a contortionist to get Fewster's throw and retire Hornsby." Richard Vidmer continued, "...and Minneapolis turned him back, saying they couldn't use him. Finer things have happened, but they don't come to mind."

And the Brooklyn Eagle said, "Babe Herman is one of the best fielding first basemen around. At least a dozen times in the last 27 games he has swept in on an attempted sacrifice and has smoothly thrown a runner out at second. Three times in yesterday's game he nipped the runner at second, the last two stopping potential Cincinnati rallies. He has one error in 27 games at first base and is better around the bag than George Kelly, Charlie Grimm, Jim Bottomly or Stuffy McGinnis. Robinson can't find a way to play Herman and Fournier at the same time. As an outfielder, Herman is a good first baseman."

Herman hit in fourteen straight games before being stopped by Willie Sherdel of the Cardinals. The following day Brooklyn split with the Braves and the Boston writers wryly chortled, with tongue in cheek, "Babe Herman was held to two singles, a double and a triple in the doubleheader."

But while Herman was banging the ball all over the league, the rest of the team was hitting only .250 and they slowly slipped into the second division.

Babe made an error that allowed the Giants two unearned runs in a 5-3 loss but at bat he was as hotter than the weather in early July. He singled twice against the Giants, then singled twice the following day. He had five hits in the July 3 double-header, including a three-run homer in the first game, and he doubled twice against the Phils on the 4th of July.

Boston moved into Ebbets Field and in four games Herman smashed out 11 hits in 15 trips to boost his average to .377 and take over the National League lead. He had clouted 22 hits in nine games and had jumped from eighth to second among National League hitters.

But a low throw bounced off his right thumb and there was some speculation that it had been broken. X-rays showed no break, but the injury put a damper on his spectacular hitting. He tried to ignore it while at bat, but in the field he would unconsciously pull on the thumb as if it pained him. He collected only two hits in his next 20 trips to the plate and was 0-for-12 before singling against the Cubs.

Babe's one-handed swing was an oddity in 1926, but it is recommended by a number of hitting coaches now.

"You can finish with both hands on the bat if it is an inside pitch," Babe noted. "But if you're going to hit the outside pitch with any power, you have to release your top hand. They claimed I let go before I hit the ball but that was baloney. My hand came off with the follow through, after contact was made.

Zach Wheat

"The only wrist action you have in hitting is the part that comes naturally. The minute you start thinking about your wrists, you'll start hitting with your hands."

Moving into St. Louis, Fournier became the first Brooklyn player to hit three home runs in one game. He smacked the first onto the pavilion roof in the fourth, hit the second into the upper right field seats in the sixth, nicking off the foul pole, and banged his third completely over the pavilion in the eighth. He had five RBI but the Robins lost 12-10.

Fournier had played six years for the Chicago White Sox before being dropped to Los Angeles in the Pacific Coast League. Successive .305, .325 and .350 earned him a ticket back to the St. Louis National League club where he hit .306 and .343 before slipping to .295.

He was traded quickly to Brooklyn by Branch Rickey, who never liked to keep a player much beyond his prime, for Hi Myers and Ray Schmandt in early 1923. He had blistered the ball for the Robins but at 34 was starting to have trouble with his legs.

Herman had moved to the outfield so Fournier could play first, but the new position wasn't coming easy to him. Babe chased center fielder Merwin Jacobson off the ball on a drive into right-center, then had the ball skip past him to the wall. The mistake cost two runs but the Robins won 5-2.

Petty was sent home from St. Louis for training violations (perhaps prompting his dismissal from the Big Four) and fined was $100 after being knocked out of the box for the first time. And the Robins bought the contract of Harvey Hendrick, who was hitting .402 in New Orleans.

Playing in Pittsburgh, Chick Fewster argued so long and so heatedly that it finally infuriated umpire Beans Reardon. Finally Reardon swung at him but missed, surprising both himself and Fewster.

Late in July, Chuck Dressen smacked a two-run triple to beat Brooklyn 2-0. A Brooklyn writer noted, "Dressen's triple might have been caught if Herman was Ross Youngs instead of a good first baseman."

Herman was hitting .345 as the season moved into August. The thumb still bothered him and on August 5 he had slipped 42 points from his season high, and was hitting .335.

Against the Cardinals that day fans saw Zach Wheat hit his final home run in a Brooklyn uniform. In the 10th inning, with the Cards leading 11-8, he smacked a shot beyond the right field wall into Bedford Avenue.

Trotting to first base, he suddenly pulled up lame and staggered to second base where he sat down on the bag to rest. After five minutes Robinson sent in Maranville as a pinch runner and he was announced, but Wheat refused to accept a runner. He finally got to his feet and limped on around the bases to complete the home run.

After losing 13 of 18 games on a home stand, Tommy Holmes wrote, "Apart from sundry pitchers, not more than three of the present team are reasonably sure of eating at the expense of the Brooklyn club next season." He named catcher Charley Hargreaves, infielder Johnny Butler and Babe Herman. "Try and pry Babe Herman, the child genius with a Louisville Slugger, loose from the Brooklyn book," Holmes concluded.

Herman was on another near-record tear. In the final series of the home stand, against Pittsburgh August 9th, he homered over the right field wall, singled to center and singled to right. On his final trip he had a sacrifice fly. On August 10th he homered to left, singled to left and then singled twice to right. And in the final game the next day he singled to center, doubled off the right field wall and came up in the sixth inning with a chance to collect his 10th straight hit and tie the National League record.

He hit a long shot to left center. Kiki Cuyler ran back to the low fence and leaped for the ball, falling into the near-empty seats. He reappeared seconds later with the ball in his hand and the umpires ruled that it was a legal catch.

Ben Sirota, a 14-year-old fan, was sitting in the left-field bleachers close to the play and saw the ball bounce out of Cuyler's glove and roll away. Cuyler quickly grabbed it and held it up to get the call.

The bogus 'catch' stopped Herman's streak at nine hits in succession, just short of the record set by Ed Konetchy in 1919 and tied by Tris Speaker in 1920.

In one respect Babe surpassed both Konetchy and Speaker. His nine safe hits were good for a total of 16 bases. Konetchy negotiated only 13 bases on his 10 hits and Speaker's 11 hits were good for just 12 bases.

But as quickly as the hitting touch returned, it just as suddenly vanished and he was 0-for-9 in the next two games. A Brooklyn paper wrote: "Herman isn't happy in the outfield, and his hitting reflects that. His well-meaning efforts in the outfield don't serve to increase his confidence at bat or in the field."

Then on August 15th one of the most talked-about plays in Brooklyn history made Herman immortal—and probably cost him a berth in the Hall of Fame.

In the seventh inning of the opener of a double-header with the Boston Braves, Johnny Butler singled to left and Hank DeBerry doubled to left to tie the game 1-1. Dazzy Vance singled and Chick Fewster was hit by a pitch to load the bases.

Boston pitcher John Wertz was taken out and George Mogridge came in to pitch. Merwin Jacobson popped out on an attempted squeeze play and Herman came to the plate.

Those are incontestable facts. From this point on, however, the story slips into the twilight zone.

The most popular impression of the succeeding events goes like this: Herman slammed the ball off the right field wall and DeBerry scored. Vance rounded third and heard the coach call out "Go back!" to Fewster. Misunderstanding, Vance returned to third. Fewster arrived at third just as Vance slid into the bag from one side and Herman from the other.

The ball arrived at third and Herman went back toward second, watching his teammates standing on the base. Fewster stepped off and was tagged out and the ball was thrown to second and Herman tagged out.

That is approximately the story as it was repeated for years around the league at banquets and in the bars, drawing laughs each time it was told. Everyone was talking about Herman tripling into a triple play.

"Nonsense," Herman said. "There was one out at the time but you couldn't write doubling into a double play, that wouldn't be so colorful.

"In the first place, I was the only one that slid into third base. Vance said later that he had messed the play up by returning to third base. 'I don't know why I did,' he said. 'I just got confused.'

"No one shouted 'stop' to get Daz to return. In fact, no one shouted at all," said Herman.

The actual account of the play started with Herman hitting the ball off the wall in right field to score DeBerry. The ball came off the wall to right fielder Jimmy Welsh who relayed it to second baseman, Doc Gatreau. He threw it to catcher Oscar Siemer. Vance ran back toward second as if to tag up on the hit and when the ball came off the wall he reversed his field and lumbered around third base, then for some reason darted back. Fewster roared into third easily and watched as the catcher chased Vance back.

Herman slid into second with a double and when he saw the throw from Gatreau go home, he glanced up to see a runner between third and home. He assumed they had caught Fewster in a run-down, (who else could it be?) so he jumped up and with his head down dashed toward third.

The catcher got the relay from Gatreau and threw to third base as Herman slid. With Vance now standing on the bag, Fewster was standing a few feet away. He had to jump to get out of the way of Babe's furious slide, and was, in effect, passed by Herman.

Umpire Ernest Quigley looked down at Babe and scratched his head. "Well, Babe, it looks like you're out for passing Fewster," he said. Herman said, "You're getting pretty technical but you're probably right."

Vance, standing on the bag said, "Ha, I'm safe!" Herman looked up at him and said, "Yea, you big dope, you're the only one."

Fewster, thinking he too was automatically out, started back with Herman to their positions. Second baseman Gatreau grabbed the ball and followed him toward second base and said, "Look what I have," before tagging him. When the umpire called him out, Fewster said, "Hell, I thought I was out five minutes ago."

The New York Times was pretty casual about reporting the play. The headlines simply noted:

ROBINS IN FORM
WIN TWO IN DAY

Richard Vidmer wrote, "Babe drove in the winning run, then made a joke of it. Herman drove the ball with a resounding smash against the right field wall, scoring DeBerry with the winning run. Vance was satisfied to take one base, Fewster through he ought to take two and Herman wanted to take three.

"Herman was tagged out, although tagging was too good for him. It didn't matter, as the Robins made two more in the 8th and didn't need those other runs. If it had been a more critical situation, the Babe would wake up this morning and find himself famous."

Robinson didn't say anything about the play to anyone in the dugout and no one made much of the story until later when a newsman heard

Herman and his teammates laughing about it during dinner. He wrote the original "Herman triples into a triple play" story but was quickly called on it by his fellow newsmen the next day when they asked him how it could have been a triple play if there was one out at the time?

In actual fact, what Herman had done was double into a double play, helped in great measure by his teammates. The Brooklyn Eagle made little of it, calling it only a "freak play."

Max Carey

The play, in addition to making Herman a household word in Brooklyn and in the rest of the baseball world, also spawned a series of funny stories.

An unusual addendum to the story is the fact that before the inning started, third base coach Otto Miller said to Robbie, "I'm really getting tired of walking down to third and back. Nothing ever happens at third when we're at bat."

Reserve catcher Mickey O'Neil jumped up and said, "Sit still, Otto, I'll coach third this inning."

Miller was well known as the Brooklyn third base coach, and was asked about the play so often over the years he finally stopped denying he was involved and took credit for the play himself. He would tell anyone who asked, "Well, I set a record anyway. Nobody else ever put three men on third."

Exactly why Herman has been given all the blame for the mixup isn't clear, with the possible exception that he was such a good-natured sort he never tried to explain who was actually at fault or why. It did, however, set the tone for many other fanciful stories about Herman that were just as funny, but quite as untrue.

One colorful story concerned a sign for an awning company painted on the wall in Pittsburgh or Cincinnati. On a blistering day, while a pitching change was being made, Herman leaned against the wall and looked up at the sign. Later he told a teammate he wished the sign had been real, because he could then have played right field in the shade of the awning.

A newsman, reworking the story to fit his needs, wrote that Herman had tried to play a ball off the awning and had it bounce away from him.

With the number of reporters traveling with the team approaching a dozen, the constant battle for innovative writing led to many flights of fancy.

Ebbets Field fans were used to unusual plays occurring in that slightly magical ballpark. In June, another gem had been enacted.

Playing the Cubs one afternoon and leading 5-2, the Chicago team had the bases loaded with Johnny Cooney at first base. Joe Kelly hit to Herman and he threw to Dave 'Beauty' Bancroft at short. Bancroft stepped on the bag to eliminate Cooney and threw to first but in the dirt. Pitcher Jess Barnes covered the bag, blocked the low throw and it rolled a short distance away.

When he picked it up, he spotted a Cub runner rounding third and heading home. He fired the ball to Mickey O'Neil at the plate well ahead of the runner, who suddenly and mysteriously swerved out of the baseline, gave O'Neil the 'come on' sign and ran into the Cub dugout.

O'Neil chased him down the steps into the dugout and tagged him behind the water cooler. Making the proceedings even more ludicrous, umpire Bill Klem was close behind to make the 'out' call.

The Robins thought it was the third out and left the field.

Cub manager Joe McCarthy walked to the plate and asked Klem, "How can you put one man out twice?"

"You can't," Klem replied.

"Well, that was Cooney they tagged," McCarthy pointed out, a small grin spreading across his face.

"Was it?" Klem asked skeptically. Then looking toward the bench his eyes popped wide in surprise. "Well, I'll be damned!"

Klem conferred with the other umpires, then waived the Robins back on the field.

"What?" screamed Robbie.

"Sorry," a red-faced Klem admitted. "They've got to go back. There ought to be a rule against such a thing but there isn't."

Kelly, who hit the ball to Herman to start the strange play, had stopped at second. When play was resumed after 15 minutes of debate, he was standing at third base not second.

Babe ran in toward Klem, shouting "Kelly should be at second, not on third." But by this time the embarrassed umpire had about enough of the whole situation. He drew a line and forbid Herman to cross it.

Babe, being a brash rookie, started to go around the line, but O'Neil tackled him and while they lay on the ground told him, "He'll fine and suspend you for a week if you go past that line."

Herman also learned an important lesson while playing in Boston. He had two strikes called on him that he thought were low, and turned to umpire E. C. Quigley and said, "Come on, get the damn thing up." Quigley bristled immediately and Babe didn't get a close call the rest of the series.

Mickey O'Neil told him, "Quigley don't like profanity or those who use it." From then on, Herman greeted him with, "Good morning, Mr. Quigley, how are you today?"

After a suitable period of time, he started getting the close calls again, but he remembered never to swear around him.

Umpire Dolly Stark quit umpiring and became a radio announcer. He interviewed Babe in Pittsburgh, and after the show Babe asked him why he had quit.

"You guys were always getting on me," he said.

"I never argued with you when you called me out," Babe reminded him.

"I know it, but I just didn't like the feeling," Stark said.

The Robins made an important acquisition, and one that would be extremely crucial, both positively and negatively, later in Herman's career, when they picked up Max Carey from Pittsburgh on waivers. In the spirit of the zany season, on his first at-bat before the Ebbets Field crowd, Carey he fouled a ball off his foot and had to leave the game.

Max became available when Fred Clarke, a former Pirate manager, became vice-president of the club and insisted on sitting on the bench. Manager Bill McKechnie naturally resented the intrusion and the two clashed.

Carey, along with other players, asked the owner of the club to keep Clarke off the bench, but instead the owner released Babe Adams and Carson Bigbee and asked waivers on Carey, despite the fact he was captain of the Pirates.

Max appealed to Commissioner Landis but before an investigation could start, he was claimed by Brooklyn. He accepted their offer and dropped his actions.

The former Pirate, now 36 years old, was known as one of the greatest base-stealers of all time, leading the league ten times between 1913 and 1925. In 1922 he had stolen 51 bases and had been thrown out only twice.

Robinson believed that he would help Brooklyn and particularly Herman, who Robinson wanted to move permanently into the outfield. He did work with Babe in the ensuing years and helped him a great deal.

The first time he played in the same outfield with Herman, he knew he had a lot of work to do. Playing center field against the Pirates, Carey waived Herman in a number of steps when Sparky Adams came to bat.

After Adams was retired, Paul Waner came to the plate and Carey was horrified to see that Herman didn't move from his shallow position.

Carey shouted at him to move up but before he could get his attention Waner cracked the first pitch on a sharp line to right field and Herman didn't have to move a step to make the catch, robbing him of a certain hit.

Waner cursed his luck and when the inning was over, Carey spoke to Babe about playing him out of position.

"What are you so hot about? I caught it didn't I?" Herman asked.

Carey said, "Yes, but you'll not get many that way and you might be killed."

Robin players constantly complained about the condition of the playing field in Brooklyn. Reporters blamed some of the team's fielding problems on the infield and outfield. Even Max Carey, an excellent outfielder, looked terrible on a ball that was hit to center field. It took a right-angle bounce and skipped by him. Later shortstop Johnny Butler was hit squarely on the chin by an erratic hop.

Herman's average slipped to .329 as August ended and a slight muscle pull sidelined him for a time.

Sitting on the edge of the dugout in Pittsburgh during a game, a drive was smashed into the left field corner of Forbes Field and outfielder Gus Felix chased it as it bounced around wildly out of sight to most in the dugout.

Robinson turned to Herman and asked, "What happened? Why did it take so long for Felix to get that ball?"

Babe said, "I don't know, Robbie, I was reading the sports page."

The story was gleefully written just that way in each of the New York papers but later Jigger Statz, who was also on the Robin bench that afternoon, told reporters, "Babe saw the play all right, but when Robbie asked, he didn't want to put the knock on old Gus." Then he added, "Robbie should have never asked him anyway."

On September 8th, Cy Williams slugged a grand slam homer in the last of the ninth to beat Brooklyn 8-4. Heinie Sand, who was on first base when the ball was hit out of the park, trotted directly to the Phillie clubhouse. Visions of the 'Merkle Boner' that decided the National League pennant in 1908 flashed through the minds of many members of the press, but no one on the field noticed as the winning run crossed the plate.

The Robins purchased the contract of Moose Claybaugh, who had clouted a remarkable 62 home runs during 120 East-Texas League games. Newsmen credited him with having said, as he stepped out into Ebbets Field for the first time, "Which is the right field wall in this park?"

In batting practice he hit seven balls out of the park. On his first official time at bat, he took the first pitch for a strike, then took a ball, a ball, a strike and another ball, running the count to 3-2. He then swung and smoked a shot directly into the hands of Bill Terry at first base who stepped on the bag and turned it into a double play.

All eyes had followed the streaking ball into Terry's glove at first base and when they swung back to Claybaugh, he was still standing at the plate holding only the last six inches of the shattered bat handle in his hands.

Claybaugh also participated in one of the most prolific pinch-hitting streaks in baseball history later in the season.

The Robins trailed 6-3 into the ninth at Philadelphia when Butler doubled and Dick Cox knocked him in with a single. It was the fourth straight pinch-hit for the Robins in the game as pinch-hitters Zach Wheat, Jake Fournier and Jerry Standaert had singled in the seventh.

Claybaugh then hit a screaming drive off the clock on the distant center field wall, smashing the glass and knocking both hands loose, causing them to drop straight down.

Jacobson singled for two runs and Carey and Felix walked to load the bases, then Herman's single scored two and put the Robins in front 8-6. Cox, up for the second time, singled again for another RBI and DeBerry doubled in two, the eighth and ninth runs of the inning. Claybaugh, also up for the second time, popped out. The Robins had received six pinch hits from five pinch-hitters in succession.

The smash to center that stopped the clock was the only hit Claybaugh could manage in 14 times at bat for Brooklyn during his short, 11-game Robin career, but it was one that players talked about for weeks.

That was the high point of the final month, and the Robins again finished the season in sixth place 17 1/2 games out of first. The club was eighth in hitting, seventh in fielding and had led the league both in errors and in being shutout.

Herman led the Robins with a .313 average and 81 runs batted in. He had been hitting .377 and leading the league on July 7 when he was injured and probably suffered a cracked bone in his thumb. From that point to the end of the season he hit only .268. Despite that, he had 15 game-winning runs batted in, eight more than his closest rival on the team, although he only had three after the month of July.

He hit .442 in Boston and completely endeared himself to the Brooklyn fans with a .441 mark in the Polo Grounds. He blasted Pittsburgh pitching for a .452 average in Brooklyn but overall hit eight points better on the road, .323 to .315.

Brooklyn won only 13 of 37 games in which Herman was held hitless. The team was 46-51 when he collected one or more hits.

Herman made 14 errors at first base in 100 games, last among players with 100 games or more, but fared a bit better in the outfield, recording only three errors in 36 games.

Brooklyn writers noted that when he was hitting, base hits rained off his bat but when he was in a slump, he seemed helpless. They reported that his failure to hit seemed to hurt his fielding and speculated that in 1927 Fournier, Del Bissonette or Claybaugh would press him for his job.

On the final day of the season, Vance fanned 15 to win 3-1 in the first game of a final double-header. Jesse Petty received a Hudson coach from admirers before the second game and the club made it a sweep, winning 6-2.

Herman, Grimes, Wheat, Butler and Claybaugh were excused after the first game to catch a train west. Herman and Butler went on a fishing trip and then played on the Santa Monica team in the California Winter League.

Babe Ruth, with the help of a newsman from each of the league's cities, selected an All-American team for 1926 and placed Herman at first base.

He was picked in preference to a number of other fine first basemen, four of which are in the Hall of Fame, including Lou Gehrig, George Sisler, Jim Bottomly and George Kelly.

Herman was also selected as the National League All-Star first baseman by the Base Ball Writers Association of America.

Fournier was released in November and signed later with the Braves. He left with many kind words for Herman. Zach Wheat was released New Year's eve and signed to play with the Philadelphia Athletics along side Ty Cobb, Al Simmons, Eddie Collins, Jimmy Foxx, Mickey Cochrane and Lefty Grove, allowing A's fans to watch eight eventual Hall of Famers on the same team during the 1927 season.

Part-time scout Nap Rucker recommended Paul Richards, a Wexahatchie, Texas, high school phenom. Richards had made Ripley's 'Believe It or Not' when he pitched and won a double-header at age 16. Not only that, he pitched the first game right-handed and the second game left-handed.

The youngster declined a Brooklyn contract until he had graduated from high school and the Robins sent him to Crisfield in the Eastern Shore League on a loan basis, semi-legal even then. When commissioner Kennesaw Mountain Landis presided at the draft meeting that fall, the St. Louis Browns promptly drafted him.

Robinson jumped to his feet and violently protested. "They can't draft him," he shouted.

"Why not?" asked Landis.

"Because we have him covered up," the red-faced Robinson sputtered.

The resulting laugh even drew a smile to Landis' stern face.

He was repurchased by Brooklyn in 1930 and played briefly for the Dodgers in 1932. He later became well known as a manager and general manager.

At the annual Baseball Writers Association banquet, the membership poked fun at Brooklyn's reputation for harboring aged athletes, as well as the lame and the halt. The skit showed the famous Casey who struck out in 1884, played by a man with a long white beard who looked 70, being brought to task by an actor representing Judge Landis. Casey was suspended for a year, then sentenced to play in Brooklyn the rest of his life.

Dropping to his knees, he pleaded, "Not Brooklyn, Judge, I'm too young to join that club." Everyone roared but Robinson, who said gruffly, "It's not quite that bad."

Babe played in the movie "Slide Kelly, Slide" that fall, doubling for Tris Speaker in center field. As the light started to fail he moved to left field to film the throws to the plate and finally moved to right field to complete the scene. He also 'played' Cardinal first baseman Jim Bottomly in the World Series scenes.

But more important than the movie, Babe returned to earn his high school diploma. He had left Glendale High without graduating when he started his professional career in 1922.

He spent the winter months completing the courses he missed and when the school board reviewed his work they expressed themselves unanimously as being pleased with both his attitude and hard work.

A telegram was sent to the Robins training camp at Clearwater, in the spring of 1927, informing him that he had been granted his diploma.

Chapter 3

Flying in the face of the writers skit about ageing ballplayers, Brooklyn added Max Carey (37), "Spittin' Bill" Doak (36), Irish Meusel (34), Butch Henline (32), Jigger Statz (29) and Harvey Hendrick (29) to the 1927 roster.

They also traded Burleigh Grimes. The last of the 1920 champions, who had won 158 games in Brooklyn, would go on to win another 112 games for various other clubs, eventually reaching the Hall of Fame.

In a three-way trade, the Robins received catcher Butch Henline from the Phillies, a deal that turned out to be one of the worst trades in Brooklyn history. Grimes was quickly shipped from Philadelphia to the Giants where he won 19 and lost 8 while Henline, relegated to the backup catching spot, hit .266.

Grimes was a no-nonsense pitcher, and became involved in a dispute with Robinson in 1925 which eventually led to his trade.

Grimes pinch-hit in the ninth inning with the Robins trailing Cincinnati by a run and singled. He advanced to third but held up on a medium fly to Elmer Smith, the Reds' right fielder. The next hitter popped out to leave Grimes stranded and Brooklyn lost.

Robinson was furious, screaming at Grimes in the clubhouse for his 'dumb' baserunning. "Everyone in the league knows that Smith can't throw," screamed Robbie. "Everyone but you, you $#@%%$ knucklehead."

Grimes fired back "I'm a pitcher. You use me as a pinch-hitter and I get a hit for you, and now you are trying to excuse yourself. If you weren't such a %*&##@ fathead, you'd have put in a runner at third for me." The argument lasted an hour and the split never completely healed between the tough pitcher and manager Robinson.

One day when Charlie Hargreaves was catching Grimes, someone hit a long home run off a pitch that Grimes hadn't wanted to throw. Complaining about it in the dugout, he was overheard by Hargreaves who asked, "Why didn't you shake off the sign?"

"I thought you knew what you were doing," snapped Grimes.

"Hell, you don't have anything on the ball anyway," Hargreaves told him, "I'll catch you without signs the rest of the game and you can throw what you want."

Grimes normally threw mostly fastballs and 'nickle' curves (the forerunner of the slider) early in his games but after the sixth inning, he'd say, "Get me a one-run lead and we're in." Then he went to his spitter, throwing it nearly every pitch.

Herman and his roomate Johnny Butler had traveled to Florida together. Herman was given the first base job immediately. He received a raise from $6500 to $8500, even then not much for a major league salary.

Burleigh Grimes

The club was prepared to train at Homosassa, Florida where manager Robinson and Dazzy Vance owned real estate, but at the last minute the deal fell through and the team returned to Clearwater where they had trained since 1922. The city had made some improvements and the new field at Clearwater was, in the opinion of many on the team, in better playing condition than Ebbets Field.

Robinson, on the urging of Max Carey, scheduled two workouts a day, a complete departure from his usual 'gentle' training camps. He usually scheduled an intrasquad game the first day.

Herman's teeth were bothering him, and he had them x-rayed before leaving for camp. They found abscesses but he decided to get by until after the season, a poor decision as it would turn out.

Before the regulars arrived, Robinson divided the pitchers into two teams and played an intrasquad game. Watty Clark led the winning team with a home run and Nap Rucker, pressed into service due to short numbers, singled three times. Jesse Barnes banged out four hits and made three great catches, then announced he would work out with the outfielders when the actual camp opened.

Robinson had built the first batting cage at the Clearwater camp in 1926 and after the regulars arrived on March 6, it was put to constant use.

Tom Rice of The Sporting News sent a dismal report on the early camp. "The Brooklyn infield, on the whole, offers a discouraging future for the team. At the present time, Partridge is the only player who it appears can both field and hit."

The first exhibition contest was against the University of Florida. The college kids were pretty good, having nearly defeated St. Louis a few days earlier. Herman hit for the cycle, slamming a two-run home run in the first, a two-run triple in the second, then adding a double and a single later in the game, good for five runs batted in.

The Florida team's uniforms didn't arrive in time for the game and they borrowed an extra set from Brooklyn. The mayor of Clearwater threw out the first ball and in usual Brooklyn fashion they forgot to raise the flag in center field until the second inning.

In an early exhibition game, the Robins played Jacksonville, managed by Tommy McMillin who had played in Brooklyn in 1908. The Robins were trying to trade for the contracts of Buzz Arlett and Ray Blades, offering pitchers. With the departure of Wheat, Max Carey was made captain of the team but he was not hitting well.

It was rumored that Ty Cobb, who had resigned as Detroit manager, would be the new Brooklyn president but Robinson had already signed a new pact. Robinson claimed Cobb was offered $50,000 to play but had joined the Philadelphia Athletics instead.

Irish Meusel, 34, had been in continual conflict with John McGraw while on the Giants, so he purchased his contract for $1,500 and sold himself to the Robins. Locals were in agreement that he was the best-dressed player ever seen in Clearwater, probably setting a standard later for Hollis John Thurston, a Robin pitcher who was nicknamed "Sloppy" because of his impeccable dress. Teammates remembering him said he would look good in a gunny sack.

Herman was not hitting, and along with many other Robin players, was having fielding troubles. Tommy Holmes noted, "The Brooklyn infield becomes hysterical at the sight of a ground ball." Herman's two errors cost four unearned runs against Cleveland, and the following day he tripled, then misunderstanding the signals at third base, overran the bag, nearly bowling over coach Otto Miller. However, in the 12th inning, as the seventeen frozen fans in attendance huddled together to keep warm, Herman singled home the winning run for a 8-7 victory. He had also singled in the seventh to key a six-run inning that tied the game 6-6. The win was the first for the Robins after 15 straight spring training losses, stretching back to the Yankee series in 1926 when the Yankees

1927 BROOKLYN DODGER SQUAD included: Back row: Milt Stock, Jim Elliott, Dazzy Vance, Jesse Barnes, Butch Henline, Jesse Petty, Norman Plitt, Jerry Standaert and Guy Cantwell. Third row: Trainer Doc Hart, Mickey O'Neil, unknown, Chuck Corgan, Bob Barrett, Merwin Jacobson, Harvey Hendrick, Del Bissonette and Babe Herman. Second row: Chick Fewster, Oscar Roettger, unknown, Jay Partridge, Hank DeBerry, Otto Miller, Manager Wilbert Robinson, Nap Rucker, Max Carey, John Butler and Bob McGraw. Front row: Billy Rhiel, Bill Marriott, Jigger Statz, Charlie Hargreaves, Rube Ehrhardt, Irish Meusel, Gus Felix, Bill Doak and Doug McWeeney.

had crushed them in a dozen straight.

The Sporting News reported "Herman is a peculiar proposition. Mechanically he is the equal of any first baseman in the world, but he is erratic."

Oddly enough, the team was drawing better against minor league opposition than they did against the Yankees during the 1926 training tour. Babe slammed two doubles and a triple, his final hit knocking in the winning run in an 11-10 win over Atlanta.

The report from Florida noted, "Herman is hitting. He is fielding mechanically but has been making one bad play per day. He is an excellent hitter and except for the daily boot, is excellent in the field."

They finished the exhibition season with a 12-6 record, including a 4-4 mark against major league competition. Returning to Ebbets Field they lost to the Yankees 6-5 after Herman's single tied the game 5-5 in the seventh. Babe Ruth's three-run homer made the difference.

They also lost the second game of the series 4-3, with Herman's double knocking home the final run in a three-run Brooklyn rally in the eighth.

Dave Driscoll had been made the general overseer of Ebbets Field and had installed a new infield, much to the player's delight. "If only we had a major league scoreboard," one of them was heard to exclaim.

Before the opener in Boston, Robinson told reporters, "We'll raise plenty of hell in this pennant race before we're finished with it. Building an entirely new team after you're satisfied that a flock of veteran players have outlived their usefulness isn't the work of a day or a week or a season. Without trying to pin any roses on myself, you can quote me as satisfied with the results to date. The Yankee series should show why.

"My team wasn't licked until the last man was out in each of the New York games and although some of them are fresh from the minors and lack big league seasoning, you didn't see a single one rattled on the field either day.

"I'm not counting on the pennant. That would be foolish with the team very much in the experimental stage. But on the other hand, I'm not counting us entirely out.

"I've got good pitchers. I could stand a little more batting punch, but I have some real hitters in Babe Herman and Harvey Hendrick. Herman may have an occasional bad day in the field, but when he is hitting, he is indispensable to the club.

"The experts have counted us out in the pennant race. Well, they counted us out in 1916 and 1920. I'm not predicting a pennant, but you can paste this in your hat: We'll be there."

The Brooklyn team would have few familiar faces from the 1926 starting lineup in the 1927 opener. Jess Petty would again be the opening day pitcher, John Butler would play short, Gus Felix would man the left field post and DeBerry, Hargreaves and Henline would again share the catching.

Jay Partridge was the new second baseman, Bob Barrett took over at third and Carey and Jigger Statz joined Felix in the outfield. Hendrick would be tried at three different positions in an attempt to get his bat into the lineup on a steady basis.

The new additions deservedly did little to change the opinions of the odds makers. Brooklyn opened as a 30-1 long shot, improved to 20-1 and then 15-1 just before the season opener. New York was a 9-5 favorite to win the National League

In the opening game at Boston, Herman doubled down the right field line, went to third on a ground ball and scored as Butler dumped a perfect bunt in front of the plate. Petty pitched a complete game and the Robins went on to win 6-2. A number of baseball people said to themselves, "Maybe Robbie knows what he is talking about."

Dazzy Vance

But then the season turned sour. In the second Boston contest a line drive bounced off Carey's knee and rolled away for an inside the park home run. For some reason no error was charged. In the third game Herman dropped a pop and the runner, who was on third after Carey had misplayed an easy fly into a double, scored. And later in the game a long shot to right field rebounded off the wall and hit Hendrick in the head, the play being scored as a double.

The Boston series set the tone for the first month, with Brooklyn losing seven in succession before winning the home opener 4-3. Herman had singled Hendrick home with the winning run in the sixth.

Earlier, in the 'unofficial' home opener, Bill Doak made his first start since 1924, but five errors cost him a 7-2 decision. The club had made 22 errors in their first nine games, losing eight of them.

On April 21st in a scoreless game the club must have convulsed the fans with a Keystone Kops routine: Herman fielded a bunt but no one covered first. Babe threw to second baseman Jay Partridge who missed the ball and it rolled into right field. Hendrick rushed in, fell down and the ball rolled through him to the fence. Later in the same inning Doak fell down fielding a bunt and the third run of the inning crossed the plate. In his final at bat, Herman smashed a shot off the Boston pitcher's chest, knocking him backwards off the mound. He scrambled to his feet and threw Babe out at first to complete the remarkable afternoon.

In an attempt to shore up the shaky infield, the Robins sent pitcher Bob McGraw to St. Louis for shortstop D'Arcy (Jake) Flowers.

As the worst month in the clubs' history ground to a close the Robins had a 4-12 record, were last in hitting with a .199 average, last in fielding with a .952 percentage and dead last in the standings.

The Ebbets Field crowd that had welcomed Herman and his booming bat as a rookie in 1926, seemed to blame him for the terrible start the Robins had in April. They apparently expected more from Babe and when he was found to have feet of clay, reacted angrily.

Thinking this might be the perfect time, a potential buyer offered $3 million for the Brooklyn club but club president Steve McKeever said no. At the same time, an offer to the Ebbets heirs of $1.2 million for their half of the stock was turned down.

The Robins won four straight from the Giants early in May. A raucous crowd of 32,000 jammed into Ebbets Field on May 1st, with another 5,000 milling around outside. Herman singled to start a two-run ninth inning rally that won the first game of the series 4-3.

Switching to the Polo Grounds, Herman smashed a pair of homers good for five runs batted in to win the second game. The first nearly cleared the left-field grandstand and the second was belted into the upper deck in left as the Robins won 10-7.

Jesse Barnes beat his brother Virgil 7-6 in the third game after Brooklyn spotted the Giants a 5-0 lead. Babe belted a triple and a homer but the Giants won 4-3. New York won the fifth game of the series 4-1 with Burleigh Grimes extracting an extra measure of revenge from his old boss Wilbert Robinson.

Brooklyn stopped St. Louis 3-0 the following day. In the fourth inning Jay Partridge homered, Herman singled and Flowers homered for the only hits and the only runs the Robins needed. Vance fanned 10 in the victory.

Babe slugs a long one to left in Ebbets Field

By the middle of the month, the club had struggled to an 11-15 record, but they made eight errors during two games with Chicago a few days later. Babe allowed two runs on a strong but errant throw to erase the effects of his two-homers.

The Ebbets Field Faithful nearly rioted when the Robins took a 9-2 lead into the top of the ninth against the Phillies, only to see them score nine times for an 11-9 decision.

Later in May Dazzy Vance won his 100th game for Brooklyn and recorded his 1,000th strikeout. Herman's 5-for-5 day led a 20-4 slaughter of the Phillies. The Robins finished the month 13-15 and edged out of the league cellar.

Herman's infected teeth started to affect his play. He was beginning to hear more boos and catcalls from the Ebbets Field crowd as his batting average dipped below .300. But Robinson and the local papers leaped to his defense.

"Herman is my best first baseman and one of my best hitters," Robinson said. "Babe will make those fans eat those boos."

The Brooklyn Eagle agreed: "Flatbush fans may have quit on

Herman but Robbie never will. And the manager is right this time.

"A great fielder and a great mechanical first baseman when he has both feet on the ground, Babe is entitled to a long and extensive trial on the strength of his batting average last year, if nothing else.

"The temperamental kid comes back into the lineup with a full realization of the fickleness of the fans who abruptly pulled away from him after his first bad days in Brooklyn. Sure, he hasn't been going too well, but who among the Robins has?

"Babe certainly did nothing to deserve the target of abuse he became over last week-end, and anybody who thinks he hasn't had a tough time handling the throws of a rubber-armed infield has another think coming.

"If Herman had the phlegmatic exterior of his predecessor, Jack Fournier, who hit like a fiend in the face of merciless and undeserved razzing, there would be nothing to worry about. But Herman is sensitive and the incessant howl of 'Hit it to Herman' isn't going to do his spirit any good.

"Be that as it may, let this young man have one good day, let two or three of his terrific line drives fall safe, and even a hostile crowd won't hold him back. We expect the time to come when the fans will pray that the opposition will "Hit one to Herman."

"Maybe we have an entirely wrong conception of things, but from what we have observed, sentiment at Ebbets Field appears to have reached the stage at which the fans absolutely gloat over each new defeat sustained by the Robins. The bitterness in the frequent Bronx cheer is obvious and seems to increase with each fresh reversal.

"The attitude toward Herman is a fair illustration. Babe is a great natural hitter. That statement goes if he never makes another base hit. He showed himself better than a mediocre first baseman through two thirds of last year's campaign. This spring he has been unsteady. What 23-year-old first baseman wouldn't be unsteady?

"He is in there trying. He hasn't been getting the breaks. He socked one of the hardest balls we ever saw at Ebbets Field the other day. It was a line drive over the right field wall and over the gasoline station on the other side of Bedford Avenue; foul by a few feet. He had to try again and was retired and the casual spectator might have thought Babe guilty of setting fire to an orphanage from the storms of disapproval that greeted his return to the bench.

"Herman's daily reception is only a slightly exaggerated example of the attitude toward the whole team. Thick, flying raspberries certainly won't get anything. Encouragement might help," the writer concluded.

Ironically, the article hit the street on "Boost Brooklyn Day," when the Robins and Phillies were at Borough Hall for a reception complete with speeches, bands and milling fans.

Late in May, Robinson heard a knock at the door of his home and when he opened it a stranger was standing there with the blackest cat Robbie had ever seen.

"Mr. Robinson, here is something to break the jinx. I found it outside," he said.

"Black cats are bad luck," Robbie growled.

"Sometimes," the stranger admitted, "but they say it takes a thief to catch a thief, and maybe it takes a jinx to break a jinx."

Robinson accepted the animal and when he carried it into the club house the next day, the reaction was about the same as his had been when the cat suddenly appeared off the street.

Max Carey shouted, "Boss, are you crazy? Don't you know a black cat is a jinx and we want to win a game again sometime?"

Robinson repeated what the stranger had said and added, "Anyway, this cat is going to get a three-day trial. And you're going to treat him right in the meantime." Then he looked down at the cat and said, "But if you don't show some quick results, I won't answer for any of your nine lives."

The cat was nicknamed "Victory" and he examined the club house from top to bottom while the team dressed. Watty Clark fixed a bed for him in a box and sent the clubhouse attendant Babe Hamberger out for a pint of milk.

As Jim Elliott walked past, Clark said, "Here, pat him on the head for luck." Elliott picked him up and stroked his fur. In his huge hands the cat was barely visible.

Then he went out and pitched a 5-2 win over the Giants. "Victory" and the Robins took four in a row from the Braves. In the final game, Herman also made up with the good-luck charm because he slammed a home run so hard into the right field bleachers it bounced off the seats and back onto the field. The shot came in the first inning with two teammates on base and was only the fifth home run hit into the distant Boston stands in 12 years. And it was one of only two that were hit in the park during 1927. The left field foul line was 402 feet in the huge park, deepest center was 550 and the right field foul pole was set at 365.

By the middle of June, Harvey Hendrick had hit in 18 straight games but was benched for 'poor fielding.' Five days later rookie outfielder Overton Tremper banged a home run on his first major league time at bat to help Vance win 2-1.

Herman had an eight game hitting streak during the final days of June, but his teeth were bothering him so badly he took time off in early July and had them pulled. He was hitting .314 at the end of May but he hit only .233 in June and .196 in July, and his average dipped to .269. After the offending teeth were pulled and the poison from his infected teeth slowly worked its way out of his system, his average slowly picked up and he hit in 10 of his final 11 games in September.

Still the object of the hostile Brooklyn crowd, Herman also seemed victimized by the scorers who seemed to overlook a ball bouncing off the knee of an acknowledged good fielder but who awarded Babe an 'e' on nearly every occasion.

In late July, with Cincinnati's Chuck Dressen on second and one out, a ball was hit to Herman at first. He checked Dressen and saw he was close to third so he turned and threw to his pitcher covering first. For some reason the pitcher was standing on the base, facing the stands, and Babe's throw hit him in the small of the back. Error, Herman.

Babe had been benched as his average plummeted and now the local papers seemed to take a different tack when analyzing him. They wrote: "The future of the benched Babe Herman is problematical. It depends more on the blond kid himself than Harvey Hendrick. Babe had the natural ability to become one of the greatest ballplayers who ever lived, but it's doubtful he'll ever be able to get it out of his system.

"He doesn't seem to have a big-league temperament. Nobody around can drive a ball further than the gangling Californian, save perhaps Ruth and Gehrig. That doesn't sum up Herman's hitting talent. His powerful, natural swing is supplemented by a good eye, but also by bad judgement. He simply cannot seem to refrain from swinging at wild pitches. And any pitcher would be a sap to cut the plate with a ball when he feels that a powerful and dangerous slugger will take a riffle at anything.

"He can move gracefully around first base, has a good pair of hands and should be able to play a high-grade fielding game at all times. There is little excuse for those fumbled grounders of the past month. Nonchalance and grace are all right in their place, but the way to get ground balls is to get in front of them and grab with both claws. Herman's boots have been due to the fact that he hasn't been set for the plays. Perhaps Hal Chase could get grounders consistently while standing on one foot, but Chase was Chase."

On the other hand, Herman received this critique later in the month. "The erratic blond didn't figure in the scoring, but he hit a triple and a single and reached base four times in four innings. And he also turned a fielding gem that saved the jolly ballgame.

"It came on a bunt of Harper's in the ninth. The bunt down the third-base line was a perfect specimen, and Bobby Barrett, plunging in, was rushed into a bad throw. It pulled Babe off the bag four or five feet. Whirling like a top, he snared the ball in the web of his mitt and tagged Harper as he went speeding by.

"Had the ball got by Herman, Terry would have scored the tying run from second and Jacobson might have scored from first. In the clubhouse after the game, more than one player ventured the opinion that Babe is the only first baseman who could make that play."

In late July Tom Rice wrote in The Sporting News: "Herman's two errors cost the Robins a 5-4 game to the Phillies. Henline had a passed ball and an error, but they were treated as misdemeanors, while

Herman's were considered felonies by the fans."

And as Babe was benched for a time in favor of Hendrick, the Brooklyn Eagle said, "Herman was benched and Hendrick took over first base. Hendrick is never as good as Herman at his best, never as bad as Herman at his worst." Then the paper added "The unfortunate Herman has been the subject of exceptionally harsh attacks in Brooklyn newspapers, and he is too young not to be disturbed by them. Normally the Brooklyn and New York writers are most amiable, but they have taken many severe wallops at Herman recently. Sometimes such criticism makes a player, but more often it breaks him."

On a blistering day in July the Robins were battling the Pirates in Pittsburgh. Veteran pitcher 'Spittin' Bill' Doak was going well for Brooklyn despite the humid afternoon.

Doak was an excellent pitcher for the Cardinals, and after the Robins made a deal for him in 1925 he did not report, deciding instead to stay in Florida and operate a lucrative real estate agency. He also sat out the 1926 season but when Florida land prices dropped in Florida, he made a comeback in 1927.

In 1923 the Robins had a pitcher by the name of Leo Dickerman, who was tagged, "The greatest pitcher who never made good in the majors." After losing his first game 2-1, he won his next five starts, and sitting by Burleigh Grimes in the dugout asked, "How many games do you expect to win this year?"

Grimes, without turning from the action on the field, said, "About 15."

Dickerman looked shocked. "What? I expect to win 25."

Grimes just smiled.

Dickerman lost 11 of his next 14 and finished the season 8-12. It was said his fastball would hop eight inches and his curve would break sharply down—but only in batting practice. In a game they were both straight as a string.

After the 1924 season the Robins traded Dickerman to the Cardinals for Doak. And after a 4-11 record in 1925 'Spittin' Bill' dropped out of the majors, only to return in 1927.

Each inning that sweltering afternoon in Forbes Field, Doak would come into the dugout, lean over and put his hands into a bucket of ice water to cool off.

The afternoon wore on, and Bill got hotter and hotter. In the sixth he came into the dugout with his face a fiery red. He put his hands into the water and passed out, his head going right into the bucket of ice water.

"Hey," Carey yelled, "There goes old Bill!"

His teammates ran over and pulled him out of the bucket before he drowned and slapped him around a bit until he came to. He was ready to go the next inning and finished his win.

Herman didn't play much in late July or early August, and when he did get in he found things hadn't changed much. In the Polo Grounds the Giants won a game when Herman 'allowed' a run to score when Butler bounced a throw to him from third and Babe could not hold it. The scoring was predictable—error: Herman.

At the same time, Hendrick returned from a Western swing with a .429 average during the 15 games.

Used mostly as a pinch-hitter, Herman made up for the errors, the bogus-errors and the wrath of the fans as best he could with a bat that still had considerable pop in it. In Chicago, trailing the Cubs 5-2 in the eighth inning, Babe was called to hit for Hank DeBerry and slammed a long shot over the right field wall to tie the game. John Drebinger wrote: "The ball cleared the right field wall and all the housetops in sight." The Robins won 6-5 when Barrett singled in a run in the ninth.

Babe also clouted a three-run double in the seventh in Pittsburgh to tie the game 7-7 but the Robins lost 10-7 as the season wound down to September.

Early in the month, Max Carey had hit an inside the park homer with the bases loaded and Brooklyn Eagle reporter Tommy Holmes noted it was "sort of a baseball grand-slam," coining a phrase that is still popular.

Robinson said he would leave the team to scout the Pacific Coast League. Then he decided to check out only the Kansas City club, and finally cancelled the idea entirely, reporting simply that it was "too hot." Then he added, "And there is probably no one out there that could help us anyway."

However, he did send a coach to Memphis to look at a hard-hitting left handed outfielder and shortly thereafter the Dodgers signed Johnny Frederick.

Robinson and John McGraw were still feuding. The two had split up after a misunderstanding in the 1913 World Series. Now, some 14 years later, the two were still going at each other. Robinson charged that McGraw was claiming all the players he put on waivers, effectively killing any chances of making a trade with any other major or minor league team. Options had been asked on Flowers, Felix, and Herman, and McGraw had refused to waive. Robinson claimed they were only 'feelers' for trade purposes and withdrew all the names.

And after losing 23 of 33 games, Robbie also announced,"I have stopped worrying about the 1927 team and I am now worrying about next year's team. I've had my scouts chasing all over the bush and they tell me there are fewer good-looking prospects in the minor leagues than ever before."

The Eagle reported that it was officially the opening of the "looking ahead to next year" period, probably the forerunner of the hallowed, "Wait Til Next Year" that was to be so popular in later years.

Herman got some playing time in September, and with his system starting to clear, his bat awakened again. He doubled and homered against the Phils and added another homer over the center field wall into Broad Street the next day. Former teammate Zach Wheat and some of his Philadelphia Athletic teammates were on hand for the game.

"Kinda looks loose and easy up there, doesn't he?" commented A's pitcher Sammy Gray.

"Yes, sir," replied Wheat. "And don't think he can't hit that old pill. That kid will drive the ball as far as Ruth or any of them. He may be an in-and-outer, but he's certainly a dangerous boy at that plate. And when he cuts, he cuts and slights nobody."

Moving to St. Louis, he boomed a two-run homer in the ninth for a 6-5 lead only to have the Cardinals win 8-6 in the 10th.

On the team's final 18-game road trip he collected 25 hits good for an astounding 54 bases, adding 10 doubles, four triple and four homers to his season total. The Robins took some satisfaction by knocking the Cubs out of first place in Chicago while drawing 115,000 fans for the four-game series.

Herman hit .313 in September and added a big double in a 10-5 victory over the Giants late in the month as Brooklyn also knocked them out of the pennant race. Babe finished the season with a .272 average and despite his problems, led the team in home runs with 14 (the team only hit 39) and in runs batted in with 73.

Brooklyn won only 10 of 39 games in which Herman was hitless. And despite his off year they recorded a 52-49 mark when he banged out one hit or more.

Late in the season, Steve McKeever blasted Robinson for the sad state of Robin affairs. He was critical of the release of Taylor, Brown, High, Fournier and Wheat and said he did not encourage young players enough when they made mistakes. He had received a number of letters demanding a new manager and he was in complete agreement with the writers' feelings.

The Brooklyn team finished sixth again, 28 1/2 games behind Pittsburgh, despite a league-leading 3.36 team ERA. Vance (3rd), Petty (5th) and Jim Elliott (10th) all finished in the top ten on the N.L. earned run average chart.

The Robins were last in hitting and, excluding Hendrick who was used at several positions on the field in an attempt to get his bat in the lineup without completely destroying the defense, the outfielders hit only four home runs, two by long-since released Irish Meusel.

According to Robinson, as in the Ty Cobb case, Brooklyn missed signing Tris Speaker by less than an hour as the Philadelphia Athletics beat them to the punch. Speaker had been cut by Cleveland and New York wags noted that he was now probably "old enough for the Brooklyn team." As with Cobb, many doubted that the Brooklyn club even made an offer.

Dazzy Vance and 'Uncle' Robbie

Looking for outfield strength, the Robins offered any two on the roster, save Vance and Petty, for Kiki Cuyler of the Cubs but were turned down. Petty had won 13 and lost 18, and in his 18 losses he was supported with one run or less 11 times. He was shutout six times and in one stretch had gone 42 innings without a run being scored for him. As he finished the season he received only seven runs in his final 11 starts.

One Brooklyn paper noted that Herman and Flowers would probably be retained. "Uncle Robbie has never lost faith in Herman, who, at times, looks like the greatest natural hitter in the racket," they noted.

But no one counted on Herman to regain his starting position in 1928. Robbie, in town for the N.L. meetings, told reporters of his proposed 1928 lineup that included Bissonette at first and Hendrick in left. No mention was made of Herman, the one-time fan favorite.

Robinson traded Gus Felix and Bob Barrett to Buffalo for Ty Tyson and traded one-time 'franchise' Johnny Butler to Chicago for Eddie Pick, then sent Pick to Milwaukee for Harry Riconda, but could come up with no other trades to strengthen the second-division club.

Team officials determined to keep player salaries a secret as negotiations began. In the spring of 1925 they had signed Vance for three years at $47,500. They had given Grimes and Wheat two-year, $15,000 contracts and Fournier one for $12,500. Ebbets thought publication of the salaries were good advertising, but when the club fell deep into the second division in 1925, the fans were up in arms that such high salaries resulted in such a low finish.

Robbie also noted they would offer no more long-range contracts, saying "When a player signs a long-term contract, funny things happen to him like chilblains, eczema, neuritis and dandruff."

Even Captain Max Carey had his $18,000 salary slashed.

Chapter 4

The battle that paralyzed the Brooklyn front office is a blood-red vein that throbs through the history of the club from 1925 to 1938. The tumultuous conflict was unlike any other in the history of baseball and it stunted the development of the Brooklyn team throughout the period.

The problem didn't come about overnight, but slowly ate its way into the front office and then spilled over onto the field. It started with the death of Charles Hercules Ebbets in 1925 and continued until the arrival of the volatile Larry MacPhail in 1938.

Charlie Ebbets joined the Brooklyn club when it became a member of the Interstate League in 1883. He started as a ticket seller, sold scorecards, worked with the books and quickly became a general handy man, taking care of all the little details that others didn't want to handle.

The club moved into the American Association in 1884. During this period of time the club was called 'Trolly Dodgers' by the press, a name also applied to the residents of Brooklyn because of the dangerous vehicles that careened around the streets.

In 1889 the name was changed to 'Bridegrooms' in deference to the six newly married players on the club. But the name only lasted for a short time and the club was again dubbed the 'Dodgers.'

They played in Washington Park, located between Fourth and Fifth Avenues and extending from Third to Fifth Streets in Brooklyn. It was so named because George Washington had fought the battle of Long Island in that general area.

Brooklyn won the pennant in the American Association in 1889 and in the fall of that year they moved to the National League, playing there for the first time in 1890. After the season George Chauncey, who had joined the front office after the fall of the Player's League, offered

Ebbets a block of stock in the company.

"It isn't because I am fond of you," he told Ebbets, "although I am. But I know that if you own stock in this baseball team you will work even harder. And that will improve my investment in the club, too."

Ebbets was made club secretary in 1896 and in the spring of 1898, when one of the three original owners of the Brooklyn franchise died, Ebbets was made club president although he was but a minor stockholder.

Little by little Ebbets purchased stock in the club until he owned it all. Then in 1908 he started planning a new field to replace Washington Park and construction began in 1912 but Ebbets ran short of money.

In August Ebbets persuaded his friends, Ed and Steve McKeever, to go into partnership with him. He turned over 50 percent of the stock in the club and they provided the necessary money to complete construction of the park to be known as Ebbets Field.

Charles H. Ebbets

Two corporations were formed, with one owning the park and land, and the other owning the baseball franchise. Ed McKeever was the president of the first, Ebbets president of the latter.

The McKeevers were the sons of a shoe maker. They became contractors and builders, operated plants and factories and were the suppliers of crushed rock for the New York Central Railroad for tracks between New York and Buffalo.

Ed was the younger by four years and although very quiet was a solid baseball man. Steve, formerly in politics, was friendly and looked the part of a politician with jet-black derby, gold watch chain and diamond stickpins and cufflinks. Steve, enjoyed the team and along with his daughter, Dearie, took many road trips with the club.

Steve McKeever and Ebbets would sit on a high bench at the back of the stands in Ebbets Field and greet all the regular fans as they filed in and out of the park. If the team won the pair would accept the congratulations of the fans, if the club lost, they would engage in hot arguments, defending the players and themselves. As these scenes developed, Ed McKeever would quietly slip away.

Shortly after returning from spring training in the spring of 1925, Charlie Ebbets died. The National League cancelled all games on the following Tuesday and most of the owners came to New York for the funeral.

A steady, cold rain fell during the services at Greenwood Cemetery. When the funeral cortege arrived at the family plot, it was discovered that Ebbets' outsized casket would not fit and the grave had to be enlarged. The mourners stood huddled in the rain for almost two hours.

Ed McKeever succeeded Ebbets as president of the club. But he was soaked and thoroughly chilled during the wait at the cemetery and quickly came down with pneumonia. The Brooklyn club, barely over the death of Ebbets, received a second shock when he died eight days later.

Wilbert Robinson had been the catcher and captain of the old Baltimore Orioles. He was also a coach for friend and long-time Giant manager John McGraw but the two had a falling out after the 1913 World Series and Robinson had been signed as Brooklyn manager in 1914, replacing Bill Dahlen.

Tipping the scales at almost 300 pounds, he was very popular in the New York area and had an almost magical touch with castoff pitchers, which was fortunate because the Brooklyn team could rarely afford young pitchers.

He was affectionately called 'Uncle Robbie' or just 'Robbie' and he would stand outside the park after games and vigorously defend his strategy with fans who had opinions that differed with his.

After the deaths of Ebbets and McKeever, no one is sure just who suggested Robinson as president of the club, but everyone seemed to agree. He was the symbol of the Brooklyn Baseball Club and would have been a unanimous choice of the fans, had they had been allowed to vote.

Later Tom Rice of the Brooklyn Eagle wrote, "This was a perfect example that the common sense of the common people is a common fallacy."

Not everyone agreed with his signing at the time. Steve McKeever was unhappy that he had not been considered for the presidency by the Ebbets heirs and although he put the decision behind him, his displeasure would show again very soon.

Looking back, the choice of Robinson was obviously not a wise one. For although he was at home on the baseball field, he was not suited for executive duties. He would come to realize that later but he tried hard from the start.

Steve McKeever originally threw his support behind Robinson and in a speech in the spring of 1925 said, "Robinson will be the president as long as he (McKeever) had anything to do with it."

Robinson's first move was to appoint Zach Wheat as 'acting manager,' but he couldn't keep his hands off the action on the field and when the club hit a slump he came back into the dugout, "for just a few days."

His presence was disruptive for the players and Wheat never got the club back. The team that finished just 1 1/2 games out of first in 1924 was badly confused and pulled themselves into a tie for sixth by winning on the final day of the 1925 season.

As luck would have it, if they had lost that final game they would have finished in last place and as such, would have had the first choice in the minor league draft. The Cubs finished 8th and gleefully picked Hack Wilson who had been left unprotected by the Giants.

Just days later Brooklyn nearly purchased Paul Waner from the Pacific Coast League but since Robinson had to check with the board of directors, and approval came too late, Pittsburgh acquired him. Within a week the Brooklyn club had missed on two players that would have certainly changed the course of the franchise.

The feud between McKeever and Robinson started to simmer after their first season together came to a close.

Robinson wanted to re-sign Zach Wheat, but for less money than his 1925 contract had called for. However McKeever brushed aside Robinson's suggestion and said they would meet Wheat's terms for 1926.

The first crack had appeared in the Brooklyn front office.

The final and irrevocable rift between Wilbert Robinson and Steve McKeever came in the middle of the 1926 season.

Robinson's two best pitchers, Burleigh Grimes and Dazzy Vance, were unable to win with any consistency. However, Jess Petty was doing very well. And when Robinson asked Vance to go to the bullpen to help out, he refused, saying "I am a staring pitcher."

Joe Villa, sports editor and columnist of the New York Sun, a close friend of Robbies from his Baltimore years, wrote a column in which he pointed out the team's ace pitcher was treating his manager badly. And Feg Murray, the Sun's sports cartoonist, drew a picture of Petty and noted below it that Petty was winning while the higher-paid Grimes and Vance were losing. "How much is Petty getting?" he asked.

Robinson saw the cartoon and was furious. He called Murphy and asked why Vila was picking on him. Murphy pointed out that they were trying to needle Vance, not criticize Robinson. But Robinson would not be placated, and he called the managing editor, Keats Speed. "Maybe you want to know the #@$**&# batboys salary, too!" he screamed.

Speed tried to explain to Robinson that neither the column or the cartoon were pointed at the Brooklyn manager. "I share their opinion that Vance hasn't treated you fairly," he said.

"Your opinion? Why you..." Robinson shouted. "What the hell do you know about baseball?" and he launched a tirade that would curl the hair of the most tough-skinned umpire.

Speed, a good baseball man himself, hung up and in a few minutes called Villa. "We no long have any relations with the Brooklyn club," he told him. "We will continue to cover the team on the road and at home, but we will not travel with the team or stay in the same hotels.

"And I do not want Mr. Robinson's name to be mentioned again in this paper."

The next day a one-column box appeared on the sports page of the Sun and read, "The Bat Boy's Salary." The final paragraph of the story noted, "The Sun does not even care to know what Mr. Robinson's salary is."

That was the formal declaration of war and was, until Robinson was fired in 1931, the final time his name appeared in the paper.

Murphy followed the instructions and covered the team but did not come into contact with any of the players or the club officials. In his stories, when the manager was infrequently mentioned, Robinson was referred to as only "the manager," and it was never complimentary.

McKeever got his first wind of the incident when the Sun returned their press passes, and his anger flared not at the Sun, but at Robinson.

"You fool," he shouted at Robinson. "Why couldn't you have settled the thing with Murphy instead of getting Speed involved. Now you have the Sun down on us."

"The Sun be damned," Robinson shouted back. "And don't call me names."

"I'll call you what I want."

"No you won't and mind your own @#**&%! business."

"My own business," McKeever sputtered, "If this isn't my own business, what is?"

From that point the breach would never be healed.

Robinson's contract expired at the end of the 1926 season and he asked for three more years. McKeever countered by attempting to fire him.

But McKeever went into the hospital for a lengthy stay and his life hung in the balance. While he was there the directors gave Robinson another three-year contract with a salary of $25,000.

When Steve returned to work, the directors explained that it was necessary to re-hire Robinson so the business of the club could continue. "Three years weren't necessary," McKeever screamed. "You could have given him one year and I would have got him next year."

Robinson's next move was a bad one, trading Burleigh Grimes to the Phillies for catcher Butch Henline. He soon found the deal was a three-cornered one, the Phils moving Grimes to the hated Giants where he won 19 games the first season. He would also come back to haunt them again in 1930 as a St. Louis Cardinal.

In 1928 McKeever attempted to pay off the final year of Robinson's contract and throw him out, but by this time the directors had taken sides on the matter.

Joe Gilleaudeau represented the Ebbets heirs who held half the stock, club attorney Frank York voted the Ed McKeever estate and Steve McKeever had the final quarter of that stock. All processes were deadlocked by the 50-50 division of the board. McKeever attempted to purchase the Ebbets stock but would not match their asking price.

McKeever commanded the big office in the rear of the Ebbets Field grandstand and moved Robbie's office to one of the small rooms in the balcony. It was not long before Robinson conducted all his business out of the Hotel St. George to avoid confrontation with McKeever.

Board meetings were events of wonder and little business could be conducted with each side automatically opposed to whatever the other side advocated.

One Brooklyn writer headlined "Brooklyn policy like a Chinese puzzle." His editor asked "Isn't that being too rough?"

The reporter said, "You can't be too rough on that club." The editor replied, "Club, hell, I was talking about the Chinese."

McKeever was angry at Gilleaudeau for siding with Robinson and, remembering that he had been willed Charlie Ebbets wardrobe to do with as he saw fit, McKeever called him "Old Clothes." Gilleaudeau, countered by calling McKeever, "Dead Horses," recalling the days when the young McKeevers had contracted for the removal of dead horses from the streets of Brooklyn.

The Brooklyn Eagle reported, "Brooklyn will not have a winning team, not only under the present management but under the present ownership. The Ebbets-McKeever corporation, with its two factions, each with their own clashing sets of ideas, is the worst-conducted big business in the United States."

In 1929, when Robinson's three-year contract expired McKeever refused to get ill and staunchly fought for his dismissal. As usual an impasse was reached and it lasted all winter.

Robinson attended the winter meetings but officially was not a member of the Brooklyn club. League President John Hydler tried to settle the matter but had little success at first. However he finally got both sides to agree on a compromise that would allow Robinson a two-year contract as manager. Frank York was installed as president and Walter Carter added as a "neutral" member of the board, giving it five members so business could be conducted without the usual deadlock.

The two sides still battled; a court decision was necessary before the 1930 park expansion could be started, but all in all things went smoother, at least in public.

In 1931, when Robinson's contract again ran out, Carter sided with McKeever and they fired the Uncle Robbie after 18 years as manager of the club. Carter urged the club to sign Max Carey as manager and since he was nearly the exact opposite of Wilbert Robinson, his suggestion was readily approved. A few months later Carter resigned and was never seen at Ebbets Field again.

And in 1932 York walked out of the Brooklyn office to go to lunch and never came back. For a time the directors searched for him but he was not found.

Tommy Holmes, in his book "Dodger Daze and Knights," said York resigned owing the ball club a considerable amount of money, but by the time he died his insurance had discharged the debt. Holmes noted he was a colorless man and had avoided the risk of making unintelligent observations about the game by making no observations whatever. He seemed like a person who would like to please, but couldn't possibly imagine why people grew excited about baseball.

After a time McKeever finally got his wish and was elected president of the club. But, for the most part, the excitement was missing from Brooklyn baseball and with the fans staying away in great numbers, the club didn't have the money needed to improve.

Only when Larry MacPhail took over as club president in 1938, at the insistence of both the National League and the bank that held the club's large mortgage, did the team start to again become respectable.

Many felt that the turning point in the history of the Brooklyn club came in the rain at Greenwood Cemetery when Ed McKeever caught pneumonia as they laid Charlie Ebbets to rest.

Holmes later wrote of the Brooklyn club of that era, "The Dodgers have been spectacular or entertaining or both and often more confusing than amusing."

Chapter 5

Robin fans knew there was little chance for improvement in the 1928 season. They had won pennants in 1916 and 1920 and had led the league for many weeks in 1924 before tumbling out of the lead. Now, again in a presidential election year, they hoped against hope that things would again break their way.

But the bookies saw things more clearly, making the Robins a 30-1 shot for the pennant. Pittsburgh and St. Louis were installed as favorites.

Steve McKeever talked of enlarging Ebbets Field and the plan gained in popularity. Proposals were made to extend the left-field side of the field with double deck stands. The club hoped to build over Montgomery Street and give the city land beyond that to relocate the street. With this plan, seating would be increased from 23,000 to 47,000.

Babe had stopped smoking after the 1927 season, his system had cleared and when 1928 rolled around he was in great shape. Although he was usually not in favor of traveling to Florida just to work out, he didn't hold out this year, driving to Clearwater with his family. He arrived with the pitchers and catchers, signing a contract quickly.

The Robins added their first real farm club by purchasing part of the Macon, Georgia team. Arrangements were also made for a working agreement with Atlanta.

Brooklyn had looked at infielders Lyn Larry and Jimmy Reese but had decided not to purchase them because of their cost. As an indication of how the bankrolls of the Brooklyn and New York clubs compared, the Yankees bought them for $150,000 and then sent them to Oakland for further seasoning.

Herman reported with both a first baseman's mitt and his outfielder's glove but Thomas Rice was not convinced he could or would play much in the outfield. "Herman was born without instinct for gauging the course of a driven ball, and we never knew a man deficient in that instinct who could overcome the deficiency by hard work," he wrote.

On the opening day of spring camp, Robbie announced a lineup that included Del Bissonette, a 28-year-old rookie who had recorded great batting averages in the minor leagues, at first base and Harvey Hendrick, Ty Tyson and Jigger Statz as the outfielders. He didn't mention Herman at all.

Bissonette was a left-handed pitcher at Georgetown University and had signed with the Athletics. But while still in school his arm went dead. However he could hit and switched to first base to protect his weak throwing arm.

Buzz McWeeney was the batting practice pitcher the first afternoon and Herman fouled off the first ball, then drove the next over the right field wall. Tommy Holmes called it a "darb of a wallop."

Holmes also reported that the fielding of Dave Bancroft, picked up from Boston where he had been player-manager, had never been equalled in a Brooklyn uniform. The club got Bancroft free from Boston, well not exactly free since they had to pay his whopping $40,000 salary. He would be the highest paid player in the franchise until Jackie Robinson drew $42,000 in the late 1950's.

Herman homered off Vance in the opening day intrasquad game and threw out a runner at second base from left field. On the second day of work, Herman hit five out of the park in five trips to the plate during a practice game. He was then 6-for-6 as his squad beat the 'regulars' 22-12. And in the final intrasquad game he had three homers and a pair of singles off Petty, Ehrhardt and Clark, adding three brilliant catches in the outfield.

After such a spectacular demonstration, Robinson began to rethink his staring lineup.

Workouts opened at 10:30 in the morning and the players worked until 12:30 when they were off for the day. Later in the season the club would also have an afternoon workout.

Babe was ripping the ball to all corners of the park. Dazzy Vance was pitching batting practice one day and bounced a curve in front of the plate. Catcher Charlie Hargreaves said, "That's the only way you are going to get a ball past Herman, bounce it under the plate."

Dan Cummerford, clubhouse attendant for the past 22 years, missed opening day action with a bad boil on his neck, setting out his first day of work since joining the club in 1906.

The mayor of Clearwater did not show up to throw out the first ball, being previously engaged with a horse race in the area. Most of the other baseball fans in the city seemed to have joined him and only a few attended the opening game.

Crowds at the Brooklyn games had been very small and the Robins had nearly moved to Homosassa, where Dazzy Vance had real estate holdings, but a 1927 hurricane had depressed land values so they returned to Clearwater.

Miami had put out serious feelers, offering the Brooklyn club a training base on the East coast of Florida, but insiders felt that the Ebbets real estate holdings in the Clearwater area would keep them there.

Dazzy Vance signed his new contract and insisted on a clause that would allow him to play golf on his day off.

Herman and Bissonette shared first base through the first three games in Clearwater, then Babe broke loose with a double and a homer in one game, two singles and a homer in the next and a double and single in the third. But he made a pair of errors at first base and the Eagle reporter said he seemed 'indifferent' in the field.

Rube Bressler, unhappy at Cincinnati, bought his contract from the Reds for $4000 and sold himself to the Robins for $4000 and a $6000 salary. Robinson said he would use him in left, Tyson in right and Statz in center.

But Herman hit .346 in the first nine exhibition games and Robbie switched him to the outfield. He had played there briefly in 1926, but with difficulty.

"Well, we can get Bissonette's bat into the lineup if you can play out there," Robinson told him.

Del Bissonette

"I'll try," Herman said and from then until he was traded in 1932, he played only two additional games at first base for Brooklyn.

He told reporters, "If Del makes good at first and I become an outfielder, the team will be strengthened at two positions. Personally I don't care where I play as long as they let me take my regular turn at bat."

Bissonette's weak arm caused him to switch to first base. He was a good pull hitter, although he was extremely slow and was unable to range far from first base while fielding. He won the job with his bat and Herman was sent to the outfield to learn a new position with the regular season just days away.

Max Carey was again appointed Captain of the Robins and Dave Bancroft was appointed assistant, with most of the players wondering exactly what that was.

The National League voted in 1928 that each team would provide two road and two home uniforms. Until that time, clubs had one of each and on the road the suits would become so stiff with sweat and dirt they could stand up in the corner by themselves. However the superstitious players didn't think much of the new two-uniform system, taking some time to get used to them.

The new road uniforms were colorful. The grey suits had dark crossbars and red piping down the leg. Red, white and blue stockings and blue caps with red piping completed the patriotic scheme.

New York Mayor Jimmy Walker and Paul Block, Newark newspaper owner, made an offer for the Ebbets half of the Brooklyn club, but Steve McKeever said he would not sell his half under any conditions, effectively killing the deal.

Nat Strong and Max Rosen, semi-pro baseball owners of the Bushwicks, also made an offer to purchase the Brooklyn club, reporting they would move them to Dexter Park and build a 125,000 seat stadium. Again McKeever beat off the attackers.

Robinson earlier noted that he was not interested in either Ty Cobb or Tris Speaker, who had been released by their American League clubs. After they had signed he expressed regret that he did not have a chance to obtain them. This strange sort of language might be interpreted as "I wanted to sign them but the directors wouldn't or couldn't loosen the purse strings."

John McGraw of the Giants told reporters that he had offered Rogers Hornsby for Vance, but Robinson denied the offer.

Babe showed some improvement in the outfield on the defensive side of the ledger and hit extremely well. He made a pair of errors in right field against the Washington Senators but pounded a homer and a double the next day, good for six RBI.

In the first Washington game Babe staggered under a high pop before catching it near the stands. First base coach Nick Altrock shouted, "Safety first, Babe. Don't get wounded," drawing a laugh from the crowd.

Herman drew a louder laugh from the fans in the box seats when he suggested that Altrock...er...chase himself around the bases or something of that sort.

After the game Robinson told reporters, "Anybody who thinks I'm going to let that long-legged kid go is crazy. Dawgone him, I'll keep him until he gets some judgement."

On get-away day he had a pair of singles and a homer against the Phils, throwing out a runner at second and two at the plate. The Eagle reported, "He covered right field like the morning dew. It was his best performance in a Brooklyn uniform."

Playing in Macon, Bissonette chased a high, wind-blown pop that descended directly on his head, bouncing away for a double.

Harold Burr, writing in The Sporting News, criticized National League exhibition games against teams from the American League. "No rivalry existed to make them respectable contests," he noted. "Intraleague games did have the necessary ingredients and were better box office attractions."

League president John Hydler agreed and was to take the matter up with league officials.

Herman carefully cultivated a phlegmatic exterior but he was both temperamental and sensitive. He had certainly lost some confidence during the terrible 1927 season.

In 1927 the general comment between the Brooklyn writers and manager Robinson was "When are you going to take Herman out?" During the late spring of 1928 their comment was "When are you going to put Herman in?"

He injured his leg in the first of three Yankee games as the exhibition season closed, spraining his ankle sliding home on the front end of a double steal. Bancroft was also injured when he attempted to steal second and shortstop Leo Durocher leaped for a high throw and came down on his hand.

The Robins had a 16-8 overall exhibition record and a 11-6 mark against major league competition. Herman hit .373 during the exhibition season, successfully fighting his way back into the Robin lineup.

He missed the first three games of the regular season but Robinson had again fallen in love with the hard-hitting youngster.

"Herman is the MVP on this club and has driven in a great many important runs. Runs that Bernie Neis used to call 'them' runs," Robinson said.

Before the second game of the new season, two youngsters tried to get into the park by climbing the right field wall but were stranded on a small ledge until park attendants went to their rescue with a ladder.

Herman slugged his first home run of the year in Philadelphia and went on a late tear to finish April with a .357 average. Now Robin fans were split on the Babe, a condition that lasted throughout most of his

Brooklyn career. Some of them were saying "Why isn't Herman the best player in the league?" and others saying, "Why is Herman in the league at all?" the Brooklyn Eagle reported.

Brooklyn led the league with a 9-4 record as April ended but slipped out of the top slot in early May when they lost the first two games of the month to the Giants.

Babe had played 35 games in the outfield in 1926 and one in 1927, being used almost exclusively at first base. Being moved to the outfield, and especially right field, on a steady basis was yet another thing.

Right field in Brooklyn faced directly into the sun, and since most games were started late in the afternoon to attract businessmen from the downtown areas, the sun could be brutal.

Ebbets Field was open-backed, allowing the sun to beam through as it went down in the West and a fly ball would cross the sun twice if you attempted to catch it at the belt.

Sun glasses were very small, about the size of large olives, and had to be carefully adjusted to do any good. As a result players were very careful how they were handled. They were placed under the player's glove in the outfield to protect them when he came in to hit.

Max Carey pointed out to Babe that he was letting the ball go through the sun twice, making it twice as hard to see. He suggested reaching up with both hands to catch routine balls above the shoulders. This simple tip helped Herman a great deal as he battled to learn the new position during the regular season.

The problems he encountered in right field during the 1928 season did much to solidify the opinion that Herman was a hopeless outfielder.

Zach Wheat, a regular since the park opened in 1913, refused to play right field in Ebbets Field because of the sun, preferring left on a steady basis. Left field in Yankee Stadium was the sun field and Babe Ruth would not play there, insisting he be positioned in right. But when the Yankees played in Brooklyn, Ruth would be found in left, out of the blinding rays.

Herman also had trouble playing balls off the right field wall, although he had made some spectacular catches earlier in the month in the spacious Boston outfield. The right field wall in Brooklyn was 19 feet high and bent at the midpoint with a vertical top half and a concave-angled bottom half.

"A right fielder in Ebbets Field must be a combination of civil engineer and mountain goat," Robinson noted. "It is one of the hardest 'sun fields' I ever have seen, and it is bounded by a slanting wall off which batted balls carom at all sorts of weird angles. A Brooklyn right fielder is more to be pitied than scorned. Everyone can't be a Tommy Griffith," he concluded.

Boston had voted in favor of Sunday baseball, cutting Brooklyn out of some lucrative week-end games that the clubs had previously

Babe Herman ... 1928

switched between themselves. However, the Phils and Pirates were still saddled with the Pennsylvania Blue Law that forbid playing on the Sabbath and would continue to play their Sunday home games in Brooklyn. Sunday baseball had been legal in Brooklyn since 1919. Despite the loss of the Boston dates, the Robins would still play a remarkable 20 of 21 Sundays at home.

Early in the season, late in a game at Ebbets Field, Herman came into the dugout and said something about it being very difficult to see in right field with the sun shining through the upper and lower stands.

Robbie heard Babe and said "We've got a good lead, let's get Tyson out there." He was talking about Al Tyson, a good-fielding outfielder the Robins had obtained from the Giants.

In the next inning somebody lined a ball into right field and Tyson lost it in the sun. It hit him on the top of the head and skipped into the right field corner.

The next day the papers reported that Herman was hit in the head by a fly ball and when Babe called them on it they said, "Gee, Babe, no one made an announcement so we just figured it was you out there."

The story about Herman getting hit on the head by a fly lives to this day and probably will as long as baseball is played. But it just never happened.

Getting hit on the head by a fly ball is a rare occurrence now, but even when the game was played exclusively in bright sunshine, it happened every now and then.

Burt Shotton, an outfielder with St. Louis and Washington and later manager of the Dodgers, was hit squarely on the junction of his cap and the bill by a fly that he never saw and was knocked unconscious. Stan Musial, Joe DiMaggio and Willie Mays are among many other illustrious players who have had the misfortune of being struck on the head by a long drive.

First baseman Del Bissonette had a habit of catching high pops with his back to the infield. One afternoon he attempted such a catch and misjudged it, with the ball hitting him in the face. A few days later Tyson was hit filling in for Herman. Bisonette grabbed Tyson when he came back into the dugout and said, "Let's go back to the International League before we both get killed."

At the Polo Grounds in early May, Jim Elliott gave up only two hits, both were in the seventh inning and both were homers as the Robins lost 2-1. Babe slammed a shot off the scoreboard, knocking a number loose. One umpire called it a fair ball and a home run, the other overruled him and called it foul.

On the first Western swing, Herman, on successive days, (a) slugged a homer to beat the Cardinals, (b) dropped a fly that cost a game, (c) was out advancing on passed ball and (d) was out for leaving third too soon

Hendricks .354, Frederick .328, Herman .340

on a fly.

The Brooklyn Eagle correspondent noted,

"Babe's daily deeds continue to mirror the rise and fall of Brooklyn's traveling empire through the West. It is positively uncanny how one man can so consistently shape the daily destiny of a ball club.

"Herman was born with a gift for slugging and under an unlucky star. That's the only way to account for his astonishing conglomeration of mixed talents and liabilities. Were Babe not the kind of fellow who's caught out in a bathing suit with no pockets when it's raining $10 gold pieces, he'd be the greatest winning asset the Robins have.

"But he never gets a break. Once in three times anyway the average player will get away with a bad play. Three times out of three, one of Herman's bad plays lose ball games. Even some of Herman's good plays turn out badly. The thumb of fate is down on him.

"Babe's feats have decided Brooklyn's last four games. He won the first of the four with a home run against the Cardinals. In the second of the four he dropped an easy fly ball. Other outfielders drop fly balls without anything happening. Five St. Louis runs followed Herman's muff.

"In the third game Herman got three hits, and drove in a run. But he made a misguided attempt to advance a base on a short passed ball and never had a chance to succeed, thus ruining a ninth inning rally.

"In the fourth game Herman found himself on third base with one out in the second inning. A fly was lifted to short center and Babe easily crossed the plate after the catch. But umpire Bill Klem ruled that

Herman left third an instant before the ball was caught so Babe was out. The average ball player gets away with that nine of ten times, but Klem had to catch Herman in the act, and the act deprived Doug McWeeney of a victory in nine innings and replaced it with a loss in 12."

On the bench, Robbie asked Herman if he had tagged. "You had plenty of time," he added.

"I thought I did," was all that Babe said.

"But, Babe," Robbie told him in all seriousness, "you know the umpire is always right."

Jess Petty was again suspended, this time in Chicago, for one of two reasons, or for a combination of both. Along with a number of other members of the team, he did not eat at the club hotel after the team arrived in town. The next afternoon the Cubs were a run ahead in the sixth with two out and a runner at second.

"I looked at the bench to see if Robinson wanted me to walk the hitter, but I got no signal so I pitched to him and he singled for the run," Petty told reporters.

"When I returned to the dugout at the end of the inning, Robinson was furious that I didn't walk the hitter. I told him to tell me before I pitched to him instead of second-guessing me afterward. We had some strong words there in the dugout," Petty said.

Robinson claimed he gave the signal to pass the hitter and that Bancroft delivered it orally but claimed Petty ignored the order. Robinson fined him $200 and sent him back to Brooklyn, but never made it clear if the suspension was for missing a meal at the hotel or for disobeying orders on the field.

Babe slugged homers over the distant right field wall in both Cincinnati and Boston but in the middle of the month, Robinson decided to platoon Herman and Bressler on a right-left basis although Babe was hitting .341 at the time. Playing on a part-time basis, Herman was only 3-for-15 and slid to .327 as June started. Robinson's experiment ended in June and Babe hit the ball at a .380 clip during the month.

Officials at Ebbets Field had planted a new infield before the 1928 season opened but due to heavy rains the grass died. Steve McKeever had workmen dig up the grass in his backyard and put it on the Ebbets infield. However it didn't take root and was rather like a thick throw rug spread over the infield.

Lefty O'Doul hit a shot toward Babe at first during an early season game and the ball burrowed into the sod, throwing a large chunk straight up in the air.

McKeever, however, thought it was a good looking infield. "Nice and green," he remarked to reporters. But an infielder walking past him said, "I just walked across it and nearly turned my ankle."

The club went on the road and when they returned, the infield had been properly resodded.

Opposing players reported that the Ebbets Field infield was the worst in the league. Travis Jackson of the Giants was knocked out by a high bounce on what appeared to be an easy double play ball.

Later catcher Frank Hogan of the Giants stepped in a hole beside the pitcher's rubber where the starting pitcher had warmed up before the game. He suffered a badly sprained ankle.

In June, Leonard Schwab of Cincinnati was hired to become the first groundskeeper in Ebbets Field history. He had worked with his brother to make Redlands Field the best in the majors.

Herman agreed the best infield in the league was in Cincinnati, partly because the river would periodically overflow and leave a deposit of rich silt on it that was excellent for the grass. In contrast, the Giants ground up peanut shells swept from the bleachers and used them for mulch on the infield. But the worst infield in the league was in St. Louis, where the sun baked the ground until it was like tile, and their lone groundskeeper would simply drag a hose over the infield dirt to smooth it.

Early in June the Robins and Pirates mixed it up in Ebbets field. Pittsburgh scored twice in the top of the ninth to break a 5-5 tie. An apparent catch by Statz in center was ruled a pickup and the fans littered the field with bottles, delaying the game. Babe had smacked a homer and triple, the first over the exit gate in center and the second off the gate, but the Pirates won 9-7 in ten innings.

Catcher Charlie Hargreaves was traded to Pittsburgh for first baseman Joe Harris and catcher Johnny Gooch early in June, and later shortstop Howard Freigau was sold to Boston. But these minor adjustments couldn't keep the club from settling back into their old sixth place slot.

Dazzy Vance fanned 15 Cubs on June 17th and allowed just three hits in a 4-0 victory as Babe belted a two-run single in the first off Charlie Root.

Playing in Philadelphia, the Brooklyn Eagle noted it was a 'normal' afternoon for Herman. His error allowed a Philadelphia run, then his single in the ninth broke a 3-3 tie and gave Petty the victory.

The Phillies won the second game of the series, an 11-10 slugfest, and Herman boomed a ball off the clubhouse wall in center field in the eighth inning. Observers say that only Sherwood McGee had hit that wall on the fly in the long history of Baker Bowl.

The field was built in 1895 and until torn down in 1950, no player ever hit a ball over the 35-foot center field fence, located 408 feet from home plate. However, Rogers Hornsby hit a ball through an open window in the fence during the 1929 season.

The club moved to Boston, and during the game workmen pulled the left field fence down to shorten the distance from the plate. After the fourth inning a ball hit in that area that rolled into the stands was a ground rule double.

Friends from Maine had a 'day' for Bissonette while the Robins were in Boston, showering him with gifts. He repaid their kindness by bouncing a homer over the fence to win the game.

Babe celebrated his 25th birthday with two singles and two doubles as the Robins swept two from the Braves. The Robins had won six in a row and suddenly were one game out of second place.

On the final day of June, catcher Walt Lerian of the Phillies struck out to end the top of the fourth, then led off the top of the fifth with a single. When the Robins finally noticed a few innings later and protested to the umpire, they were reminded it should have been mentioned sooner.

Herman was belting the ball on a steady basis, homering twice off Malone of the Cubs as the Robins split with them, and banging home four runs against the Braves in Boston. Herman was hitting .356 as June ended and Brooklyn finished the month with a 15-11 record, holding on to their first division berth.

In July at the Polo Grounds, Tyson collided with Bressler and suffered a compound fracture of his left leg. With Brooklyn leading 7-5 in the last of the 11th, he caught the ball, then dropped it upon impact with Bressler and it rolled away for a three-run homer and an 8-7 Giant win.

Babe made three errors in one game, muffing one ball hit to him and making a bad throw. The third error came when his perfect throw hit the third-base bag and bounced away from the fielder. He also homered but the Cubs won 14-8.

The following day, July 7th, McWeeney passed out after the sixth inning of the first game and Art Nehf fainted in the seventh inning of the second game in a sweltering morning-afternoon double bill in the Polo Grounds.

Babe knocked Bill Terry's glove off his hand at first base with a double in the opening game and added a homer later as the Robins won 8-3.

The Robins beat the Cubs three of the next four games and Babe was 6-for-12 against the tough Chicago staff, adding two homers and three doubles.

The move that put Herman in the outfield continued to pay dividends as Bissonette was also slugging the ball at a near-record pace. He banged his 18th home run on the 14th of July and Babe went 3-for-4 as the Cards fell 5-2 in St. Louis.

The Eagle noted the Herman hit better on the road than at home because the Brooklyn fans weren't around to rile him. In an attempt to get the boo-birds off his back they campaigned:

"Babe has hit with astonishing frequency of late. He is a good enough batter to be up with any five hitters in the league. He can run, hit and throw. On the whole, however, his running and throwing are liabilities. His value to the Robins depends on whether he happens to be hitting.

"But Herman looks about ready for stardom. He wasn't ready when he broke in two years ago and there were many times in the past when it looked like he would never be ready.

"If he comes through, it will be to the credit of Robinson. His patience with what might have been a great American tragedy would have worn out a less sensitive man.

"But Robinson's attention has cost him his reputation for treating all players alike. He explains that Herman's greatest need is confidence.

"When Babe used to drop into one of his periods of poor fielding, his simultaneous batting slump was blamed. It was really the other way around—he hit poorly through worry over his fielding mistakes. Herman has looked bad at the plate, but he has never looked worried there.

"He is ridden hard by the Brooklyn fans and as a result is a better player on the road than at home. Anybody with his talent to sock the leather is too good to be given up, and with the proper handling, Herman is a fine bet to come through.

"Give the boy a big hand when he comes home and see what happens!" the paper suggested.

The story that Robinson used a police whistle to move his outfielders apparently is just that—a story. In fact, Robinson rarely moved his outfielders at all, they mostly played where they wanted. But he was sometimes quick to criticize them when they weren't where he thought they should be when a ball was hit.

One afternoon Babe missed catching a ball after a long run, and when Herman came back into the dugout at the end of the inning, Robinson said, "Why don't you play him over a little?"

"Don't second-guess me, Robbie," Babe replied. "If you want me moved, do it before the pitch. I'll play where you want me."

Robinson fumed a while, then fined him $100 for either not playing the hitter where the manager thought he should have or for arguing with him after the fact.

Herman wasn't in the outfield the next day as the team played the Giants. Going into the ninth in a tie game, Robinson turned to Hank DeBerry on the bench and said, "You hit next."

"You don't want me to hit," DeBerry told him.

"Who's left?"

"Old slug (Herman) can hit one for us."

"I won't ask him, you ask him."

So DeBerry walked down the bench and told Babe he would hit next.

Babe hit a screwball over the gas station across Bedford Avenue and Robinson came off the bench to greet him at home plate. Leaving the bench was a rare occurrence for the Brooklyn manager, since he didn't wear a uniform during his later years with the club, and it was the first time anyone had seen him come onto the field since he started wearing civilian clothes in the dugout.

He grabbed Babe around the neck and said, "You haven't heard anything more about that $100 fine have you?"

"No," said Babe.

"Well, you won't either," said the joyous Robinson.

After a double-header loss at Pittsburgh on July 21, Robinson told reporters, "Ebbets Field ought to be jammed for tomorrow's doubleheader. Maybe these birds," waiving toward his players as they filed off the field, "will give the same kind of exhibition they gave today. And then maybe the fans will swarm out of the stands and ride these butterfingered guys out of town on a rail.

"And then maybe I'll be able to get a restful night's sleep."

Some 26,000 fans showed up, but the Robins split the two games, thus holding off the possible mob scene Robinson described. Herman broke a 1-for-22 slump with five hits in the two games, three of them doubles.

On the 25th, Brooklyn trailed Grover Cleveland Alexander 6-1 into the last of the ninth. After Harvey Hendrick doubled, Herman bunted but was nipped at first on a fine fielding play by Alexander.

The Brooklyn fans booed Herman for not slugging away, but his teammates defended his actions. "A home run would still have us four runs down. If he beats it out, a rally could have been in the making and maybe we could have gotten to Alexander," Max Carey said.

The team slipped further in the standings late in the month and completed a 14-18 July. August wasn't kind to the Robins either. The Cubs took three of four in Ebbets Field, with Herman cracking three hits in the only win. In the third game, Hack Wilson made a rare, four-base error on a long drive by Hendrick but the Cubs won 16-3.

Herman had started to win some of the writers and the fans over with his improved fielding. One Brooklyn paper noted:

"Herman had three hits and was quite a hero in the 5-2 win over Chicago. Babe has played consistently throughout the home stand and there may come a day when the oft-repeated 'Hit it to Herman,' will be a prayer and not a razzberry. He is steadily looking more natural in the field. He made three catches on the run and one—a catch of a long foul from Riggs Stephenson's club in the fourth—was a fine effort."

In Cincinnati on August 25 the Robins were tied 4-4 in the last of the ninth when Red Lucas banged a shot into the right field corner. Carey ran over to cut the ball off but a fan jumped out of the seats, grabbed the ball and headed for the exit.

Umpire Bob Hart, finding himself surrounded by hundreds of celebrating Cincinnati fans, decided to do nothing and allowed the

A pair of Babes...Herman and Ruth

winning run to score.

Robinson, when asked about protesting the game, grumbled, "Hart told me the winning run would have scored anyway."

The schedule made it difficult in the late days of August, as Brooklyn finished the month with a 10-16 record. The club completed a doubleheader in Cincinnati on the 25th and, taking a sleeper home, arrived an hour late for their game with the Giants in Ebbets Field.

Despite the long, difficult trip, they beat Carl Hubbell 4-3 in 10 innings in his first appearance in Brooklyn, as rookie Del Bissonette slugged his 20th home run and Herman went 3-for-3 off the tough left-hander.

Future Hall of Famer Carl Hubbell would have trouble with the Dodgers throughout his long and brilliant career, despite Brooklyn occupying a second-division berth much of that time. And the left-handed hitting Babe would hit the Giants' ace left-hander with apparent ease. He recorded a career .331 average against him but did even better in a Brooklyn uniform, belting out a career .408 mark, including .480 in 1929 and .476 in 1930.

Brooklyn had a winning month in September and recorded a final 77-76 record, their first season over .500 since 1924, although they again finished 17 1/2 games behind and in sixth place.

Early in the final month, the Robins made eight errors in the opening game of a double header in Boston and booted two more in the second contest. None of the errors were charged to Herman.

Despite the fact Brooklyn was going nowhere in the standings, 25,000 packed themselves into Ebbets Field for two games against the Giants. Hubbell won the first 4-0 but the Robins, with Herman banging out three hits, won the second 4-3.

In the third game of the series, Herman walked in the ninth with the score tied 2-2. Bressler bunted him to second and Jake Flowers hit a shot of Fred Lindstrom's shoulder that rolled into short left field. Herman dashed around third and beat the play at the plate with a long slide to win.

Late in the final month Robinson was looking at the youngsters on the team and pinch-hit Bill Harris for Herman against the Cardinals.

Brooklyn fans, now delighted with Herman's smoking bat, gave the Robin manager a deafeningly razzberry when he made the move, then screamed even louder when Harris popped out and the club lost 4-3 in 15 innings. Herman hit in 21 of 26 games in September.

The final games were unimportant, except for the fact that a young catcher by the name of Al Lopez made his Brooklyn debut, catching both ends of a winning double-header against the Pirates.

Del Bissonette banged a homer in each game to set Brooklyn rookie records with 25 round trippers and 106 RBI.

Babe didn't play the final game of the season in Ebbets Field but appeared in the stands before the game and received a good hand from the few thousand faithful but frozen fans in attendance. Brooklyn beat the Phils 6-1 in a game that took 1:25 to play.

The Robins finished one game over .500, the first time they had tasted that lofty air since 1924.

Herman finished with a .340 average, in a tie for fifth in the league, with 37 doubles and a dozen home runs. However he had fielded only .937 and had made 16 errors in the outfield.

Babe had hit .441 against the Phillies, .374 against Chicago, .368 against the Reds and .361 during battle with the hated Giants. His had a .553 average in Cincinnati and a .455 mark in Philadelphia, hitting .377 at home and .326 on the road.

Brooklyn won only 5 of 23 games when Herman went hitless. When he got one hit or more they were ten games over .500 at 67-57.

The Robins hit only 66 home runs, 30 at home and 36 on the road. Herman had hit a homer in every park save Pittsburgh (Joe Harris got the only Brooklyn round tripper there), and Babe was the only Brooklyn player to hit one in spacious Redland Field in Cincinnati.

Following the season, the Brooklyn Eagle solicited letters from the fans, asking what was wrong with the Robins. Of the thousands received, the paper pointed out that none listed Herman's fielding deficiencies as a part of the problem.

McKeever again campaigned for park expansion, displaying plans for a triple-deck stadium that would hold 55,000 fans and costing $1 million.

December 9th the Robinson acquired pitcher Vic Aldridge from the New York Giants on waivers, but true to the history of fierce rivalry between the two clubs, Aldridge retired rather than move across the river to Brooklyn.

Scout Nap Rucker sent outfielder John Frederick to the Robins from Memphis. Win Ballou was drafted and "Spitting Bill" Doak was released. The Brooklyn club also purchased the remaining interest in the Macon club.

Then on December 11th a trade was made with Pittsburgh in which Brooklyn swapped pitcher Jesse Petty and second baseman Harry Riconda to Pittsburgh for shortstop Glenn Wright.

Wright was a steady .300 hitter for the Pirates with good power and it seemed at the time the Robin's shortstop problem had finally been solved (again). Robinson quickly appointed him captain of the club.

But the Robins' luck in trading for shortstops held firm. Wright would tear shoulder ligaments crashing into a wall during a handball game during the winter, then reinjured it again in April. His throw from shortstop to first base, once a bullet, would travel on a gentle arc. He would play only 24 games for Brooklyn, serving mostly as a pinch-hitter, and would hit only .200 in 1929.

Robinson was furious, claiming that Pittsburgh passed on damaged goods in the trade and talked of trying to get the transaction cancelled.

During the late fall, Herman was at a golf course in California when Commissioner Landis appeared.

"Hi, Babe," he said.

"Hi, Judge," Herman replied. "What are you doing here?"

"I came to play golf with you," he said.

Babe was long off the tee but wild, while the Commissioner was short but perfectly straight down the middle of the fairway.

Finally on the ninth hole Landis purposely hit a ball in the next fairway so he could get close enough to talk to Herman.

"How much are you making playing ball out here in the winter?" Since 1923 Babe had been playing semi-pro games on week-ends for the Glendale White Sox and others. Many other major league players picked up some extra change during the winter months playing in California.

"About $80 a week."

"That's pretty good money to lose, isn't it?"

"I'm not going to lose it. Robbie gave me permission to play here."

"Listen, I'm the Commissioner, not Robbie. That's a league rule you know, major leaguer's cannot play more than 30 days after the season ends, and it must be upheld. You're getting too much publicity back east right now. I've let you play a year or so. Go ahead and play next week and then you must quit."

Herman reluctantly complied with the Commissioner's order.

Chapter 6

Herman was offered $16,000 for the 1929 season and, with his .340 average as solid leverage, asked for another $1,000, which, after some consideration the directors agreed upon.

During negotiations, Robbie had pointed to his stolen base record for 1928 when he had stolen only once.

"A great athlete like you should steal a bunch of bases," he said.

"Cripes, Robbie, you never send me," Herman replied.

At a special meeting in New York, National League president John Hydler proposed a '10-man' team concept, adding a hitter to keep pitchers from batting, in actuality proposing the designated hitter concept. The American League discarded it out of hand without discussion. During this period neither league looked favorably on any proposal by the other loop.

Numbering of players was also rejected, this time proposed by the National League, but the Yankees announced they would put numbers on players' uniforms anyway, becoming the first major league club in many years to do so.

Thomas Rice of the Brooklyn Eagle had campaigned for the numbering system years earlier. Club owners feared that numbers on the players would cut down on scorecard sales, but Rice felt the exact opposite would be the case.

One long-time fan reported he had taken his girlfriend to a game and had pointed out one of the outstanding players of the day to her. During the game the player made a number of fine plays and collected three hits. Only when the fan read the paper the next day did he realize that a rookie had filled in for the star and it had been he that had sparkled in the field and at bat. Without numbers, even a regular at the park could not always tell the players.

Rice also noted that when Ebbets Field was being built in 1912, Charlie Ebbets was reluctant to put up a scoreboard, hoping to keep the scorecard sales strong. Rice convinced him that he would be considered 'cheap' if he did not install a scoreboard and Ebbets changed his mind.

Hydler also tried to patch up the Robinson-McKeever rift and Robbie agreed quickly, but McKeever turned away without a word. Robinson's contract would run out in the fall. One newspaper noted that, "For three years it has been called 'The $3,000,000 business that runs itself.' "

The Sporting News reported that the Brooklyn club was worth $2.1 million and that profits for the 1920-24 period were: $189,785 in 1920; $151,604 in 1921; $146,372 in 1922; $116,539 in 1923 and $265,669 in 1924.

By the middle of February, only Captain Max Carey, Bissonette, Flowers and Elliott had signed, but the contracts started coming in quickly as spring training approached.

Eddie Moore would try his hand at second base during the 1929 season and Wally Gilbert would become the third baseman. Rookie Johnny Frederick would replace ageing Max Carey in center and Val Picinich joined Henline and DeBerry behind the plate. Picinich came from the Cincinnati Reds in exchange for catcher Johnny Gooch and pitcher Rube Ehrhardt.

Johnny Morrison was added to the pitching staff and he would win 13 and save eight, working mostly in relief. Clise Dudley and Ray Moss moved into the starting rotation with Clark and Vance.

Jesse Petty had been traded to Pittsburgh for Glenn Wright, apparently filling a hole at shortstop but making an even larger hole in the Robin's rotation. Brooklyn led the National League in earned run average in 1928 but after Petty's loss the club would balloon over a run and a half in 1929.

In an attempt to fill the void, they picked up pitchers Alex Ferguson, Kent Greenfield and Luther Roy but it would make little difference, for a third consecutive sixth place finish was destined.

Robinson was delayed in Georgia by a business proposition and Carey was in charge of the first days of training. Coaches Otto Miller and Nap Rucker were working with the pitchers and catchers. Jim Elliott said, "Wait until Babe finds out how much batting practice we are taking and how easy base hits are. He'll be right here." Prophetically, Herman sent a signed contract the next day and hopped a train for Florida.

The Brooklyn Eagle wrote that Herman was seeking a raise from $8,500 to $17,000. "If Babe could field half as well as he hits, he would be worth his weight in gold," Tommy Holmes noted. "To say the least, his fielding last year was not so good.

"Yet this year it might be different. According to Babe's friends, he's been working out and if he shows an improvement he will certainly be more valuable to the team."

Robinson arrived in camp March 2nd and immediately took a liking to rookie Johnny Frederick's batting style. Carey praised Al Lopez's catching. "He throws as well as anyone in the National League," he told Robinson. And of young Paul Richards: "He'll develop, although he is a year or two away."

Herman and his family arrived by train and Babe was quickly recruited for an intrasquad game, dumping a double into right field in his first trip to the plate.

Glenn Wright was appointed captain of the team on March 6th. Jake Daubert, Zach Wheat, Jack Fournier and Max Carey had preceded him.

Robinson was negotiating with Dazzy Vance but suddenly Steve McKeever announced that he was worth the $25,000 he was asking and signed him, causing Robinson a great deal of embarrassment and widening the gap between the two Brooklyn officials.

Herman's strong hitting during the 1928 spring training season paled in the ferocity of his 1929 start. He hit in the first nine games and finished by hitting in 17 of the last 18 games. He collected 34 hits in 78 trips to the plate during the spring, posting a .436 average.

Babe's one-hop smash knocked down an Atlanta outfielder in early April. Herman's line single to center ripped through Maurice Archdeacon's hands and struck him over the heart with frightful impact, knocking the breath out of him for several moments.

Tommy Holmes said he had never seen a line drive right at an outfielder playing deep that was so viciously belted that it couldn't be held. "Archdeacon deserves a medal for holding Babe to what, in my mind, is the world's champion single of all time."

Playing even deeper for him made little difference. The next time at bat, Herman slugged a long one over the outfielder's head that went for an inside the park homer.

On April 12 the Greensboro club beat Brooklyn 23-21 and Babe smacked out five hits including a triple and a double. The Robins trailed 19-3 at one point.

Rookie Johnny Frederick looked like a certainty to open the season in center field. Wright played for the first time at shortstop but injured his shoulder again. Robinson complained to the National League about receiving 'damaged goods' but he was told by the league president that there was nothing that could be done about it.

But Despite Herman's hitting barrage, scribes could see the Robins finishing no higher than sixth place, while Chicago, New York and Pittsburgh were favored to fight it out for the top slot.

Brooklyn Eagle correspondent Tommy Holmes wrote that Herman was looking for a National League batting title.

"The blond stringbean does not always do the right thing at the right time, but he is the greatest instinctive hitter in baseball history.

"Babe appears better this spring than ever before. His hard hitting last season seems to have given him the air of established confidence that he did not possess. Herman knows he's good—as far as hitting goes—and his confidence gave him a mental edge on the pitcher.

"He still takes a wide-eyed riffle at the ball. He's liable to hit a wild pitch for a home run or take a perfect third strike. He has the pitchers crazy. They've given up trying to pitch to him and they now just throw, hoping he will get a brainstorm at the plate and pop one up.

"But this year his brainstorms are few and infrequent. He consistently rains his doubles down the left field foul line, hits line singles to center and wallops home runs over the right field fence.

"The lanky one is still a fifty-fifty fielder, alternating between spectacular catches and glaring errors. There doesn't appear to be much hope for improvement and professor W. Robinson has grown more lenient in his criticisms of Herman's fielding.

"The fact is that Babe is so much a creature of instinct in his ball playing that instructions do not mean much. Let him come charging in on a low line drive and the ball may glide through him. On the other hand, he may make a sensational catch or stop. But force him to play a difficult hit safely, and the odds are that he will play it uncertainly and usually disastrously.

"This spring Herman has been playing those line drive with one hand. It looks like the most risky way in the world to tackle such a proposition. But Babe has come up with the ball every time, and not one has sifted through him.

"It's Herman's notion that he can field many balls as surely with one hand as he can with two. This quaint conceit sounds improbable, yet it is a fact that Herman knows more about his ability than anyone else.

"In 1927 some coaches attempted to improve Babe's hitting by eliminating some of his departures from the orthodox principals of scientific socking. Babe listened to instructions and tried to follow them until he grew all balled up. His batting average for the year fell below .300. Eventually Babe threw all instructions overboard and followed his own instinctive style.

"A week ago at Clearwater, Herman swung at a low, inside pitch and doubled along the right field foul line. In his next trip to the plate he hit a high, outside pitch along the left field line for two bases.

"The first ball Herman walloped would have hit him in the foot had he not swung. I doubt the second pitch was within 18" of the strike zone.

"That kind of hitting is all wrong, according to the book. But two or three such exhibitions are all in a days work for Herman."

Del Bissonette, after a sensational rookie season, was as cold in the spring of 1929 as Herman was hot. He went 0-for-20 before collecting his first hit of the spring training season.

The team finished its schedule of exhibition games with a 13-16 record against major league teams, losing to the Yankees in the both games of their spring schedule.

The Yankees won the opener 10-5 with Ruth blasting a pair of homers. The Brooklyn Eagle published this poem the next morning:

"O'er the grave of many fine games
"Reads this mellowed truth:
"Here lies a mangled pitcher
"Who threw high, inside to Ruth."

The Yanks won the second game 7-1. Vance fanned Ruth in the first for the only bright spot of the day.

The opening game at Boston was rained out, and the following day the Robins lost a 13-12 decision despite three hits by Herman. He clubbed two doubles and a two-run homer that pulled the team within one run.

Babe hit in the first eight games, recording an even .500 average on 17 hits in 34 at bats. He had three homers and eight RBI. But the club could win only four of the first 11 games.

Bissonette, who broke his slump with a homer on opening day, was hit on the head by pitcher Les Sweetland of the Phils, the ball bouncing high into the grandstand. He came back to play in April but he had only three hits in his next 26 trips.

The Sporting News said: "The Robins beat the Braves through the slugging strength of Babe Herman. He walloped an enormous home run off Brandt with a man on when Brandt tried to cross Babe with a high one outside. It was not outside far enough and went outside the park and into the left field seats.

"Herman has been hitting erratically in such respects, striking out with the base full on opening day and clouting bad balls. Then again, he has hit good pitches viciously." Bad pitches or good, Herman was hitting .467 at the time.

One of Babe's special friends in Brooklyn was Howard Pierce, son of George Pierce the inventor of the spiked baseball shoe. The Herman family shared a bungalow belonging to the Pierce family at Rockaway Point at times during the summer.

George Pierce joined the Spaulding firm, located on Sixth Street in Brooklyn, in 1887. Pierce also invented football cleats and designed various protective equipment for the Spaulding Company. The company made the first footballs and basketballs used in the United States. Competition could not match their leather, obtained from their special tannery in England.

Pierce told Babe that he invented baseball spikes and named them the 'Harper Spike' because a Mr. Harper was trying to develop a baseball spike that did not crack the sole of the shoe. He apparently paid Harper a small royalty, but he had developed the spikes himself.

In late April a Brooklyn paper noted: "Herman was the individual hero yesterday with a single, double and home run. With the Californian at bat, women and children are not safe walking on Bedford Avenue."

The following afternoon, rookie pitcher Clise Dudley, working in relief, came to bat for the first time and hit a home run against the Philadelphia Phillies on the first pitch thrown to him in the major leagues.

Glenn Wright started his first game in early April and smacked a homer but his arm made it impossible for him to be used on a steady basis. The team lost nine in succession to drop into the league basement. Herman finished April with a .415 average.

Brooklyn beat New York 2-0 on the final day of the month. In the fifth with two on and two out, Herman took what plate umpire Hart called strike three. He argued long and loudly and was ejected for his efforts.

The Robin crowd was angry at both the call and the ejection, and when the next pitch was fouled with a loud 'thump' off Hart's chest protector, the fans rose to their feet with a joyous roar.

Babe cracked out seven hits in 11 trips during a three-game series with the Giants in Ebbets Field. During one of the games, columnist Westbrook Pegler saw Herman, leaning on his bat in the on-deck circle, make crazy gestures at someone upstairs in the press box. Looking around, Pegler caught writer Garry Schmacher gesturing back with his fingers at Herman.

"What are you fellows up to?" Pegler asked.

"Oh, it's that goofy Eyetalian game we play on the road. You try to guess how many fingers the other guy is going to put up. We do not play hearts or old maid so we play this game."

The hitter reached base and Herman, with a final parting wiggle of his fingers, went to the plate and won the game with a long shot off the right field wall.

"McGraw would kill a guy doing that," Pegler said.

"McGraw didn't win the game, did he?" asked Schumacher with a smile.

Brooklyn won for only the third time in May when on the 17th Herman slammed a single, two doubles and a homer in a 14-13 victory at Philadelphia.

After the game, members of the Robins and Phillies were setting around in the hotel lobby talking about baseball. One Philadelphia pitcher said, "One thing I have learned, never throw the same pitch in the same place to a hitter."

The following day he relieved for the Phillies and threw a curve over the inside corner of the plate for a strike against Babe. Then he came back with the same pitch in the same location and Herman boomed it over the right field wall. Babe, who had five hits and five runs batted in during the 20-16 duel, smiled all the way around the bases.

On the next trip to Philadelphia, the pitcher talked to Herman before the game and said, "I didn't think you would be looking for the same pitch after my statement the night before." Again, Herman just smiled.

In late May, Herman stole second moments before Bressler crashed a winning hit. The Brooklyn Eagle noted: "In an earlier inning, Herman stole second and third, although the official scorer ruled them an error at second and a wild pitch. He had scored from second but umpire Quigley sent him back to third, taking no cognizance of the theoretically stolen base."

Johnny Frederick

June 9th, former teammate Jesse Petty should have known better when he intentionally walked Frederick to get at Herman with the bases loaded. Babe slugged a double good for two runs and a 9-6 win.

Johnny 'Jughandle' Morrison was purchased from Kansas City, despite a 1-6 record. He provided good relief pitching on a staff that desperately needed it.

In mid-June Herman made a game-winning catch to save 2-1 decision over Cincinnati. Rating his performance, the papers noted he made three good catches and one outstanding catch. He also homered in the last of the ninth to win a 7-6 decision against the Giants on the 18th as the Robins swept a twin-bill despite nine hits by Bill Terry, NY first baseman.

A pulled muscle cost Herman seven games in late June and on the final game of the month, Vance won an unusual contest. He fanned one and allowed 12 hits but beat the Braves 5-3 for a complete game victory.

The Robins split a double-bill with the Phillies on July 4th. Herman had a single and a double in the opener but was charged with an error when his perfect throw to the plate hit a sliding Philadelphia runner and bounced away.

Brooklyn beat the Washington Senators 8-6 in an exhibition game the next day in Olean, N.Y., scoring six times in the first inning on homers by Frederick, Herman and Butch Henline. Babe was leading the

National League with a .386 average and 51 runs batted in.

Herman's 14-game hitting streak ended against St. Louis on a blistering day that saw Watty Clark lose 10 pounds while beating the Cardinals 9-6.

Babe clouted his first Brooklyn grand-slam homer three days later in a 15-8 win over the Cardinals. Trailing 8-6 in the last of the eighth inning, Jake Flowers, Val Picinich and Frederick drew walks and Wally Gilbert lived on an error. Herman fouled off two pitches, then slammed the ball into Bedford Avenue to put the Robins ahead 11-8.

But Brooklyn wasn't finished. With two out Rube Bressler bounced a homer into the center field seats, Eddie Moore tripled, Flowers walked and Picinich lived on an error. Hendrick, in his second appearance of the inning as a pinch-hitter, looped a single to left and Frederick singled to right.

With the bases loaded again, Herman came to the plate with a rare chance to hit another grand slam in the same inning but the Cardinal pitcher picked Gilbert off first base to end the inning.

"That was one record I really wanted a chance at," Herman said years later. "I asked Gilbert where he was going and he told me he was trying to get a big lead so he could score if I doubled."

Playing in Cincinnati, Vance wound up three times with Red runners on base and all three of them scored to beat him 5-3. Two days later Herman banged three hits against Chicago to raise his average to an even .400.

The team was staggering, but Herman boosted his average to .404 after a nine-game hitting streak that saw him collect 16 hits in 29 times at bat, for a sizzling .552 average.

Although the club was out of contention, 22,000 Brooklyn fans showed up to watch Herman's charge toward the batting title as the club finished a long home stand.

Later in July, Babe smacked a home run over the 404-foot center field wall in Cincinnati, becoming the third player in history to hit a ball over the distant barrier. Only Babe Ruth and Ethan Allen had performed the feat previously.

League president John Heydler reacting to complaints from N.L. pitchers that the baseballs were 'slick,' set a precedent when he instructed his umpires to rub new balls with dust to take the gloss off of them.

Today baseballs are rubbed up before each game with a special mud—Lena Blackburne Baseball Rubbing Mud—taken from a secret spot on the Delaware River.

During the Cincinnati series, under a blistering sun in late July, Val Picinich and Hank DeBerry each caught a complete game without chest protectors due to the excessive heat.

Brooklyn moved into August with a 43-54 record. They were in fifth place, 16 1/2 games behind. On the final day of July, Herman banged out a single and two triples, then stole home to complete the perfect day. Clark topped the Cardinals 8-2, despite pitching with only two days rest.

The club completed an extensive road trip by losing three of four in Chicago before a near-record 140,000 fans. Herman had posted a .479 average during the trip and had added eight doubles, four triples and three homers. He held the Major League lead with a .413 average.

In the opening game, Herman hit a ball over the right field bleachers into the street, then later in the game singled and stole second base without a throw as the Cub pitcher held the ball.

The third game of the Chicago series saw

Babe and Hack Wilson

Herman save the game twice for the Robins. In the 10th he made one of the best plays of his career when pitcher Guy Bush hit against a long shot against the right field wall.

Herman grabbed the ball off the wall, quickly wheeled and made a perfect throw to second. Wright tagged the sliding Cub as he tried to stretch the hit into a double.

Then in the 12th, Herman went far to his left and took Gabby Hartnett's long drive with his back against the wall. Despite the heroics, Chicago won 9-8 in 16 innings.

On August 1st, the Cardinals installed a screen over the right field pavilion. It extended 150-feet from the four line toward center field. St. Louis pitchers called it a "rabbit cheater."

During a game in St. Louis, Herman singled and was standing on first when Cardinal first baseman Jim Bottomly said, "Are you going over to Fritz Shaw's tonight?" Shaw was a fan that made excellent home brew, and his house was a favorite gathering place for visiting players and the Cardinals in St. Louis.

Babe turned to say, "I don't know, are you?" just as the pitcher fired to first, picking Herman off the base. He started for second but Bottomly's throw to second hit him on the back of the head and bounced away. He quickly scrambled back to first.

The fans were treated to a strange sight as Herman and Bottomly stood on first and laughed so hard tears came to their eyes over the strange sequence of events.

In Ebbets Field on August 11th, the Robins trailed Pittsburgh 3-1 into the last of the eighth inning. Frederick launched a homer into Bedford Avenue, then Herman doubled, kicking the ball out of Stu Clarke's glove at second base. Hendrick slammed a drive that hit on top of the right field wall, then bounced into the street for a homer and Bissonette boomed the third of the inning into Bedford for a home run and a 5-3 win.

The following day, Herman slugged a home run off Ervin Brame of Pittsburgh that hit on top a two-story building behind Bedford Avenue and bounced up and down on the roof for a few seconds.

Brooklyn Eagle correspondent Tommy Holmes felt the homer he hit off Burleigh Grimes on July 7 was even longer.

"Herman's shot to dead center field hit the wall and bounced to the top of the tarp shed. It is 466-feet to the center field wall and the ball hit at least 10-feet higher up on the wall," he reported at the time.

On August 15th, Babe was hitting a blistering .415 after banging out four hits. Rube Bressler was ejected for arguing about a called third strike and was given a five-day suspension as Brooklyn split two with the Cubs.

Rogers Hornsby, winner of seven National League batting championships was speaking of Herman while watching him bang out line drives during batting practice.

He told reporters: "The guy that named him Babe must have known something. He will probably never make the home run record that Ruth has, but he is one of the greatest hitters you or I or anyone every looked at. There aren't five men in the league that can hit the ball as hard as Herman. And Babe hits them that way almost every day and sometimes two or three a day.

"And give him all the credit in the world. He is up there swinging at what they throw him. He hits everything. His hits aren't the product of luck. He gets clean, sharp line drives. He hits right-handers and left-handers. The change doesn't bother him. When the Babe hits, you can hear it whistle. He makes no flukes.

"A couple of years ago, his weakness was a change of pace, but now he has learned to hit the slow stuff as well as anything else. His present batting average is strictly on his merits. And there is a moral in it, too, for Herman, in the first two years he played in this league, took about as much abuse as any player I ever knew. I've heard the rooters in Brooklyn razz him unmercifully for his erratic fielding. The riding would have broken the spirit of any other kid, but Herman took it all and came back stronger than ever.

"They couldn't keep him down, for he's one of the greatest hitters who ever lived. Those who won't admit it this season will have to come around eventually, for Babe is still young and ought to be up there in the averages for the next years. You've got to give him credit, the way he has brought himself up. For two bitter years he took abuse from the fans ragged him unmercifully about his fielding, but he never let it get him down."

Guy Bush, Cub pitcher who improved his record to 17-2 by winning the first game of the double header, echoed Hornsby's comments.

"Herman is a helluva hitter," he told reporters after the game. "He's the toughest fellow I have to pitch to, and I guess the same goes for a lot of other pitchers. When a pitcher throws a ball past Herman he is lucky and when the Babe has been held to a single the pitcher should consider himself fortunate the ball wasn't hit out of sight.

"I know I am. Of the fellows I have to pitch to, I think Herman is the best hitter of the lot. He's a heavy hitting team in himself. You may fool him with a certain deliver once, but the next time you throw the same kind of a ball to him he's liable to slam it for a triple or home run."

Harold Burr added in The Sporting News: "Brooklyn bleacherites do not ride Herman about his fielding now. It has improved 50 percent over last year, competent observers claim. He made a catch in the overflow crowd in the Cub game off Cuyler that was a game-saver.

"The Robins might not have had a single victory over the champions if Herman had not leaped into the air at the right moment and hauled it down."

Late in the month Brooklyn and New York pitchers throttled both Herman and Giant first baseman Bill Terry in a three game series. Babe was 1-for-11 and Terry 1-for-13. Lefty O'Doul of the Phillies had joined the batting race and on the final day of August trailed Herman's .402 average with a .390 mark of his own. Terry was a strong third at .387 mark.

In the final Giant game Herman was called out on strikes in the first inning and set, what the Brooklyn Eagle called, "a new height record in bat throwing."

Herman, despite an even .400 average, told a reporter as the final month of the season began, "I don't know what's the matter—for some reason my timing is wrong. I feel fine and every ball looks as big as a balloon, but I don't hit them solidly."

When asked if he was trying too hard, Herman said, "I've been telling myself that for a week and sometime soon it ought to take. When I relax, or try to, the result is the same. It's an old story I guess, there isn't any reason for nine-tenths of the batting slumps

"But I have a feeling all I need to pull out of this one is to hit one really well. A good, old line shot and I'll be back in form."

What Babe obviously needed more than anything, was a couple of days off, but the Brooklyn club depended upon him so strongly that Robinson was reluctant to give him the rest he required.

The pennant race was long since forgotten by Robin and Phillie fans as they watched their favorite hitters come blasting down the stretch. Brooklyn attendance was predicated only on Babe's battle for the title.

Against the Phillies on September 1st, Herman singled past the pitchers ear for a RBI single in the second inning, then in the fourth he boomed a Sweetland pitch off the wall in the deepest part of the park and scored before the Philadelphia outfielders could run the ball down. A shower of straw hits greeted Babe as he crossed the plate with his 17th home run and a wide grin on his face.

National League opinion of Babe Herman spoke with one voice. Cub manager Joe McCarthy told reporters: "Our pitchers can't stop him. We throw him everything and he just hits and hits." Pitcher Ernie Orsatti of St. Louis said, "He's a hitting fool, that's all. Give him a ball on the outside and he'll hit to left. An inside ball he'll pull. He just don't care where he hits it."

Entering a double-header in Philadelphia, Herman had a paper-thin lead with a .3926 average to O'Doul's .3925 mark. The following day Lefty collected three hits and took the league lead by .003.

Herman had played all but three of the Brooklyn games and the heat and pressure of the batting race were taking its toll. O'Doul passed him for the final time September 4th.

The right field wall in Philadelphia, made of tin and 60 feet high but only 280 feet from home plate at the foul line, had recently been heightened by adding a 12-foot wire screen to cut down home runs. Bissonette noted that only the highest of pop flys would clear the wall now, while hard-hit drives would not have a chance. The first-baseman took his first look at it and said, "Hand me my pitching wedge."

Robinson, trying desperately to win with his contract coming due again following the season, wanted to rest Herman but decided against it. He lamely justified it to newsmen by saying, "It wouldn't be fair to Herman if I took him out and he was to win the batting title by one point. It would seriously detract from the honor. In my opinion, a rest would be the best thing in the world for him, but I'll let him stay in the lineup and work out his own salvation."

When the next day's game was rained out, Tommy Holmes wrote in the Brooklyn Eagle, "Herman is a far greater natural hitter than O'Doul, who has developed into a good hitter himself. Perhaps both started from scratch defensively, although O'Doul is handicapped by a weak throwing arm.

"However, while Herman has developed into a serviceable fly-chaser, he is not an expert one yet. O'Doul is still pretty weak. Never on his palmiest day did Herman ever pull quite as bad a play as O'Doul did the other day. He charged a short fly off Val Picinich with the score tied. O'Doul didn't come up within 10 feet of the ball, which rolled through him to the fence for a home run to tie the score."

In Cincinnati, Babe scored from first base on a hit-and-run single to center, astounding Cincinnati players and fans alike. The fans gave him a great around of applause for his remarkable baserunning.

Then in the fourth inning, showing his new-found fielding confidence, he raced toward the foul pole in Cincinnati after a Horace Ford drive. He ran full tilt into the fence as the ball bounced away for a home run. Herman flipped over the low railing and fell hard into the seats on his back. Shaken, he missed the game the following day.

The Brooklyn Eagle announced its National League All-Star team. Around the infield they picked Bill Terry at first, Rogers Hornsby at second, Rabbit Maranville at short and Pie Traynor at third. Outfielders picked included Lloyd Waner of Pittsburgh, Stephenson of St. Louis and Herman. Jimmy Wilson was the catcher, while Burleigh Grimes, Guy Bush and Red Lucas were the pitchers.

The paper noted, "Babe is the best overall right fielder in the league. Paul Waner, Mel Ott, Kiki Cuyler are all better fielders and Chuck Klein has better extra-base power, but Herman is a better hitter than the former and a better fielder than Klein."

Brooklyn lost the first two games in Chicago, but Babe pounded a grand slam homer off Guy Bush on an 0-2 count to break a 5-5 tie and give the Robins a double-header sweep, postponing the Cubs clinching pennant-clinching ceremonies.

Earlier in the game, Herman took a long fly just in front of the right field bleachers and, when throwing to third, fired the ball into the Chicago dugout on a short hop.

Almost lost in the attention given the tight batting race, rookie Johnny Frederick slammed his 50th double to tie the National League record.

Cub manager Joe McCarthy told Brooklyn reporters, "I've tried Herman in a dozen games this year and found him poisonous. Everything our pitchers throw at him receive about the same treatment. I'm glad our pennant chances do not depend on stopping a young man who hits with such authority."

He still trailed O'Doul by only two percentage points on the 22nd of September, .389-.391, after Babe went 3-for-4 in St. Louis. Less than 1,000 were in attendance for a Sunday double header as Herman slammed a two-run homer in a five-run fifth to win the first game.

Moving into Philadelphia Herman and O'Doul went head-to-head in four games. The fact that the Phillies swept four was of little concern to Brooklyn fans who had made the trip to see the series or who were watching their papers for the results.

In the first game, Babe was 2-for-5 but O'Doul went 3-for-5 and moved into a .391-.384 lead over Herman. During a double header the next afternoon, Herman was 1-for-2 and 1-for-3, while O'Doul went 2-for-5 and 2-for-4, boosting his margin a point. They deadlocked in the final contest, Babe 1-for-3 and O'Doul 2-for-6.

One of the Philadelphia writers noted, "If Herman the Great played 77 of his games in Baker Bowl in Philadelphia, his average would be higher than his fielding average."

The gentleman was nearly correct. Baker Bowl had a high, tin right field wall located only 280 feet from home plate. Babe hit a sizzling .417 during his career in the Philadelphia park, including .442 in 1927, .455 in 1928, .409 in 1929 and .587 in 1930.

In a footnote to the series, Johnny Frederick banged his 51st double of the season, setting a new National League record. The record hit was lost in the sun by the Phillie outfielder and fell for a two-bagger. He would boost the mark to 52 the following day, still a Brooklyn/Los Angeles record. With the sweep, the Phillies moved in front of Brooklyn in the battle for fifth place in the league.

O'Doul was 3-for-3 against Boston and boosted his average to .394, a full 10 points in front of the exhausted Herman. With just four games left in the season, Babe's chances were almost non-existent.

Miller Huggins, New York Yankee manager, died and the shock extended into the Brooklyn front office. Steve McKeever had made plans to offer Art Fletcher, Yankee coach, the job as Brooklyn manager but now with Huggin's death he would be needed in New York and was unavailable to the Robins.

In the final games of the season against the Giants, the Brooklyn club extracted a small measure of satisfaction from the season by pounding them twice in a double header at the Polo Grounds, dropping them into third place. The loss cost each of the Giants about $750, the difference between second and third place money.

Herman was 2-for-4 in the opener and sat out the second game. O'Doul had four hits in Boston and clinched the title. But the Phillie outfielder continued his torrid hitting, smacking eight hits in 13 trips to the plate in the final three games and finishing with a .398 average. Herman could manage only a .315 average in September as the title slipped away. Herman finished second to O'Doul with a Brooklyn club record .381.

O'Doul had hit .423 from August 16 to the end of the season and was .514 in September to earn the title, setting a National League record with 254 hits.

Herman had hit .438 in head-to-head combat with O'Doul's Phillies and had hit .488 in St. Louis and .455 average in Chicago. He hit a remarkable .447 on the road, averaging over .400 against five of Brooklyn's seven opponents.

He finished the season with 217 hits, 105 runs, 42 doubles, 21 homers and 113 runs batted in. Herman also tied for third place in the league with 21 stolen bases, showing Robbie he could run if given the chance. The Babe hit .413 against right-handers but dipped to .302 against lefties.

"Lefty" O'Doul "Babe" Herman
CONTENDERS for NATIONAL LEAGUE BATTING CROWN

The club won only three of 24 games in which Herman went hitless. They were 63-60 when he got at least one safe hit.

Herman tied for eighth in the Most Valuable Player voting and was given votes in both right field and left field on The Sporting News All-Star team.

Giant manager John McGraw, in a copyrighted newspaper article, picked his All-Star team for 1929. He included Terry, 1b; Hornsby, 2b; Traynor, 3b; Jackson, ss; Ruth lf; Simmons, cf; Herman, rf and Cochrane catching. Grove and Bush were the pitchers.

And for the second time, Herman was made a member of the Babe Ruth All-American team, selected by a writer from each of the cities in the National League. This time he was named as an outfielder on the unit. Herman polled six votes in right field, with O'Doul receiving two, Cuyler and Manush one each. All first-team choices, except Herman and Bush, are now in the Hall of Fame.

Listed in the mythical batting lineup, the Ruth team included.

Pie Traynor, Pirates, 3b
Al Simmons, Athletics, lf
Jimmy Foxx, Athletics, 1b
Babe Herman, Robins, rf
Rogers Hornsby, Cubs, 2b
Hack Wilson, Cubs, cf
Mickey Cochrane, Athletics, c
Travis Jackson, Giants, ss
Lefty Grove, Athletics, p
Joe Bush, Cubs, p

As the season closed, the bickering over Robinson's contract started anew. Speculation was that the matter would be taken to the Commissioner's office for adjudication.

At the winter meetings in New York that December, Landis tried his role as peacemaker in the bitter internal feud. National League president John Heydler had previously tried to smooth over the Brooklyn schism with little success.

During the winter meetings, Landis was invited to attend a board of directors meeting with the rival Brooklyn factions in the Hotel Roosevelt in New York. Joe Gilleaudeau and Robinson, representing the Ebbets faction, sat on one side of the table and Steve McKeever and Frank York sat on the other side, each side glaring at the other.

After a few moments of silence, those outside the room could hear shouting, quickly followed by a hatless Judge Landis bolting out the door. "Let me out of here," the Commissioner shouted. "Let me out of this. I never heard anything like this in all my life." Eyewitnesses say Landis just beat a thrown telephone book to the door.

The man who fined Standard Oil $29 million in an anti-trust lawsuit and who banished eight Chicago White Sox players from baseball never attempted to settle the Brooklyn conflict again.

After the season Robinson watched as the Yankees battered the St. Louis Cardinals in the World Series. A young reporter interviewed him and asked how he would pitch to the New York sluggers.

"How would you pitch to Ruth?" he asked.

"Walk him," Robinson replied.

"How about Gehrig?"

"Walk him."

Each player named was to be passed as far as Robinson was concerned. Finally the reporter got to the pitcher.

"Let him hit," Robinson said, with just a trace of a smile. "Let him win his own game."

After the conclusion of the series he told Dan Daniels of the New York World Telegram that the Yankee team was the greatest he had ever seen.

When asked how they would have fared against the old Baltimore Orioles, Robinson said, "They would have murdered us."

John McGraw screamed loudly at Robinson's apparent betrayal of the old club, but Robbie just puffed on his big cigar and said, "I don't give a $##@**! what McGraw says. They would have killed us."

Before Babe took his family back to California, he stopped at a local

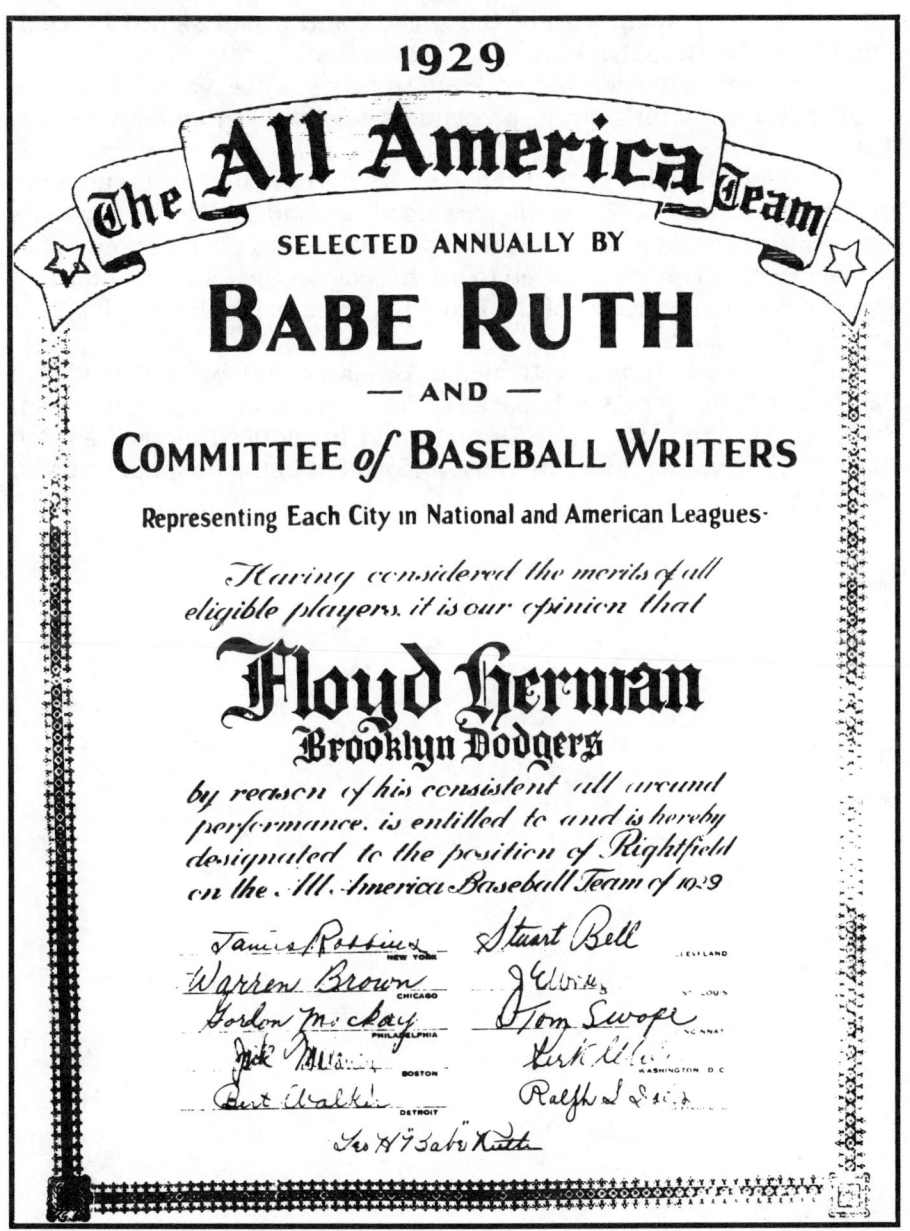

hospital to meet one of his fans.

Bobbie Hartcorn, 11, was suffering with jaundice and resulting 106 degree temperatures. Bobbie's father, Frank Hartcorn, a wealthy Flatbush broker, stopped by the Brooklyn clubhouse to see if Babe could cheer his son up.

Babe and Ann Herman, along with four-year-old Bobby, stopped to see the Hartcorn youngster, bringing with them the bat with which Babe had hit his final home run of the season and a ball signed by each member of the Brooklyn club.

Bobbie gloated over his coveted trophies while young Herman, dressed in an aviator's outfit, proclaimed his predilection for aeronautics.

The doctor in charge told reporters that Herman's visit was more effective than any of the medicines used previously. The youngster's temperature raised a little, but it was attributed to pure excitement.

The Herman family stopped to see him again the following morning and showed home movies of the Brooklyn team before leaving for their home in California.

In 1985 Babe Herman returned to Brooklyn and was inducted into the Brooklyn Dodgers Baseball Hall of Fame. While at the ceremonies in Brooklyn, a man came up to Herman and introduced himself as Bob Hartcorn, the young man who Babe had visited in the hospital some 56 years before.

Chapter 7

The front-office battle kept the Brooklyn club in the news during the off-season but they again did little to strengthen themselves for the 1930 season. They picked up pitchers Hollis 'Sloppy' Thurston on Herman's recommendation and Ray Phelps on the strength of scout Rube Marquard's reports. Catcher Al Lopez was recalled as were outfielders Hall Lee and Max West.

They purchased shortstop Gordon Slade and second baseman Neal "Mickey" Finn from the Pacific Coast League San Diego Missions at a cost of $60,000. The pair were signed on their records alone, as no Brooklyn scout had ever seen them play.

Although it didn't appear so at the time, the Robins did make a significant deal with Cincinnati in the spring, sending Doug McWeeney to the Reds for Dolph Luque. The Robin players had called McWeeney "Ace" because, they said, he was always in the hole.

Luque, the crafty Cuban, was 39 and had been in the majors since 1914, ringing up 154 victories and twice leading the league in earned run average. The Reds assumed he was through but Robinson hoped to work his usual magic on the veteran pitcher.

In another move, the club signed International League umpire Joe Becker as their Western scout. He was no relation to the Joe Becker who would later become an outstanding pitching coach for the Brooklyn club.

Glenn Wright's arm seemed strong again and he would finally become shortstop they had hoped.

The front office feud quieted somewhat in February when the National League, upon insistence from the Commissioner's office, named Frank York as president of the club for two years. Robbie was stripped of his title of president and named manager for a similar period of time. Gilleaudeau appointed Harry DeMott as director to replace Robinson and N.L. President John Heydler appointed "Dutch" Carter who had been asked to be president of the club in 1925 when Ebbets died, but had turned the offer down.

League President John Hydler emerged from the meeting with a wide grin and said, "It is the finest day's work the league has ever accomplished."

The move somewhat mollified both sides, removing Robbie as president to please the McKeever faction but re-signing him for another two years as manager to please the Ebbets faction.

Max Carey, a coach under Robinson, grew weary of the constant wrangling and quit to coach for the Pirates. He was McKeever's choice to manage the club, but when Robbie signed again, he found himself back in the coach's box and moved back to his old team. Former Dodger player and coach Ivy Olson was signed to replace him.

The Robins had finished sixth in the league in 1929 but were third in attendance, an item that angered many Brooklyn fans and caused Tommy Holmes to write, "Fans should send indignant letters to the club owners and if nothing is changed in the way of strengthening the team, should vote their displeasure by not attending the games. The Brooklyn situation will be solved when the club is sixth in the standings and sixth in attendance."

In another article, Holmes noted, "Personally I think Robbie would wash his hands of the whole Brooklyn mess except for his loyalty to Gilleaudeau. He looks tired and haggered. He lost his daughter during the winter, making his path a particularly stony one."

The team took a boat to Jacksonville, Florida on its way to spring training. Fourteen newsmen again covered the team, more than any other club in baseball including the Yankees.

Herman again conducted a lengthy holdout in 1930, finally reporting to Clearwater and immediately started to hit the ball hard. Tommy Holmes wrote: "Herman is worried he is hitting doubles and triples to left and not to right. Never mind he has been in camp just a week. But in the eighth inning he slashed a low, outside curve that might have hit him in the ankle had he not swung, and blasted a double down the right-field line. All of which indicates Herman is much closer to mid-season form than he thinks. Babe would be a .350 hitter on Christmas Eve."

Herman had held out for $25,000 and would probably have gotten it if he had stayed away from Florida another week. McKeever had told his barber when asked about the availability of Herman, "Well, we'll probably have to pay Herman what he wants."

But Thurston was leaving for Florida and Herman didn't want to make the long trip alone, so he signed for $19,000, an increase of $2,000 from 1929, as his reward for hitting .381. Vance, who slipped to 14-13 in 1929, signed for $20,000, a $5,000 cut.

Dazzy Vance and Babe Ruth argued who could hit a golf ball the longest and finally bet a box of cigars on the outcome of a driving contest. Vance reportedly overdrove the green on the first hole, a 276-yard distance. Ruth quietly withdrew and a few days later Vance received his box of stogies.

Glenn Wright, his arm seemingly strong again, was the sensation of spring training. Rookie Gordon Slade arrived in camp just in time to watch Wright range behind second base, gobble up a ball and throw the backhand to second baseman Jake Flowers for a force. "I wonder what they want with me?" he asked no one in particular. Later in the intrasquad game, Wright slammed only the third ball ever hit over the distant left field wall.

Glenn Wright

Rookie Norman Lewis "Bobo" Newsom was in camp and quickly earned the reputation as the hardest worker since Cannonball Crane. Crane, who played with Brooklyn in 1895, would arrive in the park an hour early and throw the ball the length of the field, then run down to pick it up and throw it back again. The papers also reported rookie Joe Vance wore no sox or underwear and slid headfirst, a potentially dangerous combination.

Robinson was muttering to reporter Tommy Holmes that he would trade Babe Herman if he didn't show up in camp soon. "Don't worry, Robbie," Holmes said. "If he shows up on April 1st, it will only take him a week to get in game condition."

Writers in camp felt that the Bissonette (1b), Flowers (2b), Gilbert (3b) and Wright (ss) infield was the best in Brooklyn history. They also picked the worst: The 1925 short-term unit of Jake Fournier (1b), Joe Klugman (2b), Binly Jones (ss) and Jimmy Johnston (3b). They admitted that Fournier and Johnston were all right, but the middle two were the worst ever.

The Robins beat their Jacksonville farm club with Herman collecting a triple and three sacrifice flies. He tripled and doubled against the Braves but pulled a thigh muscle.

Crowds at Macon were so good that the club considered getting into shape at Clearwater and playing all their games at the Georgia city. Attendance at Clearwater had declined for a number of years.

To emphasize what the players themselves thought about their chances in 1930, during a rainout on the way north a number of players were discussing what they would do with their share of the World Series split.

After an exhibition game, Johnny Dobbs told reporters, "Whitlow Wyatt is faster than Walter Johnson was. Faster than Johnson," and he repeated the statement in an awed voice as if he couldn't believe it himself. Eleven years later the same Wyatt pitched Brooklyn to a National League title.

Brooklyn was picked to finish second behind the Cubs by The Sporting News, while Babe Ruth picked them to finish seventh. Robbie said, "Ruth's leg has healed but his brain has gone now."

In an exhibition game with the Yankees, only his fifth of the spring, Herman singled home a run in his first at bat, then nearly amputated first baseman Lou Gehrig's leg with a double in the eighth.

Overall Babe wasn't hitting consistently, however, he made a catch on Mark Koenig in the last of the eighth in the Yankee game that demonstrated how well he had learned his outfielding lessons.

When Koenig hit the ball, some writers admitted they thought Herman would at least fall down in pursuit of the ball that was headed into right-center. The fleet Frederick couldn't catch up with it, but Herman did, taking it over his left shoulder in full flight. A New York writer noted the catch was "Classic for its speed, timing and the furor it created in a stunned press box."

And a Brooklyn writer noted, "Babe Herman must win a niche in the Hall of Fame for his bat, but he is not as awkward in the field as Frank O'Doul. O'Doul gets his feet tangled up under more fly balls than any other outfielder around."

Following an exhibition game against the Boston Red Sox in Ebbets Field just before the start of the regular season, Robinson told reporters:

"I have refused to make any statements on the chances of our team in the 1930 race until I had given the fans of Brooklyn a peek at this year's entry in the National League.

"Now that the people have seen that all the praise showered on the players in the south was deserved, I don't think I am going too far in assuring them that Brooklyn is a sure bet for the first division and a pennant possibility.

"The rest remains with the mental attitude of the players. If they show the right spirit, they can lay claim to second place, and have a good chance to beat out the Cubs."

Herman's fielding had improved during the 1929 season and he went from simply a good fielder to an excellent one in 1930. Under the coaching of Max Carey and constant practice, he soon astounded everyone.

Many days he skipped batting practice to work on fielding techniques. Pitcher Hollis Thurston hit dozens of balls a day to Babe in right field, and he would take them off the wall to learn how to play that unique boundary.

Requests for opening day tickets were the greatest in team history and on April 15 over 30,000 squeezed into a 26,000-capacity park to see the Phils win a 1-0 decision. The hilltop behind the center field wall was gone so the fans gathered on the roof of buildings behind the left field wall.

Al Lopez

After the rest of the series was rained out, the Dodgers met Boston and spotted them a 9-0 lead after two innings. Brooklyn fought back and when Herman homered in the ninth, had cut the lead to just two runs.

But from the stands came a chorus of boos following Babe's shot into the left field stands. He had popped up with the bases loaded in two previous at bats and some Robins fans let him know that a double and a homer in five trips wasn't enough for them.

But the fans were pouring into the park. Over 75,000 had attended the first three home contests.

On May 21, Del Bissonette had a grand slam homer in the first inning and added a bases-loaded triple later in the game for seven runs batted in.

The fans that booed Herman a week before, booed Robinson for pinching hitting Eddie Moore for The Babe against the Giants in a 10-4 loss. Herman was hitting .394 at the time.

Babe knocked in seven runs himself on May 29, slamming a two run homer and a two-run triple, then added four more RBIs the following day on a homer, double and sacrifice fly as the Robins swept the hated Giants.

Vance faced the Giants on the final day of April and was knocked down the first two trips to the plate. After the second trip to the dirt, he dusted himself off and said loudly enough for the rest of the Giants to hear, "You know, I throw pretty fast myself."

New York catcher Shanty Hogan said with a snarl, "Then why don't you knock somebody down?"

Vance walked and when he reached first base he was immediately surrounded by the entire Giant infield, who were quick to assure him that the pitcher had not been intentionally throwing at him and that additional knockdown pitches in his part were not necessary to demonstrate his speed.

Herman earned RBIs in the first three games of May and was hitting .468 with 29 hits and 24 runs batted over the first 16 games of the season.

Rumors that the Cardinals would move to Milwaukee circulated about the league with 'insiders' saying St. Louis was too small for two clubs. The Brooklyn Eagle reported Los Angeles and San Francisco would be in the majors within two decades. They missed their seemingly improbable prediction by seven years, an none would have guessed that Brooklyn and New York would be the National League teams making the move to California.

Brooklyn embarked on a brutal road trip, leaving on May 1st and scheduled to return May 25. In St. Louis, Bissonette homered over the right field pavilion and while watching the ball sail into the street, tripped over the first base bag and sprained his ankle.

On May 10 in Pittsburgh, Larry French wasted a high, outside fastball that seemed destined to be a wild pitch before Herman reached out and lined it into the left field stands.

The Robins moved into Philadelphia later in the month and a writer took a newspaper photo of Herman, pasting "extra outfielder" above it and "anchor" below and hanging it over his locker.

When Herman saw it his face reddened but he didn't say a thing.

He took his anger out on the opposing pitcher, slamming four singles and a homer good for six runs batted in to key a 16-9 victory that moved the team into first place. His .435 average and 33 RBI were leading the league

Four days later the phantom writer used a photo of Herman looking at his bat and pasted the words, "one-third to one-half off" and "hit on the head, knocked out" from another story below it.

Bissonette reached to take it down, but Herman said, "Leave it up. I'll show those smart guys."

He lashed two sharp singles in his first two trips to the plate, then nearly killed Boston pitcher Ed Brandt with a third shot through the pitchers box, striking Brandt squarely in the chest. Boston walked him the final two trips to the plate as the Robins won 6-3 and moved into a tie for first with St. Louis.

Later in the hotel lobby, he approached the guilty writer and said, "I suppose you think you are kidding someone. Well, just keep it up."

Rube Bressler slugged a homer in the 11th to beat Boston and end the Brooklyn road trip with an 18-6 record. Gordon Slade got into his first game and banged a home run on his first turn at bat. The Robins took three of four from the Giants and held an 6-1 season edge over their traditional rivals.

Babe was not adverse to experimentation. After the five-hit day in Philadelphia, he told Tommy Holmes of the Brooklyn Eagle he was going to try the Cobb 'hands-apart' grip.

Babe's classic swing

"Cobb's method has certain advantages," Babe explained. "For one thing, if you start to swing at a pitch and change your mind, you can check you bat before it comes around and you won't have a strike called. But when I'm swinging from the handle, it's pretty hard for me to stop before it's too late."

However he went 7-for-26 in the next seven games, and struck out three times on May 27, causing him to hastily leave the Cobb grip to Cobb.

Babe's final whiff of the game came in the last of the ninth with two on, and the next day Herman took extra long batting practice before the game, wearing out a flock of kids who were recruited to shag the balls for him.

He was checking out a new shipment of bats to find sticks with just the proper balance. When he finished hitting his hands were raw and bleeding but he had segregated three bats he would take extra care with.

He had to have his hands bandaged before the game. On his first trip to the plate he broke one of the special bats while looping a single down the right field line off Carl Hubbell. That seemed to only infuriate Babe.

With the score tied in the sixth, Herman met one of Hubbell's fast balls and it sailed deep over the right-center field wall. He grinned for the first time in a week as he trotted around the bases.

Then in the eighth he hit another over the wall near the foul pole. "That was just to prove the first one wasn't an accident," he said later. The home runs resulted in a 4-1 victory, as well as a share of first place, and the game was finished in an hour and 28 minutes.

At that, a few fans booed his second home run, still angry he hadn't hit it the day before.

A Herman sympathizer sent the following poem to the Brooklyn Eagle the next day, commemorating Babe's achievements.

The Modern Casey

Old Casey of immortal fame,
So to end the old ball game,
In Mudville long ago.
As Herman did Tuesday last,
His bat was slow, the ball was fast,
It was an awful blow.

The next time Babe stepped in the yard,
He hit the ball both far and hard,
And had a bang-up day.
Off his big bat two homers flew,
And maybe Casey came back, too,
The story doesn't say.

In the final four games of May he had eight hits, three homers and seven RBI, finishing May with a .411 average.

Playing the Phillies in Ebbets Field, Bissonette slammed a long drive to right field. Herman and Frederick had singled and were watching to see if the ball cleared the wall when Bissonette charged past both of them to nullify the shot.

The rule in effect that year allowed a sacrifice fly to be recorded in the event that any base runner advanced on the hit.

Babe, unsure if the drive would clear the right field wall, held up for a time to make certain, then seeing Bissonette charging down the line shouted to him to slow up.

Del never broke stride, roaring past both runners without noticing either of them. He later told Herman that he could not hear out of his left ear, and never realized that Babe was shouting at him.

Although Herman got most of the blame for the incident, Bissonette

Babe and Al Lopez work with Bobby Herman before a game. Note Lopez influence as Bobby bats right handed.

apologized when he noticed all the attention it drew. "Sorry, Babe," he said, "It was my fault."

The Brooklyn club entered June with a 25-15 record and a two game lead on second-place St. Louis. On June first Herman and Frederick twice hit back to back home runs as the Robins beat the Phils 10-2. One of Babe's shots was a gigantic blast off the center field wall that went for an inside the park homer. Bissonette also added an inside the park shot.

The large crowds that packed Ebbets Field caused the Board of Directors to again consider Steve McKeever's plans to enlarge the park. He suggested closing Montgomery Street behind the left-field wall to build the grandstand, deeding the extra land back to the city and increasing the park capacity by about 25,000 seats to approximately 47,000.

The Sporting News wrote: "If any proof were necessary to stamp Herman as one of the mightiest natural hitters of all time, here it is. For within considerably less than a month of the season, you find Babe running outfielders bowlegged with line drives in spite of the fact he had practically no spring training.

"The pitchers who started in February are a little ahead of him but they find out that fooling him doesn't necessarily mean getting him out. Babe's eye is so good that he succeeds in meeting balls that other hitters would miss.

"And hits were about all Herman could contribute to the team in previous years, but Babe, once the Tyro of the Outfield, has become a fine, steady fielder.

"The opposition used to cry 'Hit it to Herman.' Now it is the Robins who cry 'Hit it to Herman.' He has yet to make an error this season and has become the steadiest fielder of the whole Brooklyn team including the talented Frederick."

Pittsburgh manager Bill McKechnie told reporters: "Usually a manager knows how a hitter can be stopped, but Babe Herman...throw a curve at his ankles and he's apt to knock your right fielder down. Throw at his nose and he'll hit a line drive to left."

Babe was hitting .420 on June fifth, but went into a slump, dropping to .389 by the 15th of the month. Chuck Klein of the Phillies moved into the league lead with a .420 average.

However Babe's fielding continued to improve and on the 16th he saved a game for Ray Phelps with a brilliant catch while racing to his right in the seventh, robbing Gus Mancuso of the of Cardinals of an extra-base hit. Brooklyn tripped the Cards two of three and won their tenth straight series of the season.

The Robins split with Cincinnati on the road and headed toward Pittsburgh. On the train, coach Ivy Olson talked to Brooklyn Eagle reporter Tommy Holmes.

"No wonder we had trouble in Cincinnati," he said. "The bottom fell out of our barometer. The barometer of this ball club is Babe Herman—when he hits we win and when he doesn't we don't.

"The club has other good hitters, but Herman is the key man of our whole attack. He gets up four or five times a game. On a couple of those occasions, Frederick and Gilbert will get on ahead of him. On a couple of those occasions, Bissonette and Bressler will hit behind him.

"If Herman is hitting, the whole bunch are bound to click a couple of times a game and drive in enough runs to win."

Herman provided quick proof of Olson's theory by banging a pair of home runs, good for four runs, in a 9-6 win over the Pirates. His last homer tied the score 6-6 in the seventh inning.

In a scenario that Olson himself might have directed, Herman came up with Frederick and Gilbert on base, took two strikes from Pirate hurler Larry French, then caught a changeup and slammed it over the wall for his 15th homer. Thus inspired, his teammates scored three in the next inning to win.

In the sixth inning the following afternoon, the Robins smacked ten hits in succession, then added two more successive hits in the seventh to set a major league record. Herman banged two homers and had four RBIs.

The remarkable string of hits started with two out and one runner on base. John Frederick singled and Wally Gilbert hit an inside-the-park homer. Herman homered over the right field wall and Del Bissonette and Rube Bressler singled. Glenn Wright scored both of them with a triple and scored himself on Mickey Finn's double. Al Lopez and pitcher Jim Elliott singled and when Frederick followed with a single, Lopez was out at the plate trying to score.

Opening the seventh inning, Gilbert singled and Herman homered into the upper right-field stands. Bissonette ended the record barrage when he grounded out.

St. Louis traded Fred Frankhouse and Bill Sherdel to Boston for Burleigh Grimes. The Dodgers heaved a sigh of relief, happy the Cubs didn't obtain the former Dodger ace. But Grimes was to be the spark the Cardinals needed and his acquisition would put the Missouri team back into the pennant race.

On Babe's birthday, June 26, he made his first error of the season, overrunning a ground ball in his haste to throw a runner out at the plate. Frank York had pointed out Herman's 16 errors in 1929 when negotiations were taking place in the spring but this year Babe had gone 41 games before recording a boot.

Brooklyn lost three of four in Chicago. Guy Bush was pitching the opening game of the series and had earlier quick-pitched Glenn Wright and struck him out. Two innings later he got two strikes on Herman, and Babe stepped out of the box to get some dirt on his hands.

When he stepped back in, Bush quickly fired to the plate. Herman, reacting instinctively, cracked the ball back through the box, and a Chicago writer covering the game reported: "Bush was never nearer death than at that time. He had no chance to field the ball. Instinct brought his hands in front of his face and the ball stuck in the pocket of his glove. A split-second later and they would have packed him in ice. The ball rebounded out of the glove but Bush scrambled after it to throw Herman out."

As the month ended the Robins had a fine, 39-25 record but had slipped into second place, two behind the Cubs.

Searching for more punch, the Robins had a minor-league deal nearly completed for Buzz Arlett but he had been struck across the face with a mask in an argument with a plate umpire and suspended for 90 days. They instead purchased the contract of 32-year-old Ike Boone, who was hitting a blazing .443 in the Pacific Coast League with 21 home runs in 74 games.

Cub manager Joe McCarthy predicted that the Robinson would not contest for the pennant. "They'll blow up before long," he told reporters.

Following a series against the Braves, Boston writer Austen Lake noted: "Before the opening game of each series, it is the custom for each team to hold a meeting to discuss the batting peculiarities of the opposing players and the way to offset them.

"But they tell me when Babe Herman's name comes up, opposing managers make no attempt to analyze his tendencies, because he has none, and is just as apt to hit a ball aimed at his ear as one that cuts the plate.

"Perhaps it is because Babe is a left-hander by birth and predilection that he evades the natural grooves in which baseball action turns, since left-handers are supposed to be erratic.

"Vance tells me on the last visit to Pittsburgh, Larry French was pitching to Herman. He threw a duster that narrowly missed his chest. On the next pitch he tried to dust him again. This time the ball whizzed at Herman's chin. And yet, somehow, Babe slammed the ball against the right field fence.

"Al Grabowski threw a ball in St. Louis that should have hit Herman in the breast bone," related Vance. "Babe should have been lucky to dodge the pitch. But instead he slapped it far down the third base line for two bases. Imagine hitting a ball three feet inside to the opposite field.

"The long and short of it is, then, that Babe Herman hits everything, with no regard for a good or bad ball. He says himself he never pays any attention to the count of balls or strikes, but just swings when the spirit moves him. It seems to work, too, in Babe's case. He cuts and slashes, letting nature take it's course."

The Robins lost the last three games in June and the first game in July. As the team dressed before the final game of the series in St. Louis, Babe and Robbie were discussing the lineup for the game against the

Cardinals.

"Let me make out the lineup today," Babe said and scribbled it down on the back of an envelope. He put Bressler in the leadoff slot, dropped former leadoff man Frederick to third and hit himself fourth.

"Why not," said the Robin manger. "Bressler isn't so spry but he is the best 'waiter' on the club. It might change our luck. We can't hit any worse than we have the last couple days."

The new lineup payed off quickly, for in the second inning, with two out, Bressler walked to load the bases and Mickey Finn, promoted from seventh to second in the order, doubled to score two. The Robins stopped the Cardinals 6-5 with the team collecting 12 hits and Herman adding an important double.

In addition to playing manager, Babe put together a 15-game hitting streak, the team won six of nine and moved back into first place. He had a 12 hits in the final four games of his streak and six of them were for extra bases.

On July 6th Babe made a long run toward the stands and dove to catch a bid for a home run by Wally Berger. He caught the ball, hit the rail and was suspended on his head in the lap of a fan with his spikes in the air.

Boone's suspected fielding deficiencies began to show and he dropped a couple of easy flies in the outfield. The Brooklyn Eagle wrote, "Boone is a good judge of balls he can reach, he just can't reach many. He is hitting .529 and fielding about the same." And one of the players suggested that Robinson played Boone because there wasn't enough room on the bench for Boone, Robinson and Jim Elliott, all extremely large men.

On July 15 Herman, Wright and Clark visited the 200-member Flatbush Boys Club. Herman opened the meeting with "Ladies, Gentlemen and Rowdies...", drawing a big laugh. He drew a standing ovation when he finished and nearly every member of the club came forward afterward with something for Babe to sign.

The Cubs moved into town for a five-game series, trailing Brooklyn by three.

In the first game, Del Bissonette attempted to stretch a triple into a homer and, after being waived in by third base coach Ivy Olson, hesitated, then crashed into Gabby Hartnett who tagged him hard under the chin. He was out cold when his head hit the plate.

Third base coach Ivy Olson argued long enough to get thrown out of the game, but reappeared in the coaching box an inning later and held a runner at third on a double by Frederick.

This time Cub manager McCarthy argued that since the Robins had used an illegal coach at third, the hitter should be forced to bat again but the protest was denied.

The second game of the doubleheader was spiced with beanballs thrown by both pitching staffs and although the Robins won that game, they lost the next three of the series. The Cubs now trailed by only percentage points.

Brooklyn took three of five from St. Louis. Harvey Hendrick's pinch-hit three-run homer in the ninth won the first 9-8. Hal Lee collected his first major league hit with another pinch-hit homer. The Cards won the second game 17-10 and when Hollis Thurston stopped the Cardinals 1-0 on three hits the next day, Cardinal manager Frank Frisch, who had popped out to end the game, rushed to the mound in a rare show of sportsmanship to throw his arm around him and offer congratulations. Ageless Dolph Luque won the finale 4-1.

Pitcher Fred Heimach was purchased from Toledo, but when he arrived the Robins found that Casey Stengel had used him three straight days after the trade was made and he would be unable to work for some time.

The Robins took two from the Phillies as Al Lopez, who had only one previous home run, banging a round tripper in each game. Glenn Wright also homered in both contests.

Despite playing with a pulled muscle in each thigh, Herman had collected 14 hits in 18 trips in the final three games of July, including three doubles and a league-leading 23rd homer, accounting for eight runs batted in. He finished the month with a .397 average.

Standings showed that Brooklyn was still leading the league as Chicago, New York and St. Louis trailed.

August 1 standings:

	W	L	gb
Brooklyn	62	40	--
Chicago	59	43	3
New York	57	45	5
St. Louis	52	49	9 1/2

Moving into August, the Robins were not only in the pennant chase, but Herman was fighting for the batting title again and the fans packed the park. Chuck Klein led the league with a .411 mark. O'Doul was second at .402, Herman third at .397 and Bill Terry fourth at .396.

The first day of August Babe slammed his 24th homer and had five runs batted in. The homer broke a 3-3 tie as the Robins topped the Phils 9-4.

On August 3rd, Dazzy Vance and Carl Hubbell locked up in a scoreless dual that went into the last of the ninth. Herman led off with a looping double to left and Jake Flowers walked with the bases loaded to force in the winning run in a 1-0 contest.

"It was the toughest game I have pitched in years," Vance said after stranding 11 Giant runners. "I couldn't let up for a minute."

Brooklyn's version of 'Murder's Row'—1930. From Left: Babe Herman .393, Johnny Frederick .334, Del Bissonette .336, Jake Flowers .320 and Al Lopez .309.

And the Brooklyns won another wild contest the next day. New York scored five in the ninth to tie, after Dolph Luque enjoyed a 6-1 lead with two out and two strikes on Bill Terry who slugged a three-run homer. N.Y. also scored two in the tenth to take the lead.

Three Robins runs in the last of the ninth won for Brooklyn and Giant third baseman Freddie Lindstrom threw his glove into the stands in disgust as the winner crossed the plate on a long fly by Eddie Moore.

Moving into the road, the Robins beat Pittsburgh 7-4. Herman recorded the winning run when he tagged and scored on a short fly, jumping over the catcher who was waiting in front of the plate with the ball.

In the first game of the Cardinal series, Babe cracked out a single, a double and two homers, his 25th and 26th, in an 11-5 victory.

The following day, Babe made a miraculous catch in the fourth inning and turned it into a triple play.

The Brooklyn Eagle wrote:

"What with one thing and another, it is difficult, well nigh impossible, to keep the name of Mr. Floyd Herman out of the headlines these days. On Friday his four hits, including two home runs, featured the Brooklyn attack. Then yesterday he hit nothing at all at the plate but had the goshalmightiest catch ever witnessed by mortal man.

"Jim Bottomly was on second and Chick Hafey on first in the fourth inning when George Watkins laced a line drive headed for high on the right field wall. Messrs. Bottomly and Hafey put down their heads and started to run, intent upon scoring on the very apparent double.

"Instead of playing for the rebound off the 10-foot wall, the lean and hungry Herman ran over under the liner. His six-foot four-inch frame shot high in the air, his right arm stretched as far as it could, and in the capacious maw of his glove the ball struck and stuck.

"A few second later, Herman came down to earth. He threw a strike to Flowers at second. Jake touched the bag, which doubled up Bottomly, who, by this time, had rounded third. He then tagged Hafey to complete the triple play before the staring, unbelieving eyes of the sparse assemblage of 3,500 Cardinal rooters.

"This, however, was a purely defensive sensation and accomplished nothing towards overcoming the lead the Cardinals had established."

He banged his 27th homer in the series finale but the Cards scored three times in the last of the ninth to win 7-6 and drop Brooklyn into second place. Against Pittsburgh and St. Louis Herman had collected 12 hits in 23 trips.

Moving into Chicago in a virtual tie, the Cubs banged out three wins in the four game series played before a record 165,000 fans. After a four-hit performance in the opening game that boosted his average to .404, the Cub fans gave Herman a big hand the first time at the plate the following day. In the final game of the series, Woody English and Hack Wilson singled in the 10th inning and Danny Taylor hit a drive down the right field line.

Herman, stepping gingerly along the rope that held back the overflow crowd, leaped high in the air and into the crowd. "I had the ball in my glove," he said after the game, "but when I came down in the crowd someone rammed into me and I lost it." English scored the winning run to give the Cubs the series three games to one.

The Pirates took three of five games, dropping the Robins 3 1/2 games off the pace and the heat of the pennant race coupled with the heat of the summer began to take its toll.

On August 15, Terry led the league's hitters with a .407 mark, followed by Klein at .402, Herman at .398 and O'Doul at .394. One week later Herman crowded Terry .410 to .402, with Klein at .401 and O'Doul a strong fourth at .391.

The Robins played a double-header in Pittsburgh, then jumped onto the train to play the Sunday game in Ebbets Field.

Behind the right field wall and across Bedford Avenue, an auto showroom was located with large plate glass windows. Eight times in 1930 balls had crashed through the windows and the club had to pay each time to replace the glass.

Finally Ed McKeever ordered a screen built on top the concrete right field wall to keep at least some of the baseballs in the park and away from the expensive windows.

Robinson was startled by the proposal and told McKeever the club would be handicapped by the screen. But Ed had thought of that and was having it constructed 1/2-inch behind the wall, thus making it a home run if the ball cleared the wall and struck the screen.

The new screen would extended 19 feet above the 19-foot concrete wall and balls hit into the screen were still homers. At least that was what they thought the umpires would rule, since no one had bothered to check with league officials for a ruling on balls hit into the screen.

The screen was erected primarily to keep Herman's drives from smashing through the large plate glass windows. It cost the club $100 each time one of his rockets would arch over the wall and connect with the big display window and club officials finally felt it would be cheaper to build a screen than keep paying for windows.

The crowning blow had come when he homered during a game and the ball crashed through the window. It was quickly replaced and before the bill could even be presented to the club, Herman hit a second shot through the newly installed glass the following afternoon in batting practice.

Babe also hit a screaming foul ball one afternoon that hooked foul and crashed through a police booth on the corner of Bedford Avenue and Sullivan Place, cutting the hand of a policeman inside.

Some freak home runs have been hit because of the unusual construction of the Ebbets Field right field wall.

In 1916 a ground ball hit by Robin second baseman George Cutshaw rolled out to the base of the wall, hit the concrete and rolled right up and over the wall for a home run.

Casey Stengel was in the Brooklyn outfield that day and said of the homer, "I have seen some crazy homers and have hit a few myself, that one with which Cutshaw gave us a pennant was far and away the nuttiest of them all.

"That home run cost Erskine Mayer (Phillie pitcher) $500. He was on a bonus deal with William F. Baker, the owner. Had he won the game he would have collected. We used to call him 'Percentage,' but we couldn't after that hit.

"Here is the way it happened: Cutshaw drove a low liner past Cactus Cravath, in right field. The ball struck the base of the wall, and then began to do strange things.

"It had acquired peculiar English and climbed up that concrete wall facing as if it were something alive. I never will forget the consternation on Cravath's face as he stood by and saw that crazy baseball reach the top of the wall, look around, and then quietly drop into Bedford Avenue and a Brooklyn pennant.

"Maybe Cutshaw and that English on the ball did not do us too big a favor, because we did not do so well in the World Series. We took only one game from the Red Sox."

Phillie catcher Jim Wilson hit a similar 'climbing' home run in 1926. And in 1940 Lonnie Frey of Cincinnati hit a ball which fell off the screen on the top of the wall between the scoreboard and the right field foul pole. It bounced up and down but stayed on the ledge and never came down. Club president Larry MacPhail put up boards the next day to prevent similar homers.

During the war, when wire was unavailable to patch the screen, Dixie Walker hit a home run that went neatly through a hole and into Bedford Avenue. Walker also hit a homer that stuck in the screen and only came down when he threw a ball against it before the next inning started, allowing him to "catch" his own home run.

During the final game of the 1950 season, Pee Wee Reese hit a shot that lodged between the concrete wall and the screen, giving the Dodgers their only run off Robin Roberts. Philadelphia eventually won the game and the pennant with three runs in the tenth inning.

A daring fan crawled out on the ledge and got the ball. Reese traded him two new ones for the rust-stain souvenir of that heart-breaking afternoon.

Apparently MacPhail's boards had been removed by that time.

When the Robins arrived at home on Sunday for their game with Pittsburgh, the screen was under construction. The hot pace of the pennant race had started to tell on the players and Bissonette, Dudley, Heimach and Slade were left in Pittsburgh to rest.

Vance won a 5-0 decision as Herman slugged a homer in the first inning, his 28th, then both clubs piled back on the train and returned to Pittsburgh where the Pirates won two in succession.

"Here we are so tired we can hardly see straight and after one of the toughest sleeper jumps in the circuit we run into a doubleheader in Cincinnati," Glenn Wright said. "We've had to make more sleeper jumps than any team. We're as stale as last week's bread."

Cincinnati was the next stop, and the Brooklyn club hoped to make up lost ground against the last-place Reds, whom they had defeated 16 of 18 times, but the Robins managed to score only seven runs in the five-game series, losing all of them.

Cincinnati swept the opening double bill by identical 2-1 scores, then won the next three games to run the Robin's losing string to seven in succession. On the final day, a double header because of a rainout, Herman made fielding mistakes in each game that cost Brooklyn runs.

On a day off in Cincinnati, Robinson called traveling secretary John Gorman and handed him a wad of bills. After some whispered instructions, the returned with a number of bottles of the best prohibition booze money could buy.

Robbie called the team together and said. "You've been too tight. It's time to relax and maybe we can find our hitting eye again."

The bottles were passed around and at least for an evening, the entire team became honorary members of the Big Four as the party lasted far into the Ohio evening.

The club ended their western swing with a 5-15 record and Herman, dog tired, had only one hit in his last 23 times to the plate.

Back in Brooklyn Abe Yeager died. He had been the Eagle sports editor for 45 years. His funeral procession appropriately passed Ebbets Field on the way to the cemetery.

His son felt that Yeager had given up the long fight against cancer when the Robins lost seven straight games to the Pirates and Reds. "Maybe he associated the two cases closer than you think," he said. "He has always been bound up in baseball and Brooklyn."

Brooklyn had played 48 games on 40 consecutive days. The original schedule was made assuming that two or three days rain would interrupt the long schedule. The club had won 21 of the first 33, then slowly wore down, losing 12 of their last 15.

Everyone slept during the 18-hour ride to Brooklyn from Cincinnati, now trailing the leader by 5 1/2 games. The club split four with the Giants in NY, making the pennant dream fade even more although the team beat Hubbell in the second game of the series. A great catch by Herman off a long drive by Fred Lindstrom the next day only kept the game close but the Giants won 3-2.

On the final day of August, Babe slammed one of the longest home runs of his career. It cleared the newly-built right field screen and was chased down by a boy on Rogers Avenue one block beyond the park. The homer, his 29th, helped in a 14-3 win.

A New York paper noted, "Herman's hit may lead to a screen being built above houses on Rogers Avenue, one block over from Bedford. But apart from its sheer magnificence, the screen played only a minor role in the game."

Moving into September the standings were:

	W	L	gb
Chicago	77	51	--
New York	71	55	5
Brooklyn	72	58	7
St. Louis	71	58	7 1/2

Bill Terry led the league with a .405 mark and Chuck Klein was second at .391. Herman was hitting over .400 going into the Cincinnati series, but had slipped to .387.

The Dodgers took the train to Boston and Robinson said, "We need everything going for us to win now. We need a long winning streak and someone to beat the Cubs." The Brooklyn Eagle reporter noted, "If you believe all of that, the legend of Santa Claus is not much of a strain on your credulity."

The club lost two of three, dropping into fourth place. Columnist John Keiran voiced the opinion of most when he wrote, "The Robins are out of it."

In the first of two against the Braves, Babe took a 3-2 pitch and trotted to first base. But umpire Bill Klem shouted, "Strike three."

Herman hurried back to the plate and heatedly discussed what he considered a bad call. Press box veterans could never remember Klem allowing such a long argument from a player.

Finally Klem said, "Go ask Robbie if it wasn't a strike. If he says it was a ball, I'll buy you a suit of clothes."

"How could he tell from the dugout?" Herman countered.

"If anyone in the park says it was a ball, I'll buy you a suit."

"But it was right there," Herman said, drawing a line well inside the plate.

Klem just drew a line down the middle of the plate and looked sternly at Babe.

Realizing he has been pressing his luck, Herman just threw up his hands and loped out into right field.

With the pennant seemingly out of reach of the Robins now, rumors started concerning the 1931 season. Rogers Hornsby, seemingly out of favor in Chicago, was rumored to be the next Robin second baseman. Then rumors of a trade between the Robins and St. Louis that would allow Vance and Frank Frisch to exchange uniforms came from the usual "reliable source."

Returning to Brooklyn, the team had three off days to regroup and then they roared back with one of the greatest pennant surges in the history of the club.

They crushed the Phillies 22-8 as Herman slugged home run No. 30 over the wall and narrowly missed No. 31 inside the park when he was thrown out at the plate. He collected five RBIs in the win and his three-run shot in the first opened the gates for a 24-hit attack.

WOR radio broadcast the Giant invasion of Brooklyn the following afternoon and Babe was 3-for-4, adding a spectacular leaping catch off the right field wall on a long drive by Mel Ott, as Dazzy Vance topped Carl Hubbell 5-2. But Brooklyn was still in fourth place.

They dumped the Phils twice on the September 8 to edge back into third place, then braced for the invasion of the league-leading Chicago Cubs. The Robins had managed to win only two of the previous 16 games from the leaders.

In the Chicago opener, the Robins led 1-0 into the eighth, but

Brooklyn fans were holding their breath, waiting for Hartnett or Hack to slug one out of the park.

In the eighth inning, with Gilbert on base, Herman boomed a shot to center that Riggs Stephenson chased, then pulled up with a look of distaste on his face as the ball landed in the center field seats.

There was a moment of stunned silence, then a startled, almost unbelieving gasp. The Eagle wrote, "Then came a booming roar as the Cubs saw their game disappear though a golden shower of straw hats, sailing, hurtling, dropping on the infield."

Babe Phelps pitched a five-hit shutout and Babe made a running, twisting catch of a difficult shot into the corner off the bat of George Kelly to end the game.

Dolph Luque duplicated Phelp's five-hitter the next afternoon and Herman, hitting in his 14th straight game, added three hits in a 6-0 win as Brooklyn moved into third place just 1 1/2 games back. Babe trailed Terry by eight points, .404 to .396 in the batting race. However "Hell Old" Rube Bressler caught a smoking Hack Wilson shot on the end of his finger. The digit was both dislocated and fractured, ending Rube's participation for the rest of the season.

Bressler and Watson Clark were called the "Hell Old" twins by most of their teammates. Robbie would often say, "Hell, old Rube will hit one" or "Hell, old Watty will stop them."

Dazzy Vance fanned 13 Cubs in the third game, the top strikeout mark of the season in the National League, to sweep the series and turn the borough of Brooklyn into a madhouse. The win edged the Robins into second place, just a half game out of first. Herman walked and Glenn Wright homered in the first and that was all that Vance needed for a 2-1 victory. Wright's shot made him the first Brooklyn right-hander in history to hit 20 home runs in a season. Herman ended the game with another spectacular catch off a Wilson line drive into right-center.

Cincinnati, the Robin-killers of late August, moved into Ebbets Field for a four game set and this time the Brooklyns quickly disposed of them. Ray Moss won 7-3, Babe Phelps won 4-3 and the team passed the Cubs in the standings and now trailed only the Cardinals.

But tragedy again struck in the Brooklyn outfield as John Frederick, racing across center field in pursuit of a drive by Reds shortstop Leo Durocher, dove for the ball and tore the satorius muscle in the upper rear part of his right thigh so badly he could not walk. The lingering injury sidelined him during the rest of the 1930 season and almost ended his major league career as a regular, although he played for a number of years in Brooklyn afterward and set a major league record with six pinch-hit home runs in 1932.

Frederick was the best center fielder Herman ever played with. "I always knew where Johnny was," Herman said. "He would yell on every ball. Jigger Statz wouldn't yell and Robbie told me to let him take everything he could reach. But it was a worry, since he didn't let you know where he was or if he could get it or not.

"Kiki Cuyler was bad about not yelling and I nearly ran into Estell Crabtree at full-speed one game when he didn't call the ball. I jumped over him or we would have had a terrible collision. He dove and caught the ball but I could have caught it without diving.

"I played with some great center fielders, but Johnny was the best."

Hollis "Sloppy" Thurston and reliever Jim Elliott won 8-3 the third game of the Cincinnati series and the team moved on top of the National League for the first time since August 11. Babe had three straight hits including an RBI double.

Then Ray Moss, back on only two days rest, won 13-5 to give the Robins an 11-game winning streak and propel them into first place by a game over the charging St. Louis Cardinals. Wright bounced a homerun into the stands, and running with his head down passed Herman on the bases. Babe, remembering the incident with Bissonette on Memorial Day, was watching closely as the ball skipped into the stands but still was unable to stay in front of the hard-running shortstop. Babe had four hits but still trailed Terry .404-.398. He was one hit short of the magic .400 mark but would never be closer during the remainder of the 1930 season.

In the midst of the wild pennant drive the confident Brooklyn directors voted to build 5,000 additional seats in Ebbets Field for the anticipated World Series. That would give the park a seating capacity of 2,000 box seats, 14,800 reserved seats and 18,000 unreserved seats for a total of 34,800.

But immediately they removed the tarpaulin sheds in center field and installed 500 temporary seats in anticipation of the next series.

Often in the delightfully surprising game of baseball, the gods seem to arrange the schedule so the contending teams meet each other at the most crucial time.

Thus it happened on September 16, 1930 as the St. Louis team moved into Ebbets Field for a three-game series that all of baseball knew would decide the pennant winner.

Bill Hallahan faced Vance in the opener as Ebbets Field overflowed with Flatbush Faithful. The classic contest nearly came unwound in the fourth inning. George Watkins had singled and Charlie Gilbert doubled with two out. Then Taylor Douthit smashed a drive to right with two runners on base.

Center fielder Moore ran hard but it was apparent he would not be able to reach it. Herman cut across from right and he couldn't get it either—except he did, reaching his glove hand high over his shoulder to make the crucial catch to the delight of the huge crowd.

The game was perhaps one of the most celebrated in Ebbets Field history. Brooklyn's first hit came off Hallahan in the eighth. Vance was nearly as good but only his own heady work in the sixth inning saved the game that point.

Sparky Adams advanced to third base, then broke for home on an attempted steal with Chick Hafey at the plate. Vance noticed him and quickly fired a fastball off Hafey's leg. The resulting dead ball sent Adams back to third where he stayed as Vance retired the final hitter of the inning.

Hendrick got the first Brooklyn hit in the seventh on a line drive to center but he was promptly thrown out stealing as Robbie went for broke. Finn then singled and was out attempting to stretch it into a double, crashing into shortstop Charlie Gelbert in a collision at second base. The ball rolled away, but Finn, dazed, staggered off the base and was tagged out by Hallahan who had retrieved the ball.

In the ninth, with the game still scoreless, Lopez singled and Vance dropped down a neat bunt. The throw to second sailed into center field. However Frisch fell on Lopez so he couldn't advance to third. Eddie Moore, the best bunter on the team, popped a little foul beside the plate and Mancuso doubled Lopez off second after the catch.

In the 10th inning, former Robin Andy High pinch-hit a double off the right field wall. Eddie Moore was used in center, due to Frederick's injury, but he had a bad Charlie horse in the back of his leg. A ground ball had gone through him and Babe had to run it down early in the game.

"Let me play center, Robbie," Herman asked Robinson before the game, but he refused. Babe played toward center during the game to help cover some of the ground, and as a result High's drive down the right field line that Babe might have caught if he had been playing normally went for an extra base hit.

Taylor Douthit scored High with a single for the first and only run of the game.

Brooklyn fought back in the last of the 10th, filling the bases against Hallahan with one out. Wright doubled, Bissonette walked and Hendrick bunted them to second and third. Flowers hit for Finn and was intentional walked.

Al Lopez smashed the ball to Adams at short. The ball skipped off the grass and struck him in the chest but luckily for the Cardinals it dropped squarely in front of him. He made a quick recovery, flipped the ball to Frank Frisch at second and the relay nipped Lopez at first on a play so close that participants were still talking about it long after the season.

Lopez swore he was safe on the play and that the first base umpire had not been watching it. He claimed the umpire didn't move after the call, not realizing that the out had ended the game.

Dolph Luque was to have faced Flint Rehm in the second game but Rehm never showed up at the park. So Luque was matched against Syl Johnson and the Robins built a 3-2 lead on the strength of Ike Boone's homer. The Cards tied in the eighth and again High doubled, this time with two on in the ninth, to give the Cards a 5-3 victory.

When the Cardinals arrived back at their hotel after the game, they found Rehm, excited and a bit unsteady. He told a story about being kidnapped before the game by Brooklyn hoods who took him to a small apartment and forced him to drink great quantities of whiskey. When they released him, they said "Something worse would happen to him if he decided to pitch."

It had been a terrible experience, Rehm said. His teammates reported that he had won $200 at the track in Boston before the Brooklyn series and that "might" have had something to do with his disappearance.

Branch Rickey, when asked about the 'kidnapping' spoke for many when he simply said, "Bunk." Although he added, "You couldn't disprove the story by the way Rehm smelled."

The Brooklyn Eagle suggested that the "rowdys" who grabbed Rehm should have grabbed Andy High instead.

Some 30 years later Rehm told the "real" story at a reunion of the 1930 Cardinal team. He noted that the night before the first game, he and Bill Hallahan went out. "It wasn't a big party," he noted, "Just something to eat and maybe—I don't remember exactly— a couple drinks.

"Well, the next morning when I work up, I was sicker than I have ever been in my life. I was sick all over. Stomach, head, even the bottoms of my feet. Hallahan just looked at me and shook his head.

" 'What should I tell them,' he asked me. I told him to tell them any damn thing he wanted and rolled back over in bed. I wasn't going to the park as bad as I felt.

"Hallahan went out and beat Vance 1-0. The next day Rickey came by my room and I was still sicker than a mule. Rickey looked in and said, 'What's the matter with you? I guess somebody kidnapped you.' I was still green around the gills and told him he could call it what he liked, but that I was as sick as can be.

"The writers got the story I was sick from manager Gabby Street and built it up—I don't know if Rickey helped them or not—that I had been kidnapped and been taken to New Jersey and fed whiskey.

"All that time I was supposed to be kidnapped, I was there in a hotel room. The club moved me to another room so the writers couldn't find me. So help me, that's what happened."

However it happened, Johnson won the important second game and the Robins trailed by .002 points as the clubs moved into the final game of the series.

Former Robin, Burleigh Grimes, completed the crushing sweep with a 4-3 victory in the final game. Herman was hitless in the two previous games, but he cracked a homer and scored a second runner with a

Babe's homer in the third game of the Cardinal series was met with polite applause and a few boos.

sacrifice fly. Many in the disappointed Brooklyn crowd booed Babe as he trotted around the bases after his homer, apparently expecting him to perform miracles every day.

The Cardinals, 11 1/2 games behind Brooklyn just five weeks earlier, had won 31 of 37 games to move into first place.

The loss dropped the Robins only one and one-half games off the pace but apparently destroyed the hopes of many of the players. They cancelled the new cars they had ordered, anticipating a World Series cut, and many drowned their sorrows after the game and continuing on through an open date the following day.

Brooklyn wasn't out of the pennant chase mathematically, but emotionally they were finished. They led Pittsburgh 2-0 into the eighth on Herman's homer to deep center field, only to have the Pirates score five and go on to win 6-2.

They slipped to third the next afternoon as Pittsburgh won a 7-6 victory over Watty Clark, a 13-game winner, who inexplicably was making his first start since August 27.

Herman made a last-minute effort to turn the results around. With two out in the last of the ninth and Gilbert at second base, Herman hit a mountainous drive to center. Gilbert had crossed the plate and Babe was near second when the ball was caught against the furthest part of the center field wall to end the game.

The Giants came over the bridge and joyfully eliminated the Robins from any possibility of winning the flag. Vance lost 8-2 despite Herman's 35th homer of the year, a club record, and Philadelphia dropped them into fourth place with a 6-3 win the next afternoon.

It was all over but the weeping; Brooklyn won 8-2 in the first game of a doubleheader on the 27th behind Vance, who left immediately after the game for his home in Florida. The Robins lost the second 7-1.

Hollis Thurston got the final start of the season and made the most of it. He banged a double and a single, good for four runs batted in, to win 6-3, completing the game and ending the disappointing season in just an hour and 23 minutes.

After the Cardinal series, and while Herman was still fighting Terry for the batting title, a pitcher from an opposing team met Babe before the game by the batting cage and said, "Go ahead and bunt today, I won't throw you out. How many hits do you need to beat that guy?" Babe told him he appreciated the thought but firmly declined the offer.

Babe hit .417 from Sept. 6th until the end of the season but it wasn't enough.

Herman was beaten out of the batting championship again, this time by Terry's .401 mark. Herman was just five hits short of the magic .400 mark. Babe's .393 average, following the .381 he recorded in 1929, made him the top hitter for 1929 and 1930 combined, but didn't earn him a hitting title either year.

Herman set franchise records with his .393 average as well as in home runs, 35; runs batted in, 130; slugging percentage, .678; runs scored, 143; hits, 241; extra base hits, 94 and total bases, 416. In all the years since that most remarkable season, only the home run and RBI mark have been erased.

Babe also finished second in the league in stolen bases and credited Max Carey for his continued improvement.

"Carey really knew how to run bases and he told me, 'When you hit the ball, look over your shoulder at it and find where it is, it won't slow you down. You should do your own coaching.'

"Robbie never let you run without signals. Carey helped me become a better baserunner. He told me, 'When this pitcher looks at first, then back to the plate, run. He never looks back again.'

"So I listened to him and was leading the league in stolen bases in the middle of the season when I pulled a muscle sliding into second.

"Robbie said, 'Is it bad?'

"I told him it wasn't.

" 'What the hell are you stealing bases for anyway? We want you in the lineup for your bat,' he said.

"So I didn't steal many more the rest of the season," Babe said.

He had hit in 26 of the final 29 games, including 21 of 24 during the month of September, posting a spectacular .422 average. He tied the team record of 130 runs batted in and had 19 game-winning RBIs during the season. However, disappointed Brooklyn fans could only remember the important series with the Cardinals when he was 1-for-11. Excluding that horrendous three-day period, he had authored a .464 average for the month.

During the season Herman was hitless in 29 games and the team was 13-16 in those contests. In games when he got at least one hit, the team was 22 games over .500, recording a 73-51 mark.

He hit .471 overall against Boston, including .511 in Ebbets Field, and .529 against the Phillies, including an astounding .587 in Baker Bowl. He hit only .182 against the Cardinals in Brooklyn, but .435 against them in Sportsman's Park. His road average was .397 and he hit .389 in Ebbets Field.

The Brooklyn team with their top hitters predominantly left-handed, were again victimized by lefty pitching. Against right handers the team was 49-43 but against southpaws they slipped to 25-37.

But remarkably, Herman hit better against lefties during the 1930 season, recording a .397 average, in contrast to a 'mere' .391 against right handers. Frederick suffered from facing southpaws, hitting .301 against lefties and .346 against right-handers. And Bissonette had the same problem, recording .304 and .345 marks.

There was no 'official' Most Valuable Player voting in 1930, but Herman was fourth in the MVP balloting by the Baseball Writers

Association and fifth in The Sporting News rankings.

Wilbert Robinson, in an interview with The Sporting News, told the editor:

"That Babe wasn't so good around first base, he sometimes got tangled up in his feet. But you boys have him all wrong in the outfield. Maybe Babe don't look so good from the press box, but he's awfully fast, and he gets out for those long ones. He's got long arms and a big reach and I don't care if he pulls them in with one hand—or stands on his head, as long as he gets them."

Lewis Burton of the New York Journal-American stated unequivocally that Herman made the greatest throw ever seen in Ebbets Field.

"The score was tied in the ninth with two out and the Cubs had Kiki Cuyler, their fastest runners, on first," Burton wrote. "In this crisis situation, the next man, naturally, smacked a line drive directly over Babe's head in right field. Instead of trying to play the carom off the right field wall, he backed up to the wall, leaned against it and leaped up. The ball hit the fingers of his glove but didn't stick.

"It came down on Babe's shoulder and dropped into the grass alongside the wall. Herman located it after a few seconds, bending down with his back to the plate. He whirled up and, without any sign of taking aim, uncoiled.

"He fired a perfect strike to Al Lopez, squatting at the plate, and Cuyler was out by five feet.

"On the train that night, Dazzy Vance was still shaking his head in disbelief. 'I have trouble throwing strikes from 60 feet,' Dazzy complained, 'and that guy Herman did it from 280.' "

The Bushwicks, a strong semi-pro team in Brooklyn, had offered Babe $3500 to play a double-header following the season, but when the Robins missed the pennant and Babe's average dropped below .400 they cancelled the deal. However Gary Schumacher booked him for a game with the Glendale Farmers. Teammate Cy Moore and rookie Van Mungo pitched as 10,000 people set a new park record, breaking down the outfield fence to get in. Babe got four long shots and split the money with his pitching friends.

Shortly after he signed a $600 a week contract for a tour of the RKO circuit with pitcher Al Mamaux. Their act was such a success that they wanted the two players to extend their 13-week contract.

Babe did a monologue, with Mamaux, who had an exceptional voice, doing most of the singing. They also sung a duet. They played to standing room only crowds, breaking theatre records at each stop.

They would perform between movies and do four shows a day on Saturday and three during the week. When a friend asked Herman what he did between shows, Babe replied, "Just sit around all day and once and a while go over to the Stock Exchange and watch brokers jump out of the windows." Detroit catcher Mickey Cochrane was on the Orphium circuit at the same time playing his cornet and he and Babe became friends.

Although the money was good, Babe wanted to go home to California and, much to Mamaux's displeasure, decided to quit after the Newark booking and just before they were to play the Palace in New York. Babe didn't realize at the time how much playing the Palace meant to Mamaux.

Each night Mamaux would come on stage and talk to the crowd for a time. When Herman would come on, he'd ask, "Where were you, Babe?"

"Some kids stopped me at the stage door and wanted autographs."

"What is the celebration? I see a flower in your buttonhole."

"It's Mother-in-Law Day."

"Never heard of it. What kind of flowers are they?"

"Poison Ivy," Babe would reply.

"What delivery do you find the hardest to hit?" Mamaux asked.

"I don't know, but Willie Sherdel throws it."

Al would sing "Sonny Boy" and Babe would leave the stage.

He would come back later and tell the audience about his picks for an all-star team and the two would then close by singing a parody of "Keep your Sunny Side Up" that went:

"Keep your bats swinging up, up,
"Keep your eye on the ball.
"When the pitcher winds up to throw,
"Swing the bat and watch it go."

Then they would leave the stage in lock-step.

A reporter talked to them backstage after one of their performances and asked why they didn't appear in their baseball uniforms.

Mamaux said, "The public knows how we look in uniform. Our mission is to show them what ball players are like, off the field; to impress upon the minds of the public that a ballplayer is a fine, upstanding young man."

Babe interjected, "Yes, but is it art?"

"Keep your gags for the act," Mamaux snapped.

Reviewers noted that while the act may not have been art, it was entertaining. One wrote: "Herman is smiling all the time and soon the entire audience is smiling too at the slim, boyish blond who, in his dinner coat, appears on his way to the nearest Junior Prom."

Before Herman left for California, he was called into the Brooklyn office by Frank York who said, "I want to talk to you about a deal. Fresco Thompson and Lefty O'Doul for Clise Dudley, Jim Elliott, Mickey Finn and Jake Flowers. What do you think?"

Babe told him, "I don't like it much. In the first place, Mickey Finn and Jake Flowers are better than Fresco Thompson. Elliott and Dudley are hard-throwing kids and will get better. In O'Doul you are getting a guy that can only play left field, and in addition he is a left-handed hitter.

You've got six of them now in the lineup. And you could probably buy O'Doul outright for $25,000 because the Phillies need the money."

"Well, I didn't ask you up here to talk about that, anyway," York said, obviously displeased that Herman didn't like the deal. "I want to talk to you about your contract."

"Well, Mr. York," Babe said, "Instead of getting the press on me and all that sort of baloney, I'll sign for $20,000 right now." That was an increase of $1,000 over the 1930 salary he received.

"OK, Babe, that's fine. Come by the park Wednesday before you leave and we'll sign a contract," York said.

Wednesday Babe showed up at the Brooklyn office with his car packed and his family loaded. He noticed that someone was standing by the window, and when the Herman car pulled up the man slipped back into the office, apparently announcing his arrival to the men inside.

York met Babe and brought him into the office where Steve McKeever, Joe Gilleaudeau and James Mulvey were sitting. He said, "They don't want to give you $20,000."

"Mr. York, you're president of the club and you're the one handling the signings. You and I agreed to the terms two days ago and you told me to come by today and sign the contract," Babe told him.

"I didn't agree to any terms," York said.

"You certainly did."

"We didn't agree on any terms."

"You're a liar. We did agree."

"Is that what you think of me?"

"Yes, if you stick to that story. I'm not getting any place here and my family is waiting. I'm leaving," Babe said and walked out.

As he shut the glass door, he could hear McKeever say, "Why don't you give it to him?"

York said, "I'll never give it to him now."

When Herman arrived at his home in California, a contract for $19,000 was waiting for him. He carefully tore it in two parts and sent it back.

Chapter 8

Brooklyn and Robinson had high hopes for the 1931 season. York had made the trade he discussed with Herman. Lefty O'Doul and Fresco Thompson came over from the Phillies in exchange for Clise Dudley and Jim Elliott and outfielder Hal Lee.

It was assumed the O'Doul, Herman, Frederick outfield would give the team overpowering strength. Thompson was to plug the second base hole, although Neal 'Mickey' Finn would be more often used at that position. Glenn Wright was solid at shortstop. The club swapped Harvey Hendrick to Cincinnati for first baseman Mickey Heath and for some reason sold Ray Moss, who was 9-6 in 1930, to Boston at the waiver price.

To make up for the departure of pitchers Dudley, Elliott, and Moss, the Robins picked up pitching castoffs Jack Quinn and Joe Schaute.

Quinn was born in 1883 or 1885, making him about 46 years old. He had been pitching professionally since 1903. Schaute had formerly been an outstanding left-hander with Cleveland. Only 30, he had slipped from a 20 game winner in 1924 to working in only four games in 1930 and had been released by the Indians. He paid his own way to spring training with Brooklyn and asked for a tryout.

Also added to the roster was a big, young catcher by the name of Ernie Lombardi who would go on to win a pair of batting titles but not with Brooklyn. He joined Al Lopez behind the plate, giving the club two future Hall of Famers. Lombardi had hit .377, .366 and .370 in the PCL the previous three seasons. The Dodgers paid Oakland $40,000 for him and Lombardi was holding out, sort of, asking part of the sale price. Naturally he didn't get it.

Competing for a spot on the Dodger catching staff was young Paul Richards, destined to go on to bigger and better things later in life. Hank DeBerry was released and Picinich became the third man on the catching staff.

Cub manager Rogers Hornsby had offered to trade Hack Wilson, coming off a 56-home run, 190 RBI year, for Babe but Brooklyn turned the deal down.

F.C. Lane, writing in Baseball Magazine, noted, "Herman's antics in the outfield were once a butt of ridicule. They are no longer. His one weakness, running back on a ball hit over his head, has been largely eliminated by playing deep.

"Herman can go quite as far to one side or the other after a fly balls as the next man, and he can come in just as far, Besides, he has an iron whip. Few batters rounding first take a chance on second, if Herman is anywhere near the ball.

"Herman is the greatest free swinging hitter in the National League. Only Al Simmons can rival him in any League. Both have an eccentric stance and violate accepted batting rules, and both get results.

"Herman takes a lightning quick cut at the ball from any angle, it matters little which. He can scoop up a ball that ducks below his knees quite as readily as he can hammer one shoulder high. It requires phenomenal eyesight and quick coordination of muscular activity to bat that way."

Robbie noted, "I do not hesitate to say that the team I am going to start the season with is the strongest I have ever had in my career as manager in Brooklyn. This is the greatest hitting team in Brooklyn history and we may not win the pennant but the team that beats us will." It was high praise but the statement would come back to haunt him.

However, the Sporting News took a closer look at the Robin attack and pointed out, "They have added power to an already powerful lineup, but they lack finesse. They cannot continue to rely on big innings. The team is distinctly a poor baserunning team. With the exception of Babe Herman there is no one who can steal a base in a close game with reasonable safety. The team, almost to the man and again with the exception of Herman, is inept at bunting. However they are surprisingly good at the hit and run."

Steve McKeever, Frank York and Dutch Carter had been holding meetings through the winter to push construction plans for Ebbets Field. However, they had to go to court in February to secure permission to spend the necessary money for expansion. The Ebbets heirs fought the new plans, and when it looked like construction would actually start, the contractor had to ask the court for permission. A special referee was appointed to consider the interests of the minors who shared stock as Ebbets heirs.

No real player negotiations were held through the winter and Herman stayed in California, working out and playing golf. One afternoon he outdrove pro golfers Gene Sarazen and Charley Lacey in a best-ball foursome.

The first sign of spring came when Dan Comerford shipped the equipment to Florida in February. Comerford had been the Brooklyn equipment manager since 1907, taking care of the club as it trained in Jacksonville, Hot Springs, New Orleans, Daytona and Clearwater.

Jimmy Johnston was appointed first base coach, with Otto Miller and Ivy Olson again manning the other posts. Johnston was added to help the lead-footed Robins on the bases. He had stolen 124 bases in 1913 for San Francisco in the PCL.

The Robins took 37 men, the largest squad in baseball, to spring training. Training started with the news that Glenn Wright had injured his ankle while playing billiards, the type of incongruous injury you might attribute to a Brooklyn Dodger and particularly to one of their shortstops. He turned suddenly and something snapped. A special leather brace was fitted to his foot and he was trying to play with it.

Players also found out that the rules and the ball had been changed after the hit-happy 1930 season. The new National League ball had much thicker leather to deaden the impact and reduce the carry of the ball. Also the seams were raised, delighting the pitchers.

The American League ball had been identical to the ball used in the senior circuit, but, cognizant of the revenue that was tied to Babe Ruth's home run totals, the American League wisely did not tinker with their ball at all.

Due to the raised seams and the thicker leather, league batting averages dropped from .303 to .277 in the National League in 1931, and earned run average followed, slipping from 4.97 to 3.87. Home runs were down by 400, a remarkable total of 50 per team.

Averages dropped only slightly in the American league, from .288 to .278, ERA slipped from 4.65 to 4.38 and homers were off only 12 per club.

Late in the season Herman slugged a ball to dead center that the wind held up and Cuyler caught up against the wall. Cuyler trotted in and tossed the ball to the umpire, who looked at it and put it in his pocket.

Following the game he showed the ball to Herman. A neat 'star' was flattened in the heavy leather on one side where Babe had connected, showing just how dense the cover was.

The home run rule, which previously had counted as a homer any ball that bounced into the stands, was changed and such hits were now to be ground rule doubles.

As the season opener neared, Herman went to Florida late in the spring, five pounds lighter than at the close of the 1930 season, paying his own expenses and staying at a hotel across from the Brooklyn hotel in Clearwater.

When he showed up at the park he told his teammates that he would have to take it easy because he had reported to camp so much lighter.

He said he would probably sign a Brooklyn contract very soon.

"I thought I would just drive over from Glendale and see what was going on here," he said with a twinkle in his eye and the realization that the "drive over" was about 3,600 miles. Robbie was glad to see him and Herman took batting practice immediately, slashing line drives to all corners of the park and capping the performance with a gigantic drive over the right field wall. He then retired to the clubhouse porch to watch the first intrasquad game from a comfortable chair.

Babe played in the next intrasquad game, and when it finished the regulars had blasted out a 32-3 win over the "Yannigans." Herman had clouted two homers in the same inning. He was 4-for-4 with four walks and O'Doul was 7-for-9 after two contests.

New Robin Fresco Thompson said, "There ought to be a separate league for guys like Herman, O'Doul and Wright. I used to think that the Phillies could hit the ball, but this bunch hits harder than St. Louis in July."

York got wind of the fact that Herman and Vance were working out unsigned and telegraphed Robbie to get them out of camp. So Babe would wait for O'Doul and the two would golf together after practice.

Robinson grumbled, "How can I win the pennant when my two best players are playing golf instead of practicing?"

Before an exhibition game, Babe, attired in spotless white flannels, walked by National League president John Hydler who was sitting in a box seat.

"Why aren't you playing?" Hydler asked, peering over his glasses.

"I didn't come down here to work, I'm on vacation," Babe told him with a smile.

Herman later told his teammates, "That didn't go over too good. Landis was in the box, too, and he looked at me as if I was living a life of shame. But I'll bet they would all be around tomorrow if I signed a contract for what the club wanted me to.

"They think I'm a holdup man. But I'd sign today if I didn't think I was worth the extra thousand. I had a hell of a year last year, a $20,000 year if I'll ever have one. If I only hit .340 this year, they won't have any qualms about cutting me. But that's business and legitimate, while if a player tries to get what he's worth, he's trying to gyp someone."

Manager Robinson told the press, "I've advised both Herman and Vance to sign for their own good. If they don't get into shape, they're apt to have a bad year and regret it.

"Maybe it is poor business for the club to refuse to sign them. They could sign them both tomorrow for $3,500 extra. I wish they'd sign because Vance needs a lot of work in the spring and Herman needs some of this practice in exhibition games to start at his best."

Vance left camp for his place at Homasassa to 'do a little fishing.'

Head scout Larry Sutton came over to Babe one afternoon and said,

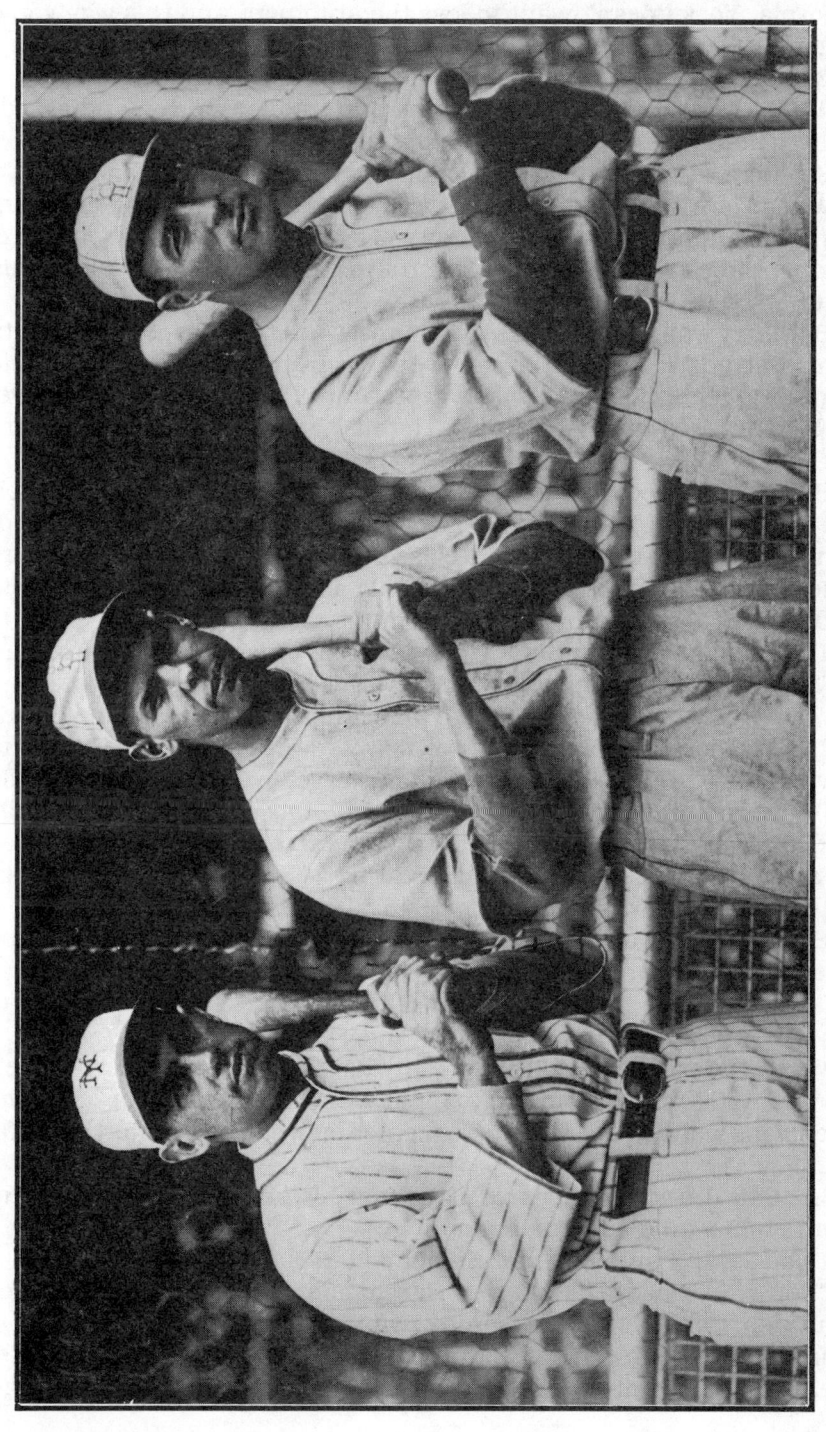

The three hottest bats in 1930 belonged to Bill Terry (.401), Babe Herman (.393) and Lefty O'Doul (.383).

"I can get you $800 expenses to move your family to Brooklyn from California. York doesn't want to lose the argument and this way you'll be just $200 off what you wanted to start with."

Babe reluctantly agreed and signed the $19,000 contract.

When they arrived in Brooklyn, he buttonholed Sutton and asked, "Larry, where is my $800 that you promised?"

Sutton looked sheepish and said, "I can't do nothing about that."

When Herman signed the contract, York was pleased and told him, "If you have an off year—drop to say .340 or so, I won't cut you next season." Babe just looked at him and muttered, 'baloney' under his breath.

Bill Terry was also a holdout that spring and the exasperated Giants offered to trade Terry for Herman even up but the Dodgers refused the deal. Casey Stengel later asked John McGraw if the deal was on the level and McGraw told him "Absolutely. Herman is more valuable to a team than Terry."

Herman slugged a double good for two runs after signing on March 14th and the Robins beat the Phillies 13-11. The Brooklyn Eagle said, "Herman gave the team a touch of class that was lacking before. Herman is the fastest man on the club but is only a fair baserunner. His faults are due only to questionable judgement."

The Ebbets heirs continued to oppose the proposed expansion plan for Ebbets Field, but this time McKeever was determined to go ahead with the program, even if he had to take it to the State Supreme Court.

The memory of screaming, overflow crowds at Ebbets Field and many more milling around outside unable to get in during the heat of the 1930 season was burned into the directors' minds and both sides finally decided it would be a good move to add the extra seats. The project was estimated at $400,000, but ended costing $750,000, the exact figure that Ebbets Field was built for in 1913.

Construction was begun in February, due to the lengthy and heated discussion, and contractors said it would be touch and go to see if it would be completed by opening day of the 1931 season, a time span of only a few months.

When the park was constructed in 1913, it was 419 down the left field line, 450 to center and 301 to right. When Babe arrived in 1926, the dimensions were 383 to left, 450 to center (moved to 466 later) and 301 to right.

In 1948 Branch Rickey told Babe that his single-season home run record of 35 would soon be broken.

Babe said, "I suppose that Snider will do it."

"No," said Rickey. "It will be a righthander. We moved the distance in but didn't change the sign on the wall."

In the final years, the measurements read 343 to left, 384 to center and 297 to right, but the left-field wall was apparently closer than that.

Home plate was moved out four feet toward the fence in 1954, then another two feet in 1957 with no change in the signs.

The double deck was extended from third base to the left field corner, then across to center field. The center field second deck hung out over the field. In addition, a new scoreboard would be installed on the right field fence. Designed along the lines of the Yankee and Pittsburgh scoreboards, it would show all National League scores, plus the Yankee scores.

The board compounded the difficulty of the unusual right field wall and there were now an estimated 289 different angles that the ball could take when belted off the wall or scoreboard. The board jutted out five feet from the wall at a 45 degree angle. It was 319 feet to the right side of it and 344 feet to the left.

At the base of the sign was an ad that offered a suit from Abe Stark for anyone hitting the sign. Most right fielders played directly in front of it, so the chances of hitting it were slight. When it did occur and the player came to claim his free suit, Stark would always ask for some autographed baseballs in exchange. Partly due to the popularity of the sign, Stark later enjoyed a successful political career.

A Schaefer Beer sign would be installed after World War II on top of the scoreboard with the 'H' in Schaefer lighting up for a hit and the 'E' lighting for an error.

The Robins schedule called for five games in Havana, Cuba, and the entire squad made the trip with the regulars (called the Robins) to oppose the rookies (called the Dodgers) in the contests.

When the ship docked they were met by Julio Blanco Herrera, owner of Tropical Breweries and Tropical Stadium. The team was showered with flowers during the drive downtown.

The players quickly threw their bags into their rooms and headed for the bar at Sloppy Joe's. That night someone threw a bomb in the toilet and when it went off the players came spilling out of the door and into the street.

Dolph Luque convinced the players to drink 'Pina de Fria' at Sloppy Joe's and manager Robinson agreed with him. The players thought the drinks were good but had little kick. Luque complimented them on being such good drinkers. It was only later in the trip that they found out they were drinking pure pineapple juice.

The first workout in the stadium saw the rookies dressing in one club house and the veterans in another. Each was supplied with a barrel of beer, donated by the sponsor of the trip. Robbie was furious when he found out and had the beer removed from the clubhouse. Then he stood by the barrel and sipped out of it himself during practice.

Before the first game, each player was introduced to the crowd, with Al Lopez getting the biggest cheer. The Cuban and American anthem was played and the game began.

Herman got the first hit, a single to right, and scored the first run moments later on Flower's single. In the second game, Max Rosenfield caught one of Herman's drives against the 500-foot marker on the right field wall and the crowd went wild.

Dictator Batista offered $1,000 to anyone hitting the ball over the distant wall, feeling quite safe about the possibility of ever paying. Then one day in batting practice Babe hit a ball over the wall about five feet foul.

The next afternoon Babe's roommate Hollis Thurston was to pitch and Babe said, "Fire that ball up there and don't try to cross me up. We'll have $1,000 to have some fun with." Batista, apparently getting word of Herman's long shot in practice, quickly called the offer off.

The Havana paper headlined, "Herman pouchardo dos veces" (Herman shutout twice) and Babe kidded, "I must be pretty good when they give me headlines when I fan." He was called 'el Bateadore Grande.'

The club drew 5,000 for weekday games and 15,000 on weekends, setting an attendance record by drawing 60,000 during their stay.

Returning to the mainland and playing against Toledo on March 27, the opposing pitcher threw Babe a curve and former Giant Johnny Rawlings, playing second base shouted, "Oh, no!" as Herman hit it into the right field corner for a double.

After the game Rawlings said that McGraw had originally ordered his pitchers to throw only curves to Herman, but during the last two seasons he had them hit so well that McGraw was finally convinced he was a good curve ball hitter. "Don't look for any curves from the Giants this year," he told Babe and Herman got a steady diet of fastballs from the New York staff from then on.

Rawlings also told Babe about a game the previous season that Kent Greenfield had pitched against Brooklyn. He threw Babe two curves and Herman fouled them off. Then he threw a fastball and struck him out.

Returning to the dugout, McGraw met him on the steps and said, "Where were you Thursday night?"

"I don't know."

"I do—you were out all night and you're fined $50.00. And the next time I tell you to curve Herman, you curve Herman," McGraw concluded. Although Greenfield had struck Babe out he had gone against McGraw's orders and was fined for it.

Playing an exhibition game against the Philadelphia Athletics in Florida, Herman asked Robinson for part of the afternoon off. Robbie said, "OK, get a hit early and I'll let you go."

Herman looked across the field at the young right-hander warming up and knew he would be out of the park in record time.

But just as the game was about to start, out from under the stands came Lefty Grove, a 28-game winner for the American League champions in 1930. Babe managed to beat out an infield hit his first trip and asked Robbie if he could leave. "Oh, get a good hit and you can go," Robinson said.

Herman spent the rest of the afternoon trying to connect with Grove's lightning-like pitches and didn't get away until after the Athletics earned an 8-7 victory in 11 innings.

Attendance at Clearwater was again miserable. Consistently empty stands made club officials discuss plans for training in California in 1932, perhaps San Diego or Stockton. And the crowds in Havana made them even consider Cuba as a training site.

Herman was only 2-for-19 in exhibition games and the opinion was that he was trying too hard to outhit O'Doul. The Eagle said, "In the past his slumps were reflected in his whole conduct. This spring has been entirely different. He isn't hitting, but he's hustling every minute, not only running out infield taps but chasing flies."

And after a game in Miami, the paper said, "Herman had only one hit, however his fielding was something to see. He covered about all the ground there is in right field to make a couple of hair-raising plays. He swooped in like a falcon to snatch one Texas Leaguer off the top of the grass, and later running back to the fence, leaping into the air, and coming down with a hard hit line drive in his gloved fist."

Vance signed for $23,000 on March 31st and when asked if the contract was all right by him, he pragmatically said, "It has to be."

Hartford beat the Robins early in April and Robinson, discussing his young catchers, told reporters, "Richards has something on Lombardi now." O'Doul was hitting .415 and Bissonette .393, but Herman was last on the club with a .133 mark. The following day they beat Hartford, but it was pitcher Watty Clark that knocked in the winning run with a single after three walks had loaded the bases. "What power we have," Herman cracked.

The Robins earned a split with Hartford on April 8 and Herman banged out four hits but an ominous note was sounded by Cardinal manager Gabby Street:

"There are too many lefties on the Brooklyn squad," he said and ticked them off on his fingers: Bissonette, Frederick, Herman, O'Doul and even Boone and Hendrick. "Everyone will feed them left-handers. And outside of Herman, no one takes an extra base on any hit. It takes wholesale batting to get most of them around the base paths. That puts them in a disadvantage in a close game."

The Robins routed their minor league opponents, winning 14 of 20 games, but Robinson knew things weren't as they should be.

As the opener neared, Brooklyn weathered home runs by Ruth and Gehrig to beat the Yankees 8-7 in Ebbets Field. The new stands were partially completed and the new scoreboard was set in right.

Babe Ruth started in right field but after losing pitcher Pea Ridge Day's fly in the sun, he quickly shifted to left, admitting that the tough sun field was something he didn't want to battle.

Clyde "Pea Ridge" Day, another of the legendary Brooklyn players, was named for the region of the south where he grew up and after beating the Yankees 8-7, let loose with a wild hog-call that delighted the fans. They quickly picked up the call and saluted him with it each time he appeared on the mound.

Brooklyn won the second Yankee game 11-7 and thousands of Brooklyn fans jammed into the park. Herman collected his third and fourth hit of the series, battering Pennock and Wenert, both lefties.

Robinson drew praise for the way he had brought Herman along. A local paper wrote: "Herman played with ten different clubs over the years before he came to Brooklyn. He worked under a dozen different managers but until Robinson took him in tow, he couldn't find a manager who would bear with his erratic tendencies.

"To my mind, Robinson's careful handling of Herman, his gradual developing of Babe from a wild, left-handed youth to a first-rate ball player who'd be a star in any baseball setting, has been the Brooklyn leader's outstanding managerial feat in the last 10 years.

"In 1926 Herman hit .319 and established himself as an idol to the wild-eyed Flatbush Fans. The next season he slumped horrifically, falling off to a mere .278

"In the spring of 1928, a disconsolate Herman reported at the Clearwater camp. He was discouraged, but Robinson wasn't.

"Robinson said, 'I don't give a hoot how Herman played last season, I'll never give up on a fellow who can hit like he can. And I know that he can do everything else on a baseball field.'

"That summer Herman hit .340. His baserunning and fielding were still pretty terrible. In the spring of 1929, Robinson delegated Max Carey to help Herman's baserunning. Babe stole 21, finishing second in the league, and hit .381.

"That left his fielding. In 1929 Babe finished second among the hitters of the league and second on the bases, but absolutely last among the regular fielders in fielding. Last year Robinson kept on Babe's heels in the matter of shagging flies. And, low and behold, before the campaign was over, Herman's improvement was downright amazing. From the worst fielder in the league he developed into one of the best—and he hit .393."

The Robins were confident that the pennant was theirs for the taking, leading Robinson to tell reporters: "The fellows act as though they expect the National League pennant to step up and kiss them or something of that sort.

"We have a good ball club, one that ought to be right up there close to the top at the finish. But if the players don't hustle more than they've hustled most of the exhibition games, they're liable to wind up a gallant sixth."

Brooklyn correspondent Tommy Holmes picked the Cardinals to win, with Brooklyn second and followed by the Cubs and Giants. He cited the fact that when you have three starters as old as Quinn (46), Vance (40) and Luque (40) you are in trouble. "This team lacks speed, with the exception of Herman, and has no finesse. It is strictly a big-inning team," he concluded.

Dolph Luque was named to open the season, but his thumb was dislocated from a shot off Wally Gilbert's bat in batting practice, sidelining him for three weeks. Fresco Thompson was spiked at second base in the Yankee series and also missed much of the opening week.

Ancient Jack Quinn drew the opening start, his first National League game in 18 years, and it would be his only start of 1931. He lost a 4-0 lead and a 7-4 decision at Boston. He was then taken out of the staring rotation and became an excellent relief pitcher, and using a low-breaking spitball led the National League in saves.

The club made seven errors the next day and a fuming Robinson unloaded on Herman after he had lost a ball in right field in the sun with the Robins trailing 8-0.

"That sun is tough," Herman said after the inning.

"Stop complaining," Robinson told him.

"You can't catch what you can't see," Herman said, sitting down on the corner of the bench.

"I should put someone else who can," Robinson muttered.

"Go ahead, if you want to," Herman told him.

"I will," said Robbie, and called to Ike Boone to warm up but then sent Boone to pinch hit for the pitcher. When the inning ended, thinking he was in for Herman, Boone went to right field.

Robbie shouted at Babe, "I don't want to take you out, for goodness sake get out there before he gets hurt."

Herman went back into the outfield but Boone would not leave. Finally, the umpires determined that Boone had been announced as Herman's replacement in right and that Babe was out of the game. Robbie was furious and sent rookie Al Cohen into right for Boone.

But Boone had hit for the pitcher and putting Cohen in for Boone should have placed him in the ninth slot and Mattingly, the new pitcher, in Herman's third spot.

But when the Robins came to bat in the sixth innings, Cohen stepped up to hit in Herman's place. Writers in the pressbox shouted down that he was batting out of turn and O'Doul asked Cohen, "Are you sure?"

"I guess so," Cohen said and singled. None of the Braves noticed the error. The following inning, the mistake was discovered by Boston manager Rabbit Maranville and after a lengthy discussion with the umpire, Cohen was allowed to hit in his proper spot. He promptly singled again. Not only that, he made a good catch and threw out two Boston runners at second base. In his final trip, the hit into a double play.

After the second hit he excitedly asked Robinson, "Do I get credit for both hits?"

Robbie looked at him, then reached inside his jacket pocket and pulled out a ticket folder and said, "It don't make much difference, kid. Here's your ticket to Hartford." However, he later changed his mind and kept the rookie on the roster for a while, but Cohen never got into another game, finishing the season with a .667 average.

After the game, Cohen asked reporters if something would be written about him in the papers, because he wanted his mother to know how well he did.

Quentin Reynolds, writing for the New York World-Telegram, used that idea and wrote the story as if the story was to his mother, then sent it off to the paper.

Awakened later that night at his hotel room, Reynolds was told by the paper that they had never received his story. He dressed and rushed down to the telegraph office to check, where he learned the confused night telegraph clerk had sent his 800 word story to Mrs. Cohen instead of the paper.

No one knows how she reacted to receiving the lengthy story of the game and her son's exploits. But it would be interesting to know, since the telegram had been sent collect.

Herman singled and homered the next day but the club lost again.

The Robins lost their first five, won one, then lost two more. When they held their unofficial home opener the newly-completed left-field stands were open but with a 1-7 record, they were quite empty.

Before the home opener, McKeever received a letter from a Brooklyn fan that read: "To the Hon. Steve McKeever: Dumb president, dumb manager, dumb secretary, dumb team, dumbest damn team in baseball. Training season a joke. Pitchers not ready. No fight, no guts." and signed it "A Flatbush Fan."

McKeever published his reply in the paper and said, "If Brooklyn wins the pennant, I'll bet that dumb guy makes more noise than any other fan in Flatbush. Dumb-it, we must be interesting."

On April 23 the Robins came home to play the Phils in the "official" home opener.

In the fifth inning Dick Bartell singled and made a wide turn at first. Herman quickly fired the ball behind him to trap him off the base, but Bartell escaped the entire Robin infield who became involved in the rundown.

Later Babe reached base on a force out, took a big lead and started to steal second. Seeing the throw had him beat, he reversed his field and slid safely back into first.

"As clean a steal of first as ever anyone saw," the Brooklyn Eagle reported. The Eagle was also critical that Herman was hitting "only" .312.

Robinson, watching his team get a steady diet of left-handed pitching, took Herman out of the game early and benched O'Doul and Frederick. "If I had a right-hander who wouldn't get killed in right field, I'd bench Herman, too," he said.

The Sporting News correspondent prophetically wrote "The .400 hitter is a thing of the past. The raised seam on the ball makes all the difference. Plus the rule eliminating the sacrifice fly. The two will cut 40 points off batting averages."

On the 25th Herman slugged a homer into the new seats in left, splitting the back of one of the wooden seats. It was the first regular season shot into the new section. It was Babe's fourth homer, tops in the National League but the Robins lost again, their seventh in eight starts against left-handed pitching.

The new stands were grey concrete and it was difficult to see the ball against it. Most of the hitters complained about the background and a green canvas was installed in center field to help. On the final day of April, Herman smashed a ball off the canvas, only a foot from going into the seats, but the ball dropped back on the field for a double.

The club finally bought green paint. "Five gallons of paint and 20 gallons of oil," Herman noted dryly, to finish the left and center field walls. It was hardly dry on April 30 when Herman slugged one off the top of the concrete in center field, missing a homer by inches.

But despite the slow start, when the Giants came to Brooklyn everyone turned out. 35,316 crowded into the new stands on May 3rd and an estimated 20,000 more were turned away at the gate and were unable to see Herman double home the winning run off Carl Hubbell in a 4-3 victory. The Giants won the next two but Phelps fired a shutout to earn a split. 95,000+ had attended the four game series, a new club record.

Harvey Hendrick, who had a .313 average during his seven years with the Robins but who could never find a position to play, was traded to the Reds for Mickey Heath and cash. Hendrick promptly spent much of the rest of the season leading the league in hitting.

The Robins lost a two-game set to the Pirates and York came into the dressing room after the second game and shouted at the players that they were the highest paid in the league, excepting the Cubs, and should be playing better. He said that a slump would kill the gate and they had better do something to get going "or else."

On the 18th Herman batted in the first inning against Cincinnati and foul-tipped a third strike that was dropped by the catcher. Given extra life, he homered over the left field wall. Babe went on to hit for the cycle, adding a single, double and triple, good for five RBIs in a 14-4 romp.

Lefty O'Doul told reporters that the new ball, with thicker leather and raised seams, would cut 25 points off averages. O'Doul was under .200 at the time.

"Fly balls don't travel like they used to," he said. "Now they sink like a spent cannon ball. And what hurts more than anything else is the fact that the umpires let the ball stay in play longer, until it's discolored and damaged. It's the discoloration that makes the ball harder to see.

"And the new ball can't take it like the one they used last year. When a ball is hit five or six times, it loses it's power. Sometimes when I connect, I think I've hit a beanbag."

Clubhouse man Dan Comerford supported O'Doul's contention that balls were being kept in play longer. He reported that only 15 of the prepared 48 baseballs had been used in Vance's last game and usually they had to use more than 48 in one of his contests.

The club was getting the lefty treatment again, facing them in 20 of the first 22 games. The team was last in hitting and fielding with Herman and Lombardi the only players over .300. There was rumors of a 25,000 name petition that had been circulated to get rid of Robinson and hire Max Carey.

McKeever replied that the directors had never considered replacing a manager in the middle of the season and that Robinson had received a two-year contract early in 1930. And for the first time McKeever announced that Robbie had promised not to be a candidate for manager when that contract expired.

The critics were riding Robinson hard, with cartoonist Ed Hughes depicting him as a bum in the Brooklyn Eagle and wondering about his control of the team after Vance had refused to pitch in little Baker Bowl in Philadelphia. And later Max Carey was seen in the stands at Ebbets Field while rumors of Robbie's removal grew in strength.

Robinson told New York reporters that some of them were welcome on the Brooklyn bench and that some were not. He also noted that none of the Brooklyn writers were welcome.

Herman belted his sixth home run on May 22 in Philadelphia and was hitting .341 but the team was 15-20 and seventh in the standings. Boone was released and Ray Moss sold as the Brooklyn front office saw attendance start to dwindle in direct proportions to the increasing payments to be made on the new, mostly empty, stands.

Late in the month, before a record 60,000 screaming fans in the Polo Grounds, Herman singled twice and Bissonette hit a three-run homer in the tenth to beat Hubbell, whom the Robins continued to handle easily. Wally Gilbert got six hits in the second game and the Robins swept the doubleheader.

On Memorial Day, the new center field seats were officially opened and a booming crowd of over 37,000 jammed into Ebbets Field to see the Robins win and tie the sixth-place Braves. Herman had five hits in the twin bill.

In early June when the Robins went on a western swing, York went along—his presence giving many players a nervous stomach. The team stopped Chicago in the first game of the series, evened their record at .500 for the first time and moved into a tie for fourth place.

The following day Herman banged two singles, a double and a homer good for five RBIs in a 9-8 loss. Babe was hitting .343 and the club was tied for fourth—but that was the high water mark for Herman during the 1931 season.

Manager Robinson was becoming tired of the mental mistakes his players were making in the field and in a team meeting told them that he was forming a "Bonehead Club" in which each player would pay $10.00 for his mistakes, the money going into a fund that would provide a team party at the end of the season.

"Hell, we'll have more money than a world series share," Robinson muttered. That same afternoon, Robinson wrote Lombardi's name on the lineup card, then sent Lopez out to catch, thus eliminating Tony from the rest of the game and becoming, himself, the first member of the new club.

No further mention was made of the club the rest of the season.

One afternoon Babe singled and suddenly set out for second, only to be thrown out by a wide margin.

Robinson was furious, shouting "I didn't send him. Let's see what his story is this time."

When Babe came back to the bench, Robbie asked him why he had tried to steal second.

Herman explained just as calmly as he could, "Why, you gave me the sign."

"What sign?"

"You touched your glasses with both hands like you said you would."

"Oh, did I?" the puzzled Robinson said. "Did I?"

Playing the Cardinals on June 8th, pitcher Dolph Luque was tossed out of the game by umpire Charles Donnelly. Moments later Al Lopez threw wildly to second on an attempted steal and the ball flew into center field. Lopez accused Donnelly of interfering with his throw. George Watkins, the hitter at the time, said:

"Forget it, that was just a rotten throw."

"I'll see you under the stands when this is over," Lopez told him.

"I'll be there," said Watkins.

Following the game, an 8-5 Cardinal win, the two mixed it up for a time before being separated. Lopez emerged with a red spot on his cheek but reported that he got one in that 'felt good.'

Before the Western swing, Robbie had asked Herman and Wright if he should pick up Jess Haines who the Cardinals had placed on waivers. They both said 'yes,' noting that his fast knuckle ball was tough to hit. Robinson was undecided. "We'll wait to see him in St. Louis and I'll decide then," he said. But before the Robins moved into St. Louis, Haines had pitched a pair of shutouts and the Cardinals hastily withdrew waivers.

Before a game with the Cardinals, Babe was talking to Dizzy Dean beside the batting cage when Dean looked up in the stands and shouted to a vendor who was selling beer, "Hi, Elmer."

"Hi Jerome," he called back.

"That's my brother Elmer," Diz told Herman. "I haven't seen him for ten years."

"Why not," Babe asked.

"Well, we were down in Arkansas driving along, with Dad and his family in one car and Elmer and my uncle in a second car. A long train came down the track and my uncle got across before we did, so we had to wait until it passed.

"My uncle turned off into a cotton field looking for work and after the train went by we couldn't see where he went. I hadn't seen him again until today." Then Dean walked away to speak to his brother.

Babe looked at Dean closely, not knowing if he should believe him or not.

Later in the season Dean pitched against the Robins and beat them one afternoon. That night Babe and some of his friends went to a House of David baseball game in St. Louis, the first night game Babe had attended.

Dean joined the Robins in the stands but late in the game the rookie Cardinal pitcher got into trouble and it looked as if the House of David team might rally to win.

"I've got to go," Dean told the Robins and jumped out of the box seats and ran down to the bullpen.

He had only thrown about five warmup pitches when manager Frank Frisch signaled to the bullpen for a relief pitcher and there came Dean.

He fanned the side to clinch the game for St. Louis.

"Dean was one of the few pitchers who could pitch the hitters high and get away with it. He had a rising fastball and in addition had an excellent changeup," Herman said.

Later, when Babe played for Pittsburgh, Dean fanned Paul Waner, Arky Vaughn and Babe in succession, each of them swinging and missing his change.

Dean told Herman that Charlie Barnett had been sent to the Ozarks to find a left-handed pitcher that could help the Cardinals.

One day on a back road he saw a left-handed kid throwing rocks at squirrels and knocking them out of the trees.

Barnett signed the kid and brought him back to St. Louis, only to see him warm up right-handed.

"Aren't you left-handed?" he asked.

"No, I'm right-handed," the kid said.

"What about the squirrel?"

"Oh, when I throw right handed at them, it tears them all to pieces

Herman beats out an infield hit against the Cardinals as first baseman Jim Bottomly waits for the throw.

and they aren't good eating then. Dad really spanks me for that," a young Dizzy Dean was supposed to have told Barnett.

In Cincinnati on June 11th, the Robins trailed 1-0 in the ninth when Herman beat out an infield hit. With two out, O'Doul slammed a shot down the right field line and Herman didn't hesitate at third.

He swooped around the bag and beat the throw to the plate with a sensational slide around catcher Clyde Sukeforth.

The play was typical Herman—hell for leather—and when it worked he was a hero but when it came up short fans would scream at him about his terrible baserunning.

The team slipped back into the second division and, coming home, Robbie switched Ivy Olson to the first base coaches box and Jim Johnston to third in the hopes he could change the teamwork luck. Another reason for the switch may have been that Olson had sent five runners home on June 17 and all of them were thrown out at the plate.

Robinson, still badgered by the New York media, told Jack Ryder of the Cincinnati Enquirer he only had 19 enemies in the world and all of them were newsmen.

"Some are trying to run the team through their columns. I wish they would come down to the field and try out some of their theories. They would find it much easier to pound a typewriter than to get results from a team of temperamental athletes," Robbie said.

He went so far as to accuse McKeever of paying the reporters to say bad things about him.

The Brooklyn Eagle received a letter from Gilbert Patten, saying the writing game wasn't going so good and he joked that he might be interested in the manager's job in Brooklyn. Patten wrote under the name Burt L. Standish about the heroics of Frank and Dick Merriwell.

Babe's bat, quiet much of the road trip, blazed to life at home and he banged out 11 hits in three days, cracking two singles, a double and a triple on June 20th to help stop the Cubs 6-5 and give Jack Quinn his first National League victory since 1913. Herman tripled in the eighth and scored on Bissonette's single to tie, then in the ninth inning he smashed a long double off the wall beside the flag pole in center field to win the game.

The rumors rumbled through the stands: Robbie was to be paid off immediately and released. Carey and/or Wheat were to take over the team. The Sporting News said Glenn Wright was to manage the team, since he had been given permission to change pitchers and players by Robinson.

Vance lost a heartbreaker later in the month after he retired the first 20 Cardinals to face him. Lopez's sparring partner, George Watkins, finally broke the string with a walk, worked his way around to third, then stole home during one of Vance's slow, deliberate tosses to first base and the Cardinals won 1-0.

Babe celebrated his birthday on June 26 with a home run and the Robins scored eight in the first to beat St. Louis 16-5.

He was kneeling at the on deck circle when a fan in the front row of the box seats called to him and said, "Think you'll ever amount to anything?"

"I'll show you this time," he replied.

"What, not a hit?"

"I'll ride one out of the park."

"I'll buy you a new hat if you do."

Babe slugged one over the right field screen and when he returned to the dugout, the batboy handed a card to him from the fan in the front row.

He was a big hat manufacturer and was ready to pay off the bet.

"I've been going bare-headed this summer, but I guess it will be a Panama from now on. It would be bad luck not grab it," Babe noted.

Robbie refused an interview with Harold Burr of the Brooklyn Eagle after the game, stating "I wouldn't give any Brooklyn newspaper a story, not after the way they have been riding me, and darn few in New York."

Then Robinson told Burr, "Do you know what I think? I think the newspapers are being paid."

"By who?"

"I don't know, but I've got my opinion." Then Robinson whispered a name, not a newsman.

"That's nonsense," said the astonished Burr.

"I don't know about that. Somebody's doing some tunnel work. Forty years in baseball and I have to go out of town to get a break from the newspapers. It's a shame, that's what it is," Robbie said sadly, walking away.

The Robins took the final four games of the Cardinal series as Frederick hit in his 11th straight game while using O'Doul's 37-ounce bludgeon. John's grand-slam in the fifth reversed a 4-1 Cardinal lead three days later.

The club finished the first three months of the season with a 36-32 record and early in July they ended a lengthy homestand that saw them win 16 of 20 games, moving into third place.

Vance and Clark fired a double shutout at the Giants before a record crowd that was estimated at 42,000 and the final victory of the homestand was a 4-3 decision over the Giants won by Quinn in relief on his 46th birthday. Babe cracked three singles and a double in the victory.

Giant manager John McGraw could easily steal the Robin signs from Robinson in the dugout, since the signs never varied from year to year. Robinson realized what was happening and hid himself back in the corner of the dugout, keeping the dugout post between himself and McGraw.

McGraw simply assigned one of his other players to watch for the signs and relay them to him. He would then signal his players on the field to counteract Robinson's moves.

One afternoon coach Ivy Olson came over to Robinson in the dugout and said, "I keep looking for the signs, but I can't find you half the time. You're not paying attention to me." Robinson just grumbled and turned away.

After infield workouts, Babe told Robbie, "Let's just play without signs today."

"Good idea," Robinson said, "OK, go ahead."

The Robins won that afternoon and also the next two afternoons but Robinson called a meeting and told the team, "Who ever heard of a team playing without signs?" and he installed them again.

The little winning streak suddenly came to an end and the idea of free-lancing on the field never came up after that.

The Robins split a short series with Philadelphia, dropping into fourth place despite a 5-1 win in which Herman collected his 100th hit of the season. Babe also made a pair of plays that saved the game. Leading 3-0 in the third and with runners on first and second, Herman raced into the corner in right field to catch a line drive and fire a perfect strike to double the runner off second. Later Chuck Klein singled and Babe threw a runner out at third to retire the side.

After beating the Braves 6-2 the up-and-down Robins moved into a tie for second place. The next day club split a pair of double headers with the Braves, the second at Ebbets Field. Herman's extraordinary throw cut down Wally Berger at the plate after he had led off with a walk but Thurston lost in the 12th.

A column by Max Kase reported it this way:

"Babe Herman was the particular bright spot in a galaxy of brilliant, scintillating plays which abounded throughout the twelve innings.

"Herman's great effort came with two out in the top of the 10th and Burger on first base, Earl Sheeley slugged a ball off the wall in right-center that Babe nearly caught. He picked the ball up as Burger rounded third and headed for home.

"Herman threw the ball to the plate, some 330 feet away. He had little time go gauge direction, but threw blindly and instinctively in the direction of the plate.

"Straight and true the ball sped as if propelled by a rifle, plunk into the big mitt of little Al Lopez, who tagged Berger with plenty to spare. For the moment it choked off the run and prolonged the game.

"The holiday crowd of 35,000 let out a roar which gathered in volume as it echoed back and across the field. It was the greatest demonstration for Herman this season.

"The Babe made another astounding throw in the sixth inning when his throw on Sheeley's single to right nailed Red Worthington trying for third from first.

"Two assists for an outfielder in one day is a real rarity, but yesterday's game was that sort of battle."

After the game Thurston kiddingly said, "Herman, you SOB, if you don't make that throw we lose the game in the 10th. But instead you made me pitch another two innings and I get the loss."

Wright hurt his ankle again on the road in St. Louis as the team again split, then they moved into Chicago to win three of four.

In the first game, Herman dropped a fly and Cuyler singled to plate the tying run in the ninth but on the hit Babe threw out Vince Barton at the plate before he could score the winning run. Slade's single in the 11th won for the Robins.

Later in the series, Robinson came under fire again from the Brooklyn writers as they complained about his strategy in a tough loss.

In the ninth, trailing 1-0, O'Doul singled and was forced by Mickey Finn. Herman walked and Lombardi flew out. Then Watty Clark was allowed to hit for himself and struck out to end the game. Many wondered why a pinch-hitter had not been used.

In Pittsburgh Herman made a great leaping catch to kill a Pirate rally but the Robins lost 10-6, then in the finale of the series Babe had an exceptional day.

He slammed a single, double, triple and home run and teammate O'Doul was 5-for-5 but despite their bombardment the Robins lost 8-7. They lost a twin-bill the next day and dropped back to fourth place. Cincinnati won three of four to end the Western trip although Herman went 11-for-17 against the Reds.

Babe recorded a .409 average and O'Doul .534 on the Western portion of the road trip but the club only won seven of 18 games and were in fourth place as the month of July ended.

In the middle of July the team moved four games over .500 but trailed the league leader by a full 15 games. They won eight of the final 10 games and the month ground to a close.

Early August headlines in the Brooklyn Eagle shouted, "Herman, Wright and Vance are Stars Who Might be Put on Block." The team had averaged 14,000 per home date in 1930 but were drawing only 11,000 in 1931.

Brooklyn directors looked at the new stands full of empty seats and wondered how they could meet the stiff payment schedule.

A Herman for Hack Wilson trade was again rumored in the papers as the Cubs came into Ebbets Field, but the Dodger management denied any interest in such a swap. Herman doubled in the ninth to beat the Cubs 4-1 in the first game and the next day the Robins swept Chicago to knock them out of first place. The second game of the double-header was won by Fred Heimach who worked 8 2/3 innings in relief of starter Dolph Luque.

On August 25 against Pittsburgh, Herman slammed a Ray Kremer pitch into the new seats in center field. The tremendous shot cleared the 13-foot wall at the 406-foot mark and was estimated to have carried over 450 feet. It was the first ball hit into that section of the park.

On the first day of September the Dodgers beat the Thomkins Bus Company 5-2 in Thompson Stadium on Staten Island in Brooklyn's first recorded night game.

President McKeever suggested a city series between the Robins,

Giants and Yankees with the proceeds going to the unemployed of the city but the New York teams seemed little interested in playing Brooklyn and instead scheduled a game between themselves.

On Monday, September 7, the Robins beat the Braves 5-4 in 10 innings in the first game of two in Ebbets Field. The Brooklyn pitcher scheduled to start the second game told Robbie that his arm hurt and he could not pitch.

But the truth of the matter was he was dating a lady wrestler and the two had been working on some difficult 'moves' on her living room floor the night before and he had suffered a number of painful rug burns from the carpet.

"Who the hell can we pitch?" Robbie asked Herman.

Babe told Robinson that he should start a young pitcher that had just arrived from Hartford after pitching a shutout to clinch the pennant for them. "Just tell him to keep the ball down," Babe said.

Robinson agreed and the rookie, Van Lingo Mungo, only 21 years of age, tripled and scored the first run, then later singled in a 2-0 complete-game victory.

Mungo had just arrived from Hartford but part of his luggage, including his baseball spikes, were still in transit. He asked around the clubhouse and the only shoes that would fit him were those of Dazzy Vance. In effect, Mungo literally and figuratively stepped into Vance's shoes to pitch his two-hit shutout.

While Mungo never put big numbers on the board, he was one of the most feared pitchers in the league. A fierce competitor on the mound, he didn't mind knocking hitters down and was big enough to stand up if that bothered them.

"I'm throwing at you," he would shout at a batter. "If you don't like it come right on out here."

"I would rather hit against a Koufax or a Ryan once a week than against Mungo once a month," Herman would say years later. "They weren't vicious but Mungo was. He would throw that big foot up in your face and take that big stride—He was a lot like Dizzy Dean."

The team was obviously out of the pennant race and McKeever asked waivers on John Frederick, Fresco Thompson, Jack Warner, Pea Ridge Day, Ike Boone and Max Rosenfield, clearing the way for possible trade talks.

Mungo stretched his shutout string to 15 innings in his next start but lost a 4-1 decision to Cincinnati. And rookie catcher Ernie Lombardi was so tough to hit in batting practice, the club actually considered making a pitcher out of him.

Babe's final big day of the disappointing season came in Chicago where he smashed a two-run homer into the wind in the first inning and the singled home the winning run in the fifth after the Cubs tied the game 2-2. Mungo was the winning pitcher.

The Robins clinched fourth place, then traveled a full day on the train to get home in time for a benefit game scheduled with the Yankees and Giants in the Polo Grounds. The two New York teams had finally condescended to include the Brooklyn team in the unusual charity game. The Robins lost 5-1 and 3-1 as 44,119 attended.

Babe Ruth excited the crowd before the game by slamming a ball off the base of the center field wall with a fungo bat, the shot traveling over 420 feet.

On the final day of the season, the Robins exacted a measure of revenge by scoring eight runs in the third inning to dump the Giants 12-3.

Bill Terry was locked in a tight battle for the National League batting title with Chick Hafey of the Cardinals. The Robins held him to one hit in four trips in the opening game as Hafey went hitless.

Studying the averages, New York officials felt that if Terry got a hit in his first time at bat in the second game, he would clinch the title. He singled in the first inning and was taken out of the game to insure his batting championship.

However, darkness cancelled the contest with the Giants leading 6-1 in the third inning and game records were nullified. That, coupled with two hits by Hafey in the second Cardinal game, gave the St. Louis outfielder an average of .34967, while Terry's average slipped to .3488, losing the title by the smallest margin in Major League history.

The 1931 team had seemingly spent its World Series money in the spring and then lost 10 of the first 12 games to fall out of the race. The weaknesses at second base and left field were to have been corrected by Fresco Thompson and Lefty O'Doul but shortstop Glenn Wright's reoccurring injuries kept him out of action much of the time.

Herman was remarkably consistent during the year, hitting .313 with 191 hits and again led the club in runs and hits as well as with 43 doubles, 16 triples, 18 homers and 97 RBI. But the deadened baseball worked as the owners hoped it would. Averages around the league were down and Herman's average plumeted 80 points. He was also off 33 runs batted in and 17 homers from his 1930 mark.

O'Doul, who was hitting only .248 going into June, had put on an exceptional spurt, hitting .367 the rest of the season to finish with a team leading .336 average although he also lost nearly 50 points off his 1930 record.

With the decrease in Herman's batting average, the club won only 16 of 40 games in which Herman was hitless. When he had at least one hit, the team was 14-games over .500 at 62-48.

Ernie Lombardi was selected on the league rookie team after hitting .297 in 73 games and his performance, in addition to the fine hitting and fielding work by Al Lopez, gave Brooklyn two of the best young catchers in the major leagues.

O'Doul tied for 10th in the Most Valuable Player voting and Herman was 15th, tied with Jim Bottomly of the Cardinals.

The full grip of the depression was being felt and baseball made moves to tighten their operations. The player limit was cut from 25 to 23, over American League suggestions that they cut to 22.

The owners adopted a resolution that player salaries be cut by 15 percent across the board. And in other moves, the owners voted against revival of the league's Most Valuable Player voting and against numbering players. They left the sale of radio rights up to each individual owner, with the intimation that it would probably be barred in all parks in 1933. And for some unknown reason, they cut the visitor's batting practice from 30 to 20 minutes, perhaps thinking that would save batting practice baseballs.

Robinson's contract to manage the Dodgers expired at the end of the season and although rumors that Burleigh Grimes would take over the club, most of his friends were confident Robbie's contract would be renewed. His opponents were equally sure that he would be retained and were resigned to the fact.

Before the season ended, Herman had warned Robinson that York had taken his president's job and would eventually get his manager's job but Robbie just said, "You don't understand York."

"I know him," Babe replied. "He's a crooked SOB."

Otto Miller had given his salary to Ebbets to keep the park open during the tough, early years and was rumored to have a guaranteed job with the Brooklyn club for life. Working behind the scenes, through Walter Carter, Miller kept pushing Max Carey as manager of the club and urging they rid themselves of Robinson.

The Robins would again return to Clearwater in the spring and talk of training in California was forgotten, apparently cancelled by the Ebbets heirs because of the additional expense. Real estate holdings in Florida seemed to be the deciding factor for the club's return, although York and McKeever had favored California because spring training gate receipts in Clearwater had been dropping each year.

A second rumor swept Brooklyn, that supposed Charlie Moore, 30-year old manager of Hartford, would take over for Robinson. Moore had won the pennant with Rocky Mount in 1929 and with Macon in 1930 before taking over the top Brooklyn club at Hartford. However, not many put much stock in that rumor.

On October 23, Brooklyn directors called a news conference and newsmen waited four hours for the director's meeting to end. Finally Frank York came out of the meeting and passed out the announcement.

They had refused to renew the contract of Wilbert Robinson, ending 18 years of service with the club. They had approved the hiring of Max Carey. The directors did, however, vote Robinson $10,000 for "faithful service," although they sent it to him by mail instead of presenting it in

Babe during batting practice in Ebbets Field

person.

The announcement ended years of infighting between Robinson and McKeever but even McKeever didn't seem to derive any joy from the move he had been working on over the last five years. The vote had been 3 to 2 for Carey, with York, McKeever and Carter voting for him and the Ebbets faction against.

Carey appeared later and responded gracefully to congratulations, but was guarded about his plans for the team. He admitted there were "a lot of things" to be done, but said future plans would have to be studied before any action would be taken. He left immediately after the news conference to bring his family back to Brooklyn. Writers thought that a more popular choice to replace Robinson would be hard to find.

Herman felt Carey was a smart manager but too technical. He insisted his players hit behind the runner and give themselves up to advance the man into scoring position. "What is the percentage in having your three-four hitters trying to advance a man when they could hit the ball into the seats?" Herman wondered.

Robinson had won two pennants, in 1916 and 1920, and had nearly won two others in 1924 and 1930. He got the most out of his players, many of whom other clubs had discarded. And although McKeever wouldn't admit it, Robinson was, in large measure, responsible for the prosperity of the club. His players, taken from here and there at garage sale prices, had put money in the cash drawer.

Opinion in Brooklyn concerning the wisdom of dropping Robbie was divided, some thinking that the baseball parade has passed him by, and other supporting him faithfully, swearing that if Ebbets had lived, he would never had considered letting him go. But he had been there for 18 years and had forever left a solid mark on Brooklyn baseball.

Murray Tynan wrote in the New York Herald, "Robbie's passing will come as a blow to many fans all over the country who loved him for his bluff honesty and the rich traditions of his background.

"He was known as a master handler of pitchers and developed many top-notchers in Brooklyn. Burleigh Grimes came up with a decidedly poor record and under Robinson's management developed into a great pitcher.

"His greatest accomplishment was his development of Vance. Daz, who had been knocking around for years, finally became a big winner when Robinson got the idea to give him four days rest between starts."

Garry Schumacher wrote in the New York Evening Journal: "The Robins will certainly play a different type of baseball than they did during the Robinson regime. A theorist and tactician, Carey was never in sympathy with the free swinging, home-run type of baseball fostered by the lively ball and now that the scientific phases of the game has been revived by the new sphere, he is sure to reconstruct the Brooklyn system of play according to his own ideas."

New York Evening Post writer Forest Cain noted, "Only the retirement of John McGraw or Connie Mack would stir the sentiment and break up ties among baseball men and fans of the land as in this case of Robinson. Unquestionably his dismissal brings a personal pang of regret for more folks than would that of any other fixture in baseball. This lovable, glamorous old character had a personal way about him. The move seems a popular one among Brooklyn fans, despite Robinson's popularity at large.

"The Robins were a slow-moving team of too many washed-up veterans and York stressed the fact that Carey, a great hustler and popular with baseball fans, is a man to inject new dash, vim and ambition into the Robins."

Joe Villa, who never mentioned Robinson's name in the New York Sun because of a feud of many years standing, broke the ban when Carey was hired and wrote: "The removal of Robinson is not only a progressive move calculated to bringing order out of chaos, but also a personal triumph for S.W. McKeever, treasurer of the club who holds 50 percent of the stock.

"Ebbets was the real manager from the time he purchased control of the club in 1909 until his fatal illness in 1925. At the death of Ebbets, a feud started between his heirs and the McKeever interests. Visualizing big business in the future at Ebbets Field, National League men are glad the Brooklyn feud is at an end."

And Dan Daniel, in the New York World Telegram, said: "No doubt it is all for the best that W. Robinson, 67 years old and conceivably tired of the grief and bickering that have been part of the Brooklyn job, should retire as manager of the Robins and challenge younger hands and maybe nimbler wits to fashion a more lustrous regime. The cruel battle of Flatbush is finally over. The selection of Carey was by acclamation. His confirmation was a glorious triumph for peace and harmony.

"Now comes the job of saving the Robins from slipping into the second division. As they stand, they cannot hope to avert the demotion. And we'll bet dollars to donuts that down at Dover Hall Robbie is laughing his head off and kicking his heels like a schoolboy on vacation."

When Carey was selected as the new manager, Herman stopped off in St. Louis on his way back to California and talked to him.

"I don't think I should take a big pay cut, Max" he said.

"Hell, no, Babe. I wouldn't," Carey told him. "I wouldn't worry about a $1,000 cut, but I wouldn't take a big cut."

"Thanks, Max," Babe said. "I just wanted to have a general idea of how you felt about it."

Then in due course, another problem confronted the Brooklyn front office. With Robinson gone, the club could no longer be called the Robins. McKeever had never called them Robins due to his constant battle with Uncle Robbie.

The Brooklyn Eagle wrote: "The Bridegrooms and Superbas died a natural death long ago. The Dodgers is a nickname that never has acquired universal popularity or come into unchallenged usage, possibly because it doesn't seem to mean very much."

William McGunnigle was manager of the Brooklyn club in 1890, and they were called "Bridegrooms," after an unusually large number of them had been married over the winter. They had previously been named "Trolly Dodgers" because of the network of trolly lines crisscrossing the area near the park.

When Hanlon arrived, one of the top vaudeville acts on the Eastern seaboard was the Hanlon Brothers who had three pieces on theatrical tour: "Le Voyuage en Suisse," "Fantasma" and the most popular of them all, "Superba." Hanlon's Superbas was an easy transition for the newsmen to make and the name caught on, staying even after Hanlon departed following the 1905 season.

Robinson's arrival in 1914 spurred them to call the team the "Robins," and that they stayed until the end of the 1931 season.

Brooklyn baseball writers, during the slow months in the off season, asked for suggestions as to what the club should now be called. One suggested "Canaries," keeping the club still in the bird kingdom and using Carey's name as a basis. "Kings" was also suggested due to the fact that Brooklyn was in Kings County.

Club officials notified the writers that they could choose a name and that they would recognize it as official. Since the club had never officially had a nickname, the project drew a good deal of comment in the papers before the writers voted January 22nd to adopt the name "Dodgers." The club accepted that as official and announced they would put the name on the front of the 1932 jerseys.

Chapter 9

Even before contracts were sent in the spring, Frank York told reporters that Herman declared he wouldn't play for less than the $19,000 he received during the 1931 season. York called him a holdout, saying, "We have no intentions of paying Herman that in 1932."

The total Brooklyn payroll was $225,000 an average of less than $10,000 per player, not including the manager and coaches, and the head office was looking for ways to cut that by another $40,000.

Baseball writers, checking the clubs' payroll, remembered that the 1909 Brooklyn team had a payroll of $30,000 with Nap Rucker the top player at $3,500.

Carey announced that he had received two dozen applications for the coaching position, including those from Zach Wheat and Casey Stengel. Carey quickly made a popular move by bringing back the popular Stengel as a coach. Casey had managed at Toledo for the past six years but the team went bankrupt and Casey was out of work. It was rumored that coaches Ivy Olson and Jimmy Johnston might be released and only Otto Miller retained.

"In my opinion, the reorganization of the pitching staff is the most important. I don't see having three left-handed hitting outfielders on the club. There isn't a player I won't trade," Carey said.

Carey attempted to trade John Frederick for Pittsburgh outfielder Adam Comorosky at the winter meetings but then the Pirates would have had three lefties in the outfield and they turned him down. He also offered Frederick for Taylor Douthit of the Cardinals to no avail. Rumors at the winter meeting had Hack Wilson coming to Brooklyn for Frederick or Vance. Another said Joe Stripp and Larry Benton of Cincinnati would be swapped for Frederick, Vance, Lombardi and Boone. Later Vance was supposed to be traded to New York for Fred Fitzsimmons and the

Cardinals were apparently offering Flint Rehm and Wally Roettger for Vance. No matter which rumor you were inclined to believe, it was apparent that Carey would shake up the Brooklyn club during the off-season and interest ran high.

Hack Wilson was traded to St. Louis by the Chicago Cubs for Burleigh Grimes and the Dodgers had their eye on the squatty outfielder, having wanted the right-hander in their lineup for some time. So they obtained Wilson by sending rookie pitcher Robert Partham and $45,000 to Branch Rickey, who never seriously wanted the hard-drinking Hack. Wilson, who made $33,000 in 1931, had been offered $7,500 by Rickey.

Hack was originally owned by the Giants and they transferred him to Toledo for additional seasoning in 1925 but someone forgot to recall him in time and he became eligible for the draft.

The Dodgers and Cubs were battling with the Phillies for last place in 1925 and the winner would have the first draft pick which, of course would be Wilson. Brooklyn lost 11 straight late in September, making a run at the league basement, but fatefully rallied to beat Cincinnati and New York before losing the last four. The two victories boosted them into a sixth place tie with the Phillies (68-85) while the Cubs finished the NL basement for the first time in history with a 68-86 mark, earning Wilson's services by a slim half-game.

The day after the season ended, Robinson was offered the services of Paul Waner, but by the time he got the necessary permission from McKeever and Gilleaudeau by telephone, the Pirates had grabbed him for the same asking price they quoted Brooklyn.

The acquisition of Wilson now gave the Dodgers an outfield that included Herman, O'Doul and Wilson and salivating Flatbush fans rubbed their hands in glee over the damage they might do to other National League pitching staffs.

Hypothetically, if each duplicated his best season, the trio would average a staggering .382 with 41 homers and 147 RBI.

	Ave	HR	RBI
Herman (1930)	.393	35	130
O'Doul (1929)	.398	32	122
Hack (1930)	.356	56	190

But Wilson had hit .261 in 1931 for the Cubs, but the home run and RBI figures he recorded in 1930 are still National League records almost 60 years later. Herman had slipped to .313 and O'Doul to .336.

Carey noted: "This is a 'might' proposition, but Herman is much faster than Wilson and gets a better jump on the ball than O'Doul, so he would seem the logical man to play center field with Wilson shifted to right where I believe he would do a good job.

"It may not work that way, but I'm confident of this much—Babe is a pretty good ball player, much better than most believe. I don't have to tell anyone that Babe has all the physical requirements that a great ball player needs and I believe he will improve right along with some sympathetic coaching.

"I worked a lot with Herman when I was with the club a few years ago, and while I don't want to pin any medals on myself, I think I helped him in certain directions.

"I gave him a few hints and he swiped something like 20 bases that year. The next year he asked me to watch him in the field and tell him the things he did wrong. He wasn't a Pavlova in fielding grace when I finished with him, but he certainly did improve fast before I left the club.

"I think most people have the wrong slant on Herman. He's ambitious, willing, eager to learn and easy to teach. You've got to like the fellow who pastes a ball as he does.

"But the prospect of Herman in center is an idea that just occurred to me. Nobody can tell how it would work out until it's tried. First we have to see in the south if we need him there. Then we'd have to see if he could do it."

The Dodgers, who were attempting to sign Herman for $15,000, agreed to pay Wilson $16,500 for the 1932 season, although most officials around the league felt that the former Cub outfielder was nearly finished. It turned out they were right.

Dolph Luque, 42, and Rube Bressler, 36, were released but 46-year-old Jack Quinn was signed with a raise. O'Doul signed for $11,000, a cut of $1,000 after hitting .336. 'Official' holdouts were Vance, Wright, Lopez, Clark, Gilbert, Thompson, Day, Moore, Lombardi, Shaute, Slade and Herman, all resisting the proposed across the board pay cut.

However, when training camp opened on Feb. 23, only Herman, Frederick, and Gilbert were unsigned. Vance soon relented and accepted a pact for $17,000, down $5,500 from 1931. Herman was again offered $15,000.

York said, "Our so-called holdout list doesn't mean much. Perhaps Vance and Herman will prove a bit stubborn but I don't believe it will take them much longer to realize it's for their own interests as well as that of the club to get an early start this season. At present, their demands and the final offer of the club are close enough to assure an early capitulation. Vance, particularly, must realize he is not the star he once was."

Carey installed callisthenics in the Dodger camp and set a 9:30 curfew, and both moves were shocking to the once-rollicking Dodger camp. He had tried to set up workouts with Robinson in previous years but after the first session Robbie felt the team hit with less than robust power in batting practice the next day and called them off.

Robinson always opened spring training with a game between the regulars and the yannigans. He simplistically thought the best way to condition a baseball team for baseball was to have them play baseball.

York had insisted that all players would be signed by spring training, but it soon became obvious he was wrong.

A similar scenario in the Cincinnati camp saw Tony Cuccinello and Joe Stripp holding out against big salary cuts. Rumors of a deal for one or both floated in the Florida air.

Gilbert and Herman were still not in sight and Carey said, "If Herman doesn't sign, we'll get along. I'm not convinced Ike Boone wouldn't help us, he's a great hitter."

Babe, holding out as much to miss the spring training games as to boost his eventual contract, was working out in California, oblivious to the festering politics of the Dodger camp. York's obvious animosity toward Herman made the atmosphere different in Clearwater than it had been in previous springs.

Tommy Holmes, analyzing the feelings of club officials in Florida, wrote in the Brooklyn Eagle, "Herman's holdout this year will probably prove costly to him. He has maneuvered himself into a spot on which the club doesn't give a hoot, for the present, whether he signs or not and some of the officials really believe what they say when they assert that they hope he does not.

"When he reports and goes to work, he isn't gong to operate as he did in times past. If old Wilbert Robinson had a pet on the Brooklyn team, that pet was Herman. At any rate, Babe did as he jolly well pleased. You can lay your money on the line that Max Carey will handle Herman differently, and it is at least doubtful that the skittish outfielder will prosper under a regime that will stress strict discipline from the bench in the course of the game.

"You can also bet that Herman, unless he bats better than .313 this coming season, won't be with the club a year from now even if the Dodgers can't get anything more than broken bats for him in a trade.

"In other words, Babe has just put himself on a spot."

Carey had approached Cincinnati owner Sid Weil at the National League meetings early in the year and offered to take Cuccinello and Stripp off his hands, offering Clark and Frederick in return.

On March 5th, York talked to Weil and manager Dan Howley in Tampa. The Reds wanted Lombardi, the Dodgers Stripp and/or Cuccinello. Five days later a rumor spread through both the Dodgers and Reds camp that Cuccinello and Stripp would be traded for Lombardi, Frederick, Boone and Gilbert.

On March 11th York, Carey, Weil and Howley were locked in a non-stop meeting at the Fort Harrison hotel and players in the Dodger camp were extremely nervous. Weil had set a one p.m. deadline on his final trade offer to keep negotiations from dragging on all spring. The Dodgers finally made a decision and called him just at one.

The deal was announced and it was a shocker. The Reds sent Stripp,

Cuccinello and Clyde Sukeforth to the Dodgers for Herman, Lombardi and Gilbert.

Then Brooklyn erupted.

Screams of anguish echoed from Jackson Heights to Coney Island, from Bay Ridge to Canarsie and all points beyond and between. The Brooklyn switchboard was swamped.

Babe had received calls or telegrams from Gilleaudeau, Mulvey and McKeever the day he was traded, asking if he would sign for the offered $15,000. Babe told them he hadn't changed his mind.

"I'll sign as soon as you send me the contract we agreed to with Mr. York," Babe told them.

Ernie Lombardi

"That's not definite enough," McKeever said.

"It's pretty definite to me," Babe replied.

While having dinner at his home in Glendale with a number friends and most of the New York newsmen who were in California to cover the Giants, he received a call from Dan Howley at 11 p.m.

"You're a big red," Howley told him.

"I've been called worse than that," Babe replied, not knowing what he was talking about.

"I don't mean a Bolshevik, Babe, I just made a deal for you. How much salary do you want?"

"You know what I want."

"You'll have to talk to Sid Weil about that," Howley said.

Herman called Weil in Tampa, Florida and asked for $19,000 but was told the club couldn't afford that much. Weil listed the salaries of the other players and said money was very tight.

Babe said, "OK, I'll play for $16,500 and if you don't draw more people than you did last year you don't owe me a cent extra. If you draw more, pay me an extra $3,500." Weil quickly agreed to that contract condition. However, Herman would not collect the bonus money as Reds' attendance fell below the 1931 figures.

Cincinnati fans had been hostile to the general trade talks when the Brooklyn outfielder rumored to be included was John Frederick, and flooded the front office with angry mail. But when Herman's name was announced in the trade, fan response made a 180 degree turn, becoming overwhelmingly favorable.

Carey said, "I think we made a good trade. Of the three players we gave Cincinnati, only Herman could be counted as a regular. We got two regulars, Stripp and Cuccinello. We can spare Babe because I'm pretty sure an outfield of O'Doul in left, Wilson in right and Frederick in center is a good combination."

"Herman is a great fellow to drive in four runs when his team is six runs behind, but if his team is only one run behind he never seems to drive in any. I haven't lost anything in giving up a sulky, dissatisfied, headstrong player like Herman for a team player like Cuccinello. I think I got the best of it," Max Carey told a New York newspaper.

"And Herman only hit well in games when a lot of runs were scored," Carey said, but reporters laughed and corrected him. "You've got it backwards. When Herman hits, a lot of runs are scored," one said.

Tommy Holmes noted, "Herman, without doubt, was the most discussed of the players in the trade. Some were with him, some against him, but between his boosters and his detractors, he was a uniform drawing card.

"Nor is the deal universally acclaimed as a Brooklyn success by baseball men in Clearwater. There is a tendency to regret the passing of Herman's great power. 'Gee, how he can hit,' was the main quote from Brooklyn players. But in the next breath, the players admit that it seemed Herman's own fault he was traded."

Carey said, "I'm pleased the club stood behind me in this deal. It amounts to a $100,000 transaction for which I'm taking the full responsibility. I'm sure it will help our club, and the fact that I was able to put it through assures me that I'm going to have the full cooperation of the front office."

Ed Hughes wrote in the Brooklyn Eagle: "That Carey intends to preserve as little as possible of the 'merry clown' personality of the old Robin outfit is becoming more and more apparent.

"The comparatively strict discipline that he immediately established to replace Uncle Robbie's free and easy tactics was the first step. Now it is the personnel itself that is being removed. Babe Herman was sold down the river yesterday.

"That is sad news to many Flatbush fanatics. The gangling, colorful, hit-or-miss Babe was a Brooklyn institution, a subject that has been more or less a specialty with Robin teams of the past. Uncle Robbie himself was a 16-cylinder institution.

"But all institutions crumble and collapse in the rush of time. They wear out physically and sentimentally. It took Robbie a long time to ramble to the end of this tether, but he got there.

"Now it is the youthful Herman as far as Flatbush is concerned. With Carey and a new scheme of things it somehow doesn't seem surprising that Herman is now found among the missing. Herman was Robbie's 'fair-haired boy,' as they say. You would almost feel that the spirit and personality of Robinson still hovered over the team with Babe in the lineup. However, that isn't why Babe was turned loose. Carey doesn't deal in such fantastic baseball items as that. He knew Herman was a good ball player, and had the Babe been less hoity-toity about signing up, very likely this wouldn't have been written.

"Nevertheless, Babe is gone from Flatbush, and no matter how the replacement works out, there will be many who'll sincerely miss the colorful kid. Babe had a lot to recommend him at that. He had the inward stuff, real determination. From a clown outfielder he made himself into something akin to a ball hawk.

"Robbie has been given credit for developing him. In reality, all that Wilbert had to do with Babe's remarkable improvement was to extend his boundless patience toward the youth.

"That wasn't extremely hard for Wilbert. In fact, it was the round fellow's amazing patience with all sorts of diamond faults and shortcomings that cost Flatbush pennants and creditable showings.

"Still it was to Robinson's credit that he personally and professionally liked Herman, for he endured in Flatbush to witness Herman regarded as a first-class ball player in spite of an occasional dementia on the base paths.

"All in all, I think Flatbush is sorry that Herman has passed. He was a good fella, a good entertainer and a good ball player."

Cincinnati writers felt that Weil had out-traded Brooklyn on the deal and while it perhaps helped both clubs, the Reds had gained a big edge.

Frank Grayson of the Cincinnati Times-Star noted, "The Reds gained one of the leading batsmen of the county in addition to a gigantic young catcher who has one of the most magnificent throwing arms in the game." And Jack Ryder added: "There was much joking about his awkward fielding at first base but Herman is now an accomplished performer on defense."

Manager Dan Howley was pleased. He said, "This deal will make the club. Herman will add terrific punch to our lineup. I know the Babe, he will hustle for me and produce plenty of base hits. And don't think he can't go snag 'em, just because he looks awkward."

Cincinnati fans were wary, thinking that Herman would be quickly sold to Chicago. Weil and Howley emphatically denied that. Dodger business manager Dave Driscoll noted that the trade stipulated that the Babe must play one season with Cincinnati before being traded.

From the outset, Dodger fans were certain it was a bad trade. The discussion centered mostly around the departure of Brooklyn's Babe. None of the Cincinnati refugees could match his color and it is color that draws crowds.

Lefty O'Doul said, "Babe is a great hitter and I think he's likely to hit about .400 if he spends a season in that big Cincinnati park."

Frederick noted, "I always thought Herman's fielding was greatly underestimated. I played beside him for three years and I think he's a good outfielder."

Bissonette added, "I think the club has been helped, even though we will miss old Babe in there cutting and slashing next season."

Letters of protest poured into the Brooklyn offices as the fans who had jeered Herman when he was one of their own, now reacted violently, furious at the front office that had traded him away.

Herman had many critics, but the situation reversed itself after the trade and suddenly the Herman boosters came out of the closet and became deafening. In letters to Brooklyn papers they declared York another Harry Frazee, the man who sold Babe Ruth to the Yankees, and cries were heard that they had sold Herman down the river for a mess of nothing much.

The newspapers were mostly of the same opinion. Gary Schumacher spoke for many when he wrote, "The deal whereby Brooklyn obtained Cuccinello and Stripp for Herman scarcely merits disapproval in that two right-handed hitters of ability have been added to the roster.

"Yet it isn't possible to escape the conclusion that the club sacrificed an exceedingly valuable and certainly a very colorful player. Other terms could have been arranged; one or both the two new infielders obtained and Herman retained at the same time.

"From that standpoint it was a bad deal.

"President York is likely to discover, too, that the box office reaction will be decidedly unfavorable. As a Brooklyn player, Herman was the most colorful in the National League, the player who created more fan interest and discussion than any other. Left to a decision of the fans, the deal would have not been completed, and their opinion, ignored now, is sure to be forcefully impressed upon the club officials before the season has run it's course.

Regardless of the quality or merit of his play, it never failed to provide entertainment, and as such it created and maintained in a team that until recently had little else to recommend it.

"As the front man, if not the sponsor for the deal, Max Carey must stake his managerial future upon the results. To justify it, he must win the pennant or come close to it. Failure will discredit him completely and lay him open to criticism he will not be able to answer.

"Even as a disciplinary measure, if one was necessary, the wisdom of the trade is to be doubted. Herman is certain to wind up in Chicago and there throw up another bar to Brooklyn's progress toward a pennant."

Joe Villa, still high from the removal of Robinson, who had been a thorn in his side, thought the Dodgers were made pennant contenders by the trade. "It is understood that Herman was unpopular with team officials. He was considered the managers pet and allowed to do as he pleased," Villa noted.

Harry Sylvester of the Brooklyn Eagle interviewed Abe Bettan, a long-time Herman critic about the trade. Bettan told him, "Ever since the Babe came to Brooklyn I have been razzing him along with the rest of the Brooklyn team in general. It is my pleasure to do so; I pay my admission.

"But they made a great mistake in letting the Babe go. He was worth $150,000 on the open market, and a lot more than the three players Brooklyn received in the trade. There aren't many better hitters in baseball and his fielding the past two years has been much better.

"No, now I will root for the Babe. Hack Wilson is the guy I will pan. Herman is worth as much as him any day. Even when Wilson hit 56 homers he did not bat as high as Babe. No, it was a bad trade. Now if Wright doesn't hold up, the only place for Brooklyn will be in Jersey City.

"Babe is my pal now. I'll root for him every time he comes to Ebbets Field. But Wilson—phooey!" he said.

When the season started, Brooklyn outfielders and infielders would wince as implacable, inevitable, stentorian, the blasting fog-horn that Abe Bettan used for a voice started to remind them and the world in general of the nature of their shortcomings.

Martin Bracken, well known Borough Hall figure said: "In Herman they let a good, willing, colorful player go. In return they received Cuccinello who is slow; Stripp who is fast of foot but not of mind and Sukeforth on whom they must gamble as his injuries have hurt him permanently. In addition, a promising catcher was lost."

But Uncle Robbie, from his home in Georgia, said, cheek, "You know what I think about Babe Herman as a hitter, but I think Carey unquestionably lost more than he gained in the trade."

Westbrook Pegler noted that the Dodgers were now "Mother Carey's chickens." He wrote prophetically: "I hope the Dodgers win the pennant this year or the inmates won't turn out to watch them. Max Carey stands for discipline, which may be all right in armies, political parties and eye-rolling organization of the pious type. It is his theory of life and conduct that traded Babe Herman to Cincinnati.

"Babe is the champion baseball comedian of all time, because he is a great baseball player on one hand and incredibly clumsy on the other.

"Babe Herman developed under Wilbert Robinson into a great hitter, a champion outfielder and no mean strategist. He once even set up a batting order that won a number of games to break the team's slump."

Borough Hall Taxi Drivers Association, Long Island Depot Taxi Drivers Association members and the Three Hundred Blue Club wrote letters of protest, stating that Herman had been rated near Ruth in their books in total worth to the team. "We are sore and we don't mean maybe," they added.

Vincent J. Wilham submitted this poem to the Brooklyn Eagle.

The Voice of the Bleachers

They promised for the last 10 years
We'd have the winning team.
But when October rolled around
It proved e'ar but a dream.

We didn't kick, we didn't cry
Each year we went and paid.
We didn't mind no winning team
As long as we had Babe.

Although last year, with new stands built,
No bleacher seats were made.
We gladly paid twice as much,
As long as we had Babe.

Although they lied and fooled us,
We went most every day.
But they sold Babe down the river,
So now we'll stay away.

The team's character didn't change immediately after Herman's departure. In an early exhibition game Gordon Slade bunted and was easily thrown out with two down and two on and the team trailing by five runs, then later Ike Boone and Hack Wilson found themselves on third base at the same time. This time no one could blame Herman.

Ed Hughes of the Brooklyn Eagle, after watching the Dodgers for a time, wrote: "The infield was strengthened but it was a costly business. Herman, I should say, should most certainly have been retained. The Babe could maul that pill and he could cover the tricky right field. He had his faults, of course, but I think his gifts clearly overshadowed them."

Rumors had Cincinnati just a stopping off place for Herman on his way to Chicago. Despite the alleged agreement that provided he wouldn't be sold or traded before the opening of the 1932 season, Rogers Hornsby announced that the Cubs wanted Herman badly and would try to convince the Reds that they were serious.

Predictions about the fate of the Dodgers proved correct. 'Carey's Canaries' were pretty much colorless and although they finished third in 1932, they were never really in the race and Brooklyn fans indifferently avoided the new outfield stands. The trade would be later rated as the worst in Brooklyn history. They not only lost the booming bat of Herman, but swapped a Hall of Fame catcher, Ernie Lombardi, who would become the only catcher in history to win two batting titles (1938 and 1942). He was the N.L. Most Valuable Player in 1938.

A sixth-place finish in 1933 doomed Carey and he left in favor of Casey Stengel, who left in favor of Burleigh Grimes and the club floundered in the second division until Larry MacPhail arrived to resurrect the franchise in 1938.

Herman said leaving the Brooklyn club was not too traumatic for him. He missed the fans and his fellow teammates but being traded was part of the game and no one realized it more than he. And although he didn't say it, distancing himself from the revengeful Frank York was no hardship.

"I'll miss my many friends in Brooklyn, but that is the way it is," Herman said. "Brooklyn fans are the best in the league. They are completely partial to their own players."

"I could always tell who the gamblers were betting on," he said. "When we left the dugout, if they shouted 'You're a clown, Herman, you're no good,' I knew they were betting against Brooklyn that day. When they yelled, 'Let's go, Herman, hit a couple today,' I knew they were betting on us.

"I was the one they booed in Brooklyn. Vance got all the publicity before I came but as I became more popular with the fans it split them into two camps, one with Dazzy and one with me. Neither of us could do anything about it."

Babe would hit with a vengeance in Ebbets Field during the next five years. He was particularly vicious in 1932 playing with the Cincinnati Reds, banging Brooklyn pitching around for a .519 average in front of the Flatbush Faithful. He hit .444 in 1934 and .417 in 1936, leaving the National League early in 1937 with a .370 average in his old park and compiling an overall .330 average against the Dodgers.

However, the Babe was never quite the same after he left Brooklyn. Attribute it to less media attention, to the natural ageing process or, as some have intimated, to a broken heart, he would continue to play well in the field and hit with authority, but never reach the glorious heights he did on the field and in the hearts of Brooklyn.

Chapter 10

Herman reported to Macon and trained with the Georgia club until Cincinnati came through on March 22nd. Manager Dan Howley of the Reds said, "Herman, I think, is going to be a great asset to the team. His fielding has been press-agented up and down the league but he is far from a joke. I'm going to turn right field over to him because I'm sure he will play it satisfactorily. And I know his bat is going to do us a lot of good."

Babe asked the manager when he wanted him in the lineup. "When you're ready and not a day sooner," he said. "You have been playing long enough to know and I'll count on your opinion."

Babe told reporters, "I was never treated with so much consideration. Each year with Brooklyn I played nine innings the first day in camp and last year I pulled a muscle early and never got over it. It will take me about a week to get ready."

Sid Weil, with a thought to Herman's future salary, said to him, "You won't hit all the home runs you hit in Brooklyn."

"I'll make a deal with you, I'll hit as many in Cincinnati as I did in Brooklyn," Babe said. This was quite a statement, since there were a total of only 10 home runs hit in spacious Cincinnati during the entire 1931 season.

Redland Field (It would be named Crosley Field in 1934) was a left-handed hitters nightmare, with a right-field fence that measured 377 feet at the foul pole, while center (407) and left (339) were of more normal distance.

Despite the fact that the Reds had finished seventh, seventh and eighth the three previous years, baseball fever reached its pitch in Cincinnati when Chick Hafey was obtained for Harvey Hendrick and Benny Frey. Club president Sid Weil noted, "We're ready for one more trade—we'll deal anyone but Herman or Hafey."

Old friend Harvey Hendrick would later replace Mickey Heath as the Cincinnati first baseman. George Grantham was at second, former teammate Wally Gilbert at third and Leo Durocher covered shortstop.

Herman joined Estel Crabtree, Wally Roettger, Taylor Douthit and Chick Hafey in the outfield. Ernie Lombardi would do the bulk of the catching.

Si Johnson, Red Lucas, Ownie Carroll, Ray Kolp and Larry Benton were in the starting rotation. Spot starters included Eppa Rixey and later Benny Frey would join the club.

Jack Ryder wrote, "While Herman, originally a first baseman and a good one, was studying to be an outfielder, he performed some unusual acrobatic stunts and was frequently referred to as a clown.

"Undoubtedly he was awkward in the pasture for a season or two but he kept at the job of perfecting the finer points of outfield play and today he is a finished performer.

"No one who has seen him judge long flies accurately and spear them off the right field wall in Ebbets Field can any longer call him a clown."

True to his word, Herman was ready to go in about a week and in his third exhibition game, against the Philadelphia A's, he demonstrated that hitting was not his only talent.

He singled to center in the fifth, took third on another single and then stole home with a long slide as the Reds won 10-9.

Two days later, with two on base, he slammed a shot directly at the Louisville first baseman who was playing close to the base expecting a bunt. The drive was turned into a triple play. It would have been a cinch double or triple had the fielder been in normal position. Babe had finally hit into a triple play.

The Reds were picked as 1000-1 shots to win the pennant, 400-1 to finish second and 200-1 to finish third. Dan Howley apparently agreed with the odds and told newsmen, "Even with Herman and Lombardi, this is the worst team I have ever handled."

Opening day the Reds surprised the Cubs with four runs in the ninth to win 5-4. Despite a bitterly cold wind, 25,869 were in attendance at Redland Field. But after the booming crowd on opening day, the next two games drew only 2,100 each day.

Herman doubled once in four trips but make his mark in the game with his glove. "Where are those New York scribes who used to say Babe Herman can't field?" Ryder noted in the Cincinnati paper. "The Babe made two of the prettiest catches of the day, both on difficult running chances, which he handled with ease and grace."

The Cubs were impressed and offered 20-game winner Pat Malone for Herman but the Reds turned the deal down.

Babe singled and scored the first run against the Pirates on April 17 and threw a runner out at the plate in the fourth. But in the ninth he fired a throw over the catcher's head as the Reds lost 4-3.

He made up for the error the next day although the Reds were held to only five hits by lefty Larry French. Herman scored a pair of runs and knocked in three others in the 5-0 victory. He doubled to right in the fourth to plate the first run, then singled and scored in the seventh. In the eighth he banged an inside-the-park homer into the right field corner, scoring two ahead of him, and crossed the plate standing up before Paul Waner could get the ball back to the infield.

Herman opened the season with his longest hitting streak of his major league career, 17 straight games, finishing April with a .362 average and 13 extra base hits, including six doubles, five triples and a homer. The surprising Reds were 8-8 during that period.

He stole home on April 27 in a 6-4 win over the Cardinals and banged a bases-loaded single and a homer in a 7-6 win at Pittsburgh the next day. The home run was a long shot into the top row of the second deck.

"New Reds Day," scheduled to introduce the Cincinnati players to the fans, was cancelled early in April because of the cold weather. It was held May 1st and 21,000 showed up. Pittsburgh scored four in the third before Herman threw a runner out at the plate to end the inning.

He singled twice, knocking in a run, and was picked off first but dashed to second ahead of the throw. "The Babe had plenty of color, and there isn't a shade of yellow in it," Ryder wrote.

Babe's hitting streak ended on May 4th as his wife, Ann, and his two sons, Bobby and Don, arrived from Glendale, California. They left their home Sunday night, arriving in Pittsburgh by train early Thursday morning.

The next day Herman celebrated their arrival with a two-run double as the Reds beat Boston 9-6 and moved into first place. Ernie Lombardi boomed a homer and a triple off the distant scoreboard.

The winning streak reached five before they dropped one to the Phillies.

Brooklyn arrived in town and found Lombardi hitting .500 and Herman batting .334 with 21 RBI in 27 games. Babe tripled home a run in the first, then scored but that was it for the Reds as the Dodgers won 5-2.

The following day Herman crushed a ball that carried into the distant right field stands off Dazzy Vance but the Dodgers won again. Babe tripled off his old friend Hollis Thurston to win the third game of the series 5-3 and the Cincinnati paper noted that "a fine crowd of 4,200 was in attendance."

The Reds split the first two with the seventh place Giants. Before the first game Reds shortstop Leo Durocher was suspended for three days for punching Dick Bartels of the Phillies earlier in the month.

Cincinnati won the third game of the series 2-1 as Herman threw out Bill Terry at third attempting to stretch a double into a triple. New York manager John McGraw told Cincinnati newsmen, "The Reds now constitute a threat to every club in the National League."

Phillie manager Burt Shotton was equally impressed and said, "The Reds are by miles the best team I've seen in the National League. By July 4th

Chick Hafey and Herman

they'll be so far ahead there won't be a race."

Lombardi was hitting .463 and the Babe had a .336 mark but the club, with little other hitting help and burdened by poor pitching, started to slip in the league standings.

Against Chicago late in May, Herman smashed balls off the left-field scoreboard in Cincinnati on successive days, getting an inside-the-park homer on the first and a triple on the second. The triple came in the first inning and Babe scored when the ball was mishandled.

In the fifth Herman walked, and on a 3-1 pitch to Chick Hafey he started for second base and Hafey took first. But the Cubs threw the ball to second and tagged Herman before he arrived, claiming the umpire called the pitch a strike.

Babe argued that the first base umpire had called ball four. While the umpire never admitted that he had said it, Herman's case must have been air-tight because he was allowed to return to first base safely.

Despite slipping a bit in the standings, pennant fever ran hot in Cincinnati and a local sportsman bet $500 at 20-1 odds that the Reds would win the pennant and $1,000 at 2-1 odds that they'd finish in the first division.

Late in May, playing in Pittsburgh, Herman twice fumbled ground singles, then twice threw runners out at the plate attempting to score on the bobbles. Herman finished the month hitting .312, with 13 doubles and eight triples. Of the nine Cincinnati homers, Herman had four and Lombardi three.

But their lack of any sort of offensive punch to compliment Herman and Lombardi began to tell in early June, and the Reds started to slip in the standings. They were at the .500 mark for the final time on June 1.

On June 6th they lost 5-1 in an exhibition game to the Philadelphia A's. The game was played in only 1:15 to allow the visitors to catch a train.

Against the Giants in the Polo Grounds Herman boomed a gigantic shot into the left-center field seats. If the ball had been pulled, it would have cleared the right field roof.

A New York writer noted, "Many of Babe's local critics said that he never hit with men on or in the clutch, but his long drive, that should have won the game, proved them wrong."

Cincinnati, tied for sixth place with the Dodgers, moved into Ebbets Field for the first time since the trade and the Brooklyn natives gave Herman a standing ovation when he appeared for his first appearance at bat. Babe was on a 13-for-24 (.542) tear after a series with the Giants and Phillies.

The Evening Graphic headlined, "Help! Murder! Herman Comes Back to Flatbush" Homer Metz continued, "Babe made his first appearance of the season as a Red at Ebbets Field yesterday and did everything but knock down the stands in his zeal to show Max Carey and company they made a mistake in turning him loose this spring."

On his first time at bat he was greeted with tumultuous applause, mingled with a few ill-natured boos. He lined the first pitch thrown to him into the center field seats. He got a standing ovation from the Brooklyn fans and tipped his cap as he crossed the plate.

The second time at bat he doubled to left to plate a runner. The third time he tripled to left, again knocking in a teammate. All the hits came off left-hander Watty Clark. His final trip to the plate he backed Taylor against the wall in right field to catch his long drive.

He banged a two-run double in the first inning of the second game, again won by the Reds. Brooklyn won the final two games of the series but Herman had a RBI in each.

In the four game series in Brooklyn, Babe had eight hits in 16 times at bat with seven runs batted in.

Moving to Boston, Cincinnati beat the Braves 9-3 as Babe cracked out four hits, including a homer in to the left-field seats. But the Harvard-Yale college game across the river out-drew the Reds-Braves game.

The Reds were playing Wilkes-Barre in an exhibition game on June 23rd when president Sid Weil wired the club to have numbers sewed on their jerseys according to the new National League rule.

"Fans will be able to tell Leo Durocher (5-10, 160) from Ernie Lombardi (6-2, 220) without much trouble from now on," he told newsmen with a smile.

Chick Hafey, Andy High, Herman, Wally Roettger, Taylor Douthit in Cincinnati dugout.

The Reds played against Pittsburgh while wearing numbers for the first time the next day. Cincinnati numbered the players by their batting position initially, while Pittsburgh had no single numbers at all. Neither team had a number 13. Batting third, Babe wore number 3.

Returning home before the month ended, the Reds lost to St. Louis. Thousands of ladies, who had made Herman their favorite, took advantage of the 10¢ admission charge on 'Ladies Day.' The Cincinnati paper noted, "It may be well to advise Babe's admirers that he is married to a charming lady, has two bright young sons and is very domestic by nature."

Despite Herman's heroics, the Reds were only 7-21 in June. After an early 21-17 start, they slowly dropped out of the first division, and were 31-46 going into July.

On the first day of July, the half-way mark of the season, the Reds were in eighth place by 11 games and were 7 1/2 games out of seventh place.

Weil talked Branch Rickey into parting with Benny Frey and Harvey Hendrick. They had both gone to St. Louis in the Hafey deal. That improved the club's batting attack but did nothing for the pitching problems.

Babe was hot against St. Louis in July, banging out seven hits in eight drips in the first two games and boosting his average to .349. Included was a long shot that landed on the Pavilion roof off leftie Jesse Haines. The Reds won three of four from the Cardinals and the fourth game ended in a 3-3 tie after 13 innings. The three wins were more than the club had against St. Louis during the entire 1931 season.

BROOKLYN'S BABE—PAGE 173

Brooklyn came to Cincinnati, and their impressive ten-man press corps astounded the Reds players. Babe made his fifth error of the season in the third game as the Dodgers scored seven runs in the first inning.

Cincinnati won the first three games of the Giants series. Herman slugged a three-run, first-inning homer to give the Reds a 3-1 victory in the opener and after a double-header sweep the following day, Cincinnati had rallied to squeeze past the Giants into seventh place.

Hubbell had a no-hitter through six in the final game of the series but Herman doubled for the first hit and also drove in a run with two out in the seventh. However, NY rallied to win 4-3, dropping the Reds back in the basement to stay.

Bobby Herman, Babe's young son, became tired of serving as the team mascot and moved into the stands to sell scorecards.

Against the Phillies, Harvey Hendrick suffered fractured ribs in a collision and Cincinnati stock dipped even lower. Herman had seven putouts in the second game of the series, two of them on fine running catches, but the Phils won 11-6. In the final game he had six putouts and an assist, playing what most in the National League felt was the worst sun field in the loop.

Babe made a noble effort to carry the team but with Hafey in and out of the hospital, and Hendrick hurt, the load was more than he could handle.

Herman banged out seven hits in the four game series at Philadelphia, including a trio of homers and a pair of doubles but the best the Reds could do was split.

In a 4-3 win the paper noted, "A sensational catch by Herman, one of four as he patrolled the short right field wall, helped Cincinnati triumph. On a long smash, he leaped to catch the ball in front of the wall and convert it into a double play with two on. He made another great catch in the ninth to save the game."

In Boston on August 4th, he made an error in right field on a ground ball that allowed a Brave run, then homered but the Reds lost 3-2. He suffered a lacerated ankle in the game and missed nine days of action. After he healed he had a successful pinch-hit against the Dodgers to tie the game in the ninth and the Reds won in the 10th. But the following day, again pinch-hitting, his 12-game hitting streak was broken.

Attendance in Cincinnati continued to slump and an Oldtimer's Day game drew only 6,000 fans. National League president John Hydler told the sparce crowd: "There will never be night baseball in the major leagues. If we ever get as low as that, we might as well close the gates on our ball parks." Oddly enough, only a few years later Cincinnati would be the first team in the majors to put lights in their park and the resulting attendance surge made every baseball official rethink his position.

Babe slugged five hits in a double header against the Dodgers as the teams split on Sept. 17. The following day against the Cubs he dashed in on a looping single off the bat of Billy Herman and the ball bounced away for a triple to tie the game. The Reds lost 4-3 in 15 innings despite Herman's three hits.

Late in September, as the tough season ground to a close, a three-game total of only 1,600 fans showed up at Sportsmans Park in St. Louis to watch a series with the Reds. Babe had a pair of hits in the first two games but headlines in the Cincinnati Enquirer told the story of the support by the paper and the Reds fans.

After a 3-1 loss in the opener, the headlines read: "Who cares? Reds lose another." After a 2-0 loss in the second game they reported, "As usual, Reds take a beating." and after the 8-5 defeat in the final contest said "Usual act put on by Reds."

Herman finished the season with a .326 average, cracking out 188 hits, good for 312 total bases. Among the hits were a league-leading 19 triples, as well as 38 doubles, 16 home runs and a team-leading 89 RBI. He hit an astounding 16 homers and 19 triples, banging them into all corners of the huge Cincinnati park. Lombardi knocked in 68 runs and the two ex-Brooklyn sluggers were responsible for 46 percent of the Cincinnati runs for the season. Herman was 12th in the Most Valuable Player voting conducted by the Baseball Writers of America.

Remarkably enough, Babe Herman, the man who had been associated with ineptness in the field, set a National League record for right fielders during the 1932 season that has never been surpassed.

Babe Herman made 392 putouts while roving the vast right field area in Cincinnati during the 1932 season, to this day more than any right fielder in the history of the National League. The total was also a major league record until Del Unser of Washington caught 394 in 1971.

In addition, Herman's 423 total chances in right field also was a National and Major League record until 45 years later when Dave Parker handled 430 chances while playing for Pittsburgh in 1977.

Cincinnati had a 60-94 record, finishing exactly 30 games behind the pennant-winning Cubs and were an even dozen games behind the seventh-place Cardinals. The Cincinnati club lost money during the 1932 season; in fact only Chicago, Boston and Brooklyn managed a profit as the depression deepened.

Weil had invested and lost a great deal of money on the Tennessee Valley project and the banks had called in his loan. He had to liquidate his holdings and to that end had to sell Herman to get working capital for the 1933 season. The money didn't last long and during 1933 he was forced to liquidate his holdings in the club.

Rumors that the Cubs wanted to swap pitcher Pat Malone to the Reds for Herman was laughed at by Weil and Bush. "We will get two players like Malone or we will keep Babe," they said, but most knew a move, with a lot of cash on the side, was inevitable.

Weil called Herman into his office after the 1932 season and said, "I don't want to sell you but you are the only player we can get any money out of. Would you like to go to New York or Chicago?"

New York had finished sixth in 1932, while the Cubs had just won the National League pennant, then were mauled by the Yankees in the World Series. The Cubs seemed to be a good bet to repeat and Babe chose them.

On November 30, the Cubs sent pitcher Bob Smith, catcher Rollie Hemsley, and outfielders Johnny Moore and Lance Richbourg plus $75,000 to Cincinnati for Herman. Papers reported that it was a $140,000 deal.

Lee Allen, in his informal history of the Reds, noted, "Tremendous clouting by Chick Hafey, Babe Herman and Ernie Lombardi gave the fans more entertainment than they had since 1926.

"The fans were sorry to see Herman leave, as he had lived up to all his clippings in the one season he spent with the club. The butt of many a joke and the inspiration of many a wild yarn, the Babe was never so strange as he was painted. Though usually thought of as being slightly lacking in wisdom, the Babe always won his winter battle for more money. His reputation for dumbness only added to his color and made him more of a gate attraction."

New manager Donie Bush (Dan Howley had been fired) said, "He is a good hitter and a valuable man, but he would not fit into my scheme of running the club here." Bush developed an infected foot during spring training and later developed bronchial pneumonia and pleurisy, spending much of the season at home. The Reds would finish in eighth place, 33 games behind the league leader in 1933 and Bush, along with his 'scheme of running the club' received their walking papers at the end of the year.

"Great news, anyway you take it," Babe said to newsmen between daubs of paint on his garage back in Glendale. "Eighth place club to first place is all right."

Chapter 11

Brooklyn fans were very interested in the trade that sent Herman to the Cubs. The Brooklyn Eagle reported: "There is a tremendous interest because in six seasons at Ebbets Field, Herman succeeded in convincing everybody that he was a pretty good ball player, with an accent on hitting. The rumor factory has Babe returning in a Brooklyn uniform.

"Fifty percent of the Brooklyn fans, more or less, thought he was a world beater. The other half, more or less, thought he was a lemon. Fist fights resulted from arguments on the wisdom of the trade that sent Herman to Cincinnati. But there seems to be no way of making Herman's boosters and his detractors meet halfway in the matter. The situation has built up Herman's color several degrees more brilliant than a sunset. No angle of baseball has been so thoroughly over-emphasized as Herman's eccentricities on the ball field.

"To read the metropolitan papers, one would think Babe is hit on the head with fly balls each afternoon. I watched Herman for six years and never saw him close to being hit. There is a current story that Herman stole second base with the bases loaded while a Dodger. When did that one happen, and where was your correspondent?

"Babe's feat of hitting a double into a double play has become highly magnified so that fans now read Babe tripled into a triple play. That particular play was an example of bad baserunning—not on the part of Herman, but on the part of Dazzy Vance who was on base ahead of him. Vance could have scored standing up, but for some unaccountable reason he wheeled halfway to the plate and turned back to third. Herman reached third before the ball, and Vance, who was on second when it was hit, got no further than third. And yet, to read the story in its present version, one would believe Babe lucky to be at large.

"Yes, Herman is colorful and Chicago will probably slip him into the spot of idolatry once held by Hack Wilson, and that is fair enough. I think the Chicago fans and their enthusiasm will result in pepping up the gangling young slugger, who was a pretty pepless individual in the closing days of the 1932 season.

"Herman was unhappy in Cincinnati. In Brooklyn the fans cheered him and the fans booed him but the Redland rooter, perhaps deadened by a long line of second-division clubs, considered him just another member of just another tail-end club."

Weil told reporters, "We received enough cash to reestablish the Cincinnati team's credit and it is highly important we did so." The deal was announced the night of November 30th.

Chicago papers noted that the news Babe would join the Cubs was received joyfully in Chicago, although there were those who hated to see Johnny Moore included in the trade. There was reason to believe Babe would be a great favorite in Wrigley Field, not only for what he could do with his bat, but because the Cub fans have craved a showman ever since Wilson left.

And Dan Daniels wrote, "The Dodgers may train in Miami this year but they won't be the Dodgers again until they get Babe Herman back. Lefty O'Doul, with his green suit, may make a stir in Miami—but give me Babe for real color."

Club president William Veeck came to Los Angeles especially to sign Babe to a reported $20,000 contract. Babe, pleased with the new pact, reported with the pitchers and catchers on Feb. 23 instead of waiting for the rest of the defending champion Chicago squad on March 4.

He arrived on Catalina Island, where his professional baseball career had started by accident in 1922. He was in excellent shape and hit the ball hard from the start.

He had coached a team of National League players in an exhibition game against Glendale High to benefit the baseball program at the school. Included on the team were Pie Traynor, Freddie Fitzsimmons, Sloppy Thurston, Herman Bell, LeRoy Parmelee, Eddie Marshall, Frank Shellenback, Truck Hanna and Johnny Bassler. Babe's major leaguers won an 11-7 contest.

The defending National League champions had manager Charlie Grimm at first, Billy Herman at second, Billy Jurges at short, and Woody English at third.

Herman joined Frank Demaree and Riggs Stephenson in the outfield and Gabby Hartnett was the catcher. Former Yankee Mark Koenig, Kiki Cuyler and Hendrick were strong second liners.

Guy Bush anchored the pitching staff, with Lon Warnecke, Charlie Root, Bud Tinning and Pat Malone filling out the rotation. Burleigh Grimes was on the staff but was swapped to St. Louis for Taylor Douthit later in the season.

Herman slugged a pair of homers and a single in the first intrasquad game, batting in six runs, then he got three hits the next day against the Giants in the first official exhibition game at Wrigley Field in Los Angeles.

An earthquake shook the city the night before but Herman homered and singled off Carl Hubbell the next day and added two homers in the third Cub-Giant contest.

An aftershock shook the city the following day and one of the Cub players was so terrified that he ran out of the hotel barbershop half shaved and with the barber's apron still on him. The frightened player slept that night in the park across the street from the hotel. If it bothered Babe, it wasn't noticeable in his play. He homered in his third consecutive game that afternoon.

The Cubs suffered a blow just before they left the West coast when Kiki Cuyler broke his leg sliding into second base in a game against the Hollywood Stars.

In early April, playing the Pirates in Tucson, Herman said, "My stride has been wrong for some time. I wasn't depressed, because I've never had striding problems for more than two weeks. Strangely enough, I knew I had the proper stride when I struck out the second time." His stride was apparently correct, because he slugged a long homer and a double later in the game against Pittsburgh.

Moving East toward the season's opener, the Cubs were playing an exhibition game in San Antonio, and discovered that the small park had a very short right field wall. It was so short that a marker was placed on the wall, halfway toward center field. Balls hit over the fence between that marker and the right field foul line were only two bases. Balls hit on the other side of the line were home runs. Back of the fence were rows of homes with large yards. Then came a street and then more houses with yards and another street.

In the middle of the game, Babe unloaded on a fast ball thrown by a San Antonio hurler. It went over the right field fence, over the first row of houses, over the first street, and landed on the roof of one of the houses in the second block. Those present claim that no man who ever lived could have hit a ball further than the distance that incredible shot travelled.

But the ball cleared the fence on the wrong side of the marker. It was recorded as a simple two base hit, without a doubt the longest in baseball history.

Cold cancelled a pair of games in Kansas City, and Babe injured his leg sliding into the plate in the opener on an inside-the-park homer. He didn't play or even dress in the final exhibition games against the White Sox as Al Simmons banged a homer in the first game for a 1-0 victory and the Sox took the second 12-6.

Dizzy Dean beat the Cubs 3-0 in the opening game of the 1932 season, and Herman was unable to get the ball out of the infield. But in the second game, against left-hander Bill Hallahan, he doubled on his first three trips to the plate and only a great catch in right field by George Watkins kept him from collecting his fourth two base hit. He also made an exceptional catch late in the contest and Chicago writers wondered in print where his 'bad field' tag had come from.

Shutout in Pittsburgh, Herman slammed a two-run double to beat Dizzy Dean 3-1 at St. Louis. The next day a ball rolled through his legs in right field for an error. Herman retrieved it and threw the runner out at the plate but the Cardinals won 4-0. Injuries continued to dog the club as shortstop Bill Jurges sprained his ankle and was lost for three weeks.

Despite collecting his first Cub homer off Hallahan late in the month, Herman finished April with only 12 hits in 51 trips and a .235 average. Injuries to Cuyler and Jurges were being felt and the Cubs slipped into eighth place on the 25th, then finished April with a 5-9 record.

Babe warmed up in May, starting with 10 hits in his first 25 trips, including four doubles, a triple, a homer and seven RBI as the Cubs played New York and Boston.

Moving into Brooklyn later in the month, a heavy fog enveloped Ebbets Field but it was only after less than 1,000 fans showed up for the game that it was called and rescheduled as part of a double header. However, cold weather persisted and finally the Dodgers cancelled the entire series.

Herman pulled a groin muscle in Philadelphia and the club continued to struggle. Newspapers reported that Chicago had offered $200,000 to the Phillies or $100,000 and Babe Herman for Chuck Klein.

President Veech said, "The club never comments on amounts offered for players but would make an exception this time and deny such an offer."

In New York the Cubs shifted Herman from third to fourth in the batting order and he responded with a game-winning home run off Fitzsimmons into the right-center field bleachers.

Returning to Wrigley Field, Herman attempted a diving catch on a line drive by Phil Collins of the Phillies but the ball skipped past him for a three-run triple. For the first time in a Chicago uniform he heard boos.

Ed Burns wrote, "The wolves, who have been patient with Babe in his hitting efforts, lost their restraint when he made his dive for Collins' ball in the seventh. They gave him a pretty heavy razz, which isn't nice—for Babe's embarrassment was attributed only to zeal, and baseball zeal rarely rates a Bronx cheer."

He turned the fans around two games later by punishing the Braves in a three-game set. He singled home a run in a 3-0 win, slammed two homers in the second 4-3 win and singled home a run in the opener of a twin bill.

Against the Pirates, Herman came in to make a scoop of Paul Waner's short fly in the fifth against Pittsburgh but umpire Cy Pfirman ruled it no catch. As the Cubs crowded around Pfirman to argue, Babe tossed the ball to Bill Jurges standing at second base and when time resumed, Jurges tagged pitcher Hal Smith as he led off. It was the Pirates turn to argue, claiming that Cub pitcher Bud Tinning had taken the mound without the ball, but they had no more luck than the Cubs in changing the decision.

The Cubs swept Pittsburgh but bad luck struck the club again as outfielder Riggs Stephenson broke his finger.

Despite many injuries suffered by the club, the Cubs were finally winning and had pulled themselves back into second place, trailing by only three games as May ended.

The Cardinals came to Chicago and Dean again stopped the home team, helped along by five Cub errors. Herman tripled two runs home and scored the winning run the next day to earn a split.

Babe in Chicago

Babe hit in 14 of the next 16 games, recording a .409 average, and the team won 10 of them. Herman boosted his average to .301 in Pittsburgh, slugging a homer off Hal Smith in a 5-0 win.

Babe smacked a double, triple and a homer into the upper deck in Pittsburgh on June 17th, then made four great fielding plays against the Giants the following afternoon in the Polo Grounds.

The Cubs were bobbing between second and fifth as they moved into Ebbets Field.

In the first game of the series Herman slammed a double off the right field wall in the first inning and scored. Trailing by a run in the fifth inning, he boomed a mammoth homer, good for three runs, off Walter Beck, to spark a 7-2 win. In addition he threw out a Dodger runner at the plate. He tripled off the center field wall the next day in a 6-3 Brooklyn win.

Brooklyn took two of the next three, winning the final game as Al Lopez stole home in the last of the ninth while Charlie Root held the ball on the mound.

Late in June, the Cubs moved into Philadelphia. The Phillies were drawing badly and with a light mist falling, they cancelled a game 'because of rain' so they could schedule a doubleheader the next day, hoping to boost attendance.

Ed Burns wrote, "Many thought the Phillies had no tarp to cover the infield—so they could call a single game because of dew on the infield and change it into a doubleheader. But they do have a tarp. In fact, they have nine tarps. They were obtained from a stranded hoochie-koochie show, a defunct jigsaw puzzle shop and the covering from five banana carts."

The unexpected day off was spent buying wedding gifts for shortstop Bill Jurges.

On the morning of July 4th the Cubs were an even 37-37. They had played 36 games without a day off through May and June and were in fourth place, 8 games behind the first place Giants.

Cuyler returned from his broken leg but was still very tentative.

The Cubs took two of three from the Reds, then swept a four game series from New York, moving within four games of the Giants. Babe was of little help in the NY series, managing only one hit in 14 trips to the plate. His slump continued against Brooklyn although he boomed a monster triple to key a six run eighth inning as the Cubs trailed 1-0 in the series opener.

His average slipped to .288 in mid July and he was benched as manager Charlie Grimm replaced Babe and Jim Moslof with Cuyler and Riggs Stephenson.

The Cubs won three of four with Babe on the bench, and club general manager William Walker called owner Phil Wrigley and told him he wanted to get rid of Herman.

Walker was a holdover from Federal League days and had joined the club when Charles Weeghman had taken over. Walker's stock holdings in the club were good sized.

Home attendance had plummeted and would finish some 400,000 below the 1932 figure. Walker felt that Herman should be traded and told owner Wrigley how he felt.

Wrigley, who was not a William Walker fan, said he would come to the park and watch Herman play, then let him know how he felt about the proposal.

In one of the most unusual 'tryouts' in baseball history, Herman was inserted into the lineup against the Phillies with their top winner, Ed Holley, on the mound.

He singled sharply in the first inning. In the third Herman homered over the left-center field wall with Cuyler on base. In the fifth inning Herman homered again, this time to right center, again scoring Cuyler in front of him. In the eighth inning with the bases loaded, Herman hit his longest shot of the game for his third homer, a blast deep into the right field stands, tying the National League record for homers in a single game. He had eight RBI as the Cubs won 10-1. The runs batted in put him only three behind the team leader, Gabby Hartnett, who had 58.

Wrigley met a chagrined Walker leaving the park after the game and said in a low-key voice, "Herman looks like a pretty good player to me."

The next day, Wrigley called Babe and asked him to come down to the gum factory before the game and have lunch with him. Mrs. Herman and the kids were invited and were given a tour of the plant as well as all the gum they could chew.

At lunch, a smiling Phil Wrigley shook Babe's hand and said, "Geeze, that really did me good yesterday."

Babe and Gabby Hartnett

Herman was in the lineup for good as the Cubs finished a 16-3 homestand, trailing the Giants by two games. But the Chicago club couldn't seem to catch the speeding New Yorkers as the battle raged through August.

Herman heated up, slugging a pair of homers good for four runs off Tex Carlton in St. Louis, then in early August he cracked a two-run shot off the Pirates and added his 14th the next day off Grimes of the Cardinals.

He was 3-for-3 off Larry French in Pittsburgh and ranked 10th in the league with a .293 average. He had 14 homers and 71 RBI.

In early August the team returned from a road trip. The Cub management had been feuding with an afternoon paper in the city and the paper had begun printing player numbers each day, apparently hoping to cut down the scorecard profits the club received. On August 6th, the players were instructed to switch their uniform jerseys with a teammate and they took the field with completely different numbers, showing the paper who was in charge but hopelessly confusing the fans.

By the middle of the month, the battle with the paper was almost the only exciting thing going on in Wrigley Field. The pennant race was over, as far as the Cubs were concerned.

The team was a world champion at home, winning 42 and losing only 14, a blistering .750 percentage. But on the road they were of the Mudville genre, winning 19 of 56—a dismal .339 mark.

One afternoon, Boston outfielder came over to Babe and pointed out a man sitting in the left field box seats.

"Do you know who he is?" Jolly asked.

"Nope," said Babe.

"That's John Dillinger, the famous bank robber," Jolly told him.

Dillinger, his girl friend and a cluster of what appeared to be body guards attended the games throughout the entire week. Other members of the Cub team told Herman that the local police knew that he was there but wouldn't tell the Federal Agents.

In a related incident, Woody English of the Cubs had the same type of car that Dillinger drove and was stopped four nights in succession by agents with drawn guns.

Babe was used sparingly because of an injury through late August, although he made a game saving catch off a long drive by Hack Wilson at the scoreboard in Brooklyn and drew his first cheers in weeks. He was in a 4-for-34 slump and his average tumbled to .279 as the month ended with six-straight doubleheaders.

As September opened, William Veeck of the Cubs suggested interleague play as a method of boosting attendance. And on September 7 the Cubs changed numbers for the second time to further thwart the paper's scorecard and again confuse the fans.

Herman played the peaks and valleys within a two day span.

On the 8th he had four hits in four trips, including a double, and batted in three runs in a 5-3 win over the Braves. The following day he dropped a long, wind-blown fly in the third inning that cost the Cubs a run, then fumbled a hit in the 13th to allow the winning run to score. In between he was 0-for-6. Dolph Camilli took over for him at first base the next day.

He played only briefly for ten days. Against the Giants he pinch hit and slammed a double to spark a two-run rally in the last of the ninth to gain a 4-3 win.

Back in the lineup again, he went on a tear, hitting in 10 of the final 11 games. He rang up 19 hits in 38 trips to the plate, an even .500 average, and had 10 RBI.

On the 30th he teed off on Dizzy Dean and banged out a triple in the first inning and a homer over the right-field roof in the sixth off the future Hall of Famer. He added a double and a single in the ninth inning to hit for the cycle the third time in his career. He raised his average from .276 to .289 as the season ended and finished with a team-leading 93 RBI, the sixth best total in the N.L. Averages tumbled all around the league.

Lefty O'Doul hit .284 and Mel Ott .281.

"We didn't have it in 1933," Charlie Grimm would write years later. "But it wasn't Herman's fault. He hit .289 and knocked in 93 runs."

He was third in the league in slugging percentage (.522), trailing Chuck Klein of the Phillies and Wally Berger of Boston.

Chicago finished third, one game behind second place Pittsburgh and six back of the winning Giants. They were 56-23 at home but only 30-45 on the road. However their overall 49-29 record after July 4th was the best in the league.

Attendance suffered and the Cubs drew only 595,000 fans, down almost 400,000 from the previous season.

The White Sox swept the city series as Babe went 2-for-16. William Veeck died on Oct. 5th, the clubs postponing the fourth game so the Cub team could attend the funeral. The losers share of the city series was $465.70. The winning White Sox took home $637.79.

With Veeck's death, the handwriting was on the wall for Herman when William Walker was made the new president of the club.

When Herman's 1934 contract arrived, he was upset with the slash in salary but refused to talk to reporters about it. One paper quoted him as saying, "They didn't cut my contract, they put a cleaver to it."

Babe sent a telegram to Chicago denying he said it, hearing that Wrigley was reportedly angry at the remark. He then disconnected his telephone and avoided reporters

The Cubs beefed up their attack when they traded Mark Koenig, Harry Hendrick and Ted Kleinhaus plus $120,000 to the Phillies for Chuck Klein.

Grimm was again at first base, Billy Herman at second, and Jurges at short but newcomer Stan Hack took over at third. Herman, Cuyler and Klein were in the outfield with Hartnett behind the plate. Lon Warneke, Bush, Malone, Bill Lee and later Jim Weaver manned the rotation. Bud Tinning and Bush worked in relief.

Klein had led the league in hitting in 1933 with a .368 average, but he found out that hitting in eighth-place Philadelphia and hitting in pressurized Chicago were quite different. He would finish the season with a .301 average complaining about the pressure and remark, "Here they watch you on every pitch."

He also apparently missed the cozy right field wall, located only 190 feet behind the first baseman. Klein hit .411 and .467 in Philadelphia during the 1932 and 1933 seasons but only .267 and .280 on the road. He would hit .301 and .293 in Chicago before being traded back to the Phillies in 1936.

Klein was also plagued with knotted muscles known then as a 'Charlie horse.' They became so bad that trainer Andy Lotshaw finally admitted that they were, in his words, 'probably cronicle.'

The Cubs offered Cuyler, Pat Malone and Jim Mosolof plus $60,000 to the Reds of Chick Hafey but were turned down.

Plans originally called for Klein to open in center, Herman in right and Cuyler or Stevenson in left. Klein told the club he was not interested in playing center so Cuyler took his place between he and Herman.

Babe hit well during the exhibition season. And when the season opened Cuyler was again not available. This time he was suffering from an infected hangnail and unable to play.

Klein started hot, smacking five homers good for 13 runs in the first 10 games. Herman opened on the flip side of the coin, getting a hit opening day but then suffering through a 1-for-18 slump the first four contests.

But the Cubs got seven complete games from their pitching staff to open the season and soared into first place with a 7-0 mark. They lost the first three in May but righted themselves and rolled into New York still in first place.

The Cubs asked for waivers on both Babe Herman and Charlie Root anticipating a trade, but Brooklyn quickly claimed them both and the waivers were suddenly withdrawn.

Dolph Camilli beat out three bunts against the Giants and took over first base from manager Charlie Grimm. After the sluggish 1-for-18 start, Herman hit in the next nine games in succession, boosting his average to .258 but Rookie Tuck Steinbeck replaced Herman in right field and rumors circulated that Babe was being offered around the league for a pitcher.

The team slumped and Grimm was rumored on his way out with Jack Lelivelt of the Chicago minor league club in Los Angeles said to be his successor.

On May 28 the Cubs decided Steinbeck needed more minor league experience and moved Herman back into the lineup the next day. At the time Babe was playing very little and hitting .261, but he collected seven hits in the next three games, adding four doubles and four RBI.

In early June, Herman knocked in runs in seven consecutive games and over that period hit .419, boosting his average to .301. He continued to slash the ball to all fields and his average soared to .343 late in the month. He collected 27 RBI during June.

He slammed homers in the first and second game of the St. Louis series on June 5, then knocked in Billy Herman with the winning run in a 1-0 victory on the final day, dropping the Cardinals out of first place.

June 11th Babe awakened in his Cincinnati hotel room and found Don Hurst, former Phillies first baseman, sleeping in the other bed.

Looking around for his roomate Dolph Camilli, Herman asked, "Where did you come from?"

"I don't know, they just traded me for Camilli," Hurst said.

The trade was one of the worst in Chicago history. Camilli went on to lead the league in RBI for the Phillies that year while Hurst hit only .199 for the Cubs.

Walker had made the deal without Charlie Grimm's knowledge and when Hurst reported to the Chicago dressing room that afternoon, the manager thought he was there looking for tickets to the game.

Four days after the trade, Camilli homered in the ninth to tie the game and the Phillies won in the 10th.

Mungo fanned 12 in Ebbets Field, but Herman homered and the Cubs won 5-1. Babe added a single and double in the second game, good for three RBI, to key an 8-0 win in the nightcap. He added three more hits in the final two games in Brooklyn as the Cubs swept the four games. On June 28 he was hitting .343 with 35 RBI.

Babe and Bobby at first All-Star Game in Philadelphia, 1933

On July 2 in St. Louis the Cubs loaded the bases and Chuck Klein hit a ball a mile high behind the plate. The catcher ran back to catch it and the wind blew it back toward fair territory, hitting a few feet in front of the plate.

The ball bounced high in the air and Dean grabbed it but was too late to make a play on Klein at first and the runner scored from third.

As Herman came to the plate, Cardinal Manager Frank Frisch came out of the dugout to talk to plate umpire Bill Klem. Klem saw him coming and said, "Get out of here you counterfeiter."

"Bill, that was an infield fly," Frisch told him.

"I didn't call an infield fly."

"I don't care what you called it, it is an infield fly."

"The man was never in a position to catch the ball, that's why I didn't call it."

"It's still an infield fly."

"Well, it's not."

By this time Frisch was standing on home plate and Klem looked at him and said, "Frisch, you're out of the ball game, dead or alive." However, Frisch protested the call and the league upheld it, ordering the game to be replayed from the third inning on.

Cuyler and Herman kept the Cubs in the pennant chase before the All-Star game. After the three-day break, Herman heated up again, hitting in 13 of 15 games. He drove in 19 runs in the next 14 games and his average moved to .338.

Charlie Parker wrote in the N.Y. World-Telegram,

Babe and Riggs Stephenson

"They laughed when he sat down at the piano.

"They laughed when the waiter addressed him in French.

"They laughed when he engaged in his profession.

"But they are not laughing at him now. Herman has been the mightiest figure in the Cubs drive that has carried them from sixth to fourth place.

"Babe Herman is a vital cog in the Chicago machine that has returned today to his old stomping grounds at Ebbets Field for a four-day visit.

"With the Bedford Avenue wall becoming to him—and he has pumped more home runs over that barrier than any other player—Babe had a chance in the current series to drive his team into the league leadership."

Babe again destroyed Brooklyn pitching, reaching base four times in the opening game on two walks, a single and a double. He was on base all four times in the second game on a single, double walk and force play.

CLASS OF SERVICE DESIRED

DOMESTIC		CABLE	
TELEGRAM		FULL RATE	
DAY LETTER		DEFERRED	
NIGHT MESSAGE		NIGHT LETTER	
NIGHT LETTER		WEEK END LETTER	

Patrons should check class of service desired; otherwise message will be transmitted as a full-rate communication.

WESTERN UNION

NEWCOMB CARLTON, PRESIDENT J. C. WILLEVER, FIRST VICE-PRESIDENT

CHECK

ACCT'G INFMN.

TIME FILED

Send the following message, subject to the terms on back hereof, which are hereby agreed to

Brooklyn N.Y. 5/8-34

John A. Heydler President
National League
1907 R.C.A Bldg
New York N.Y.

Brooklyn claims Charles Root and
Floyd Herrman from Chicago

Stephen W. McKeever
President

WESTERN UNION GIFT ORDERS SOLVE THE PERPLEXING QUESTION OF WHAT TO GIVE.

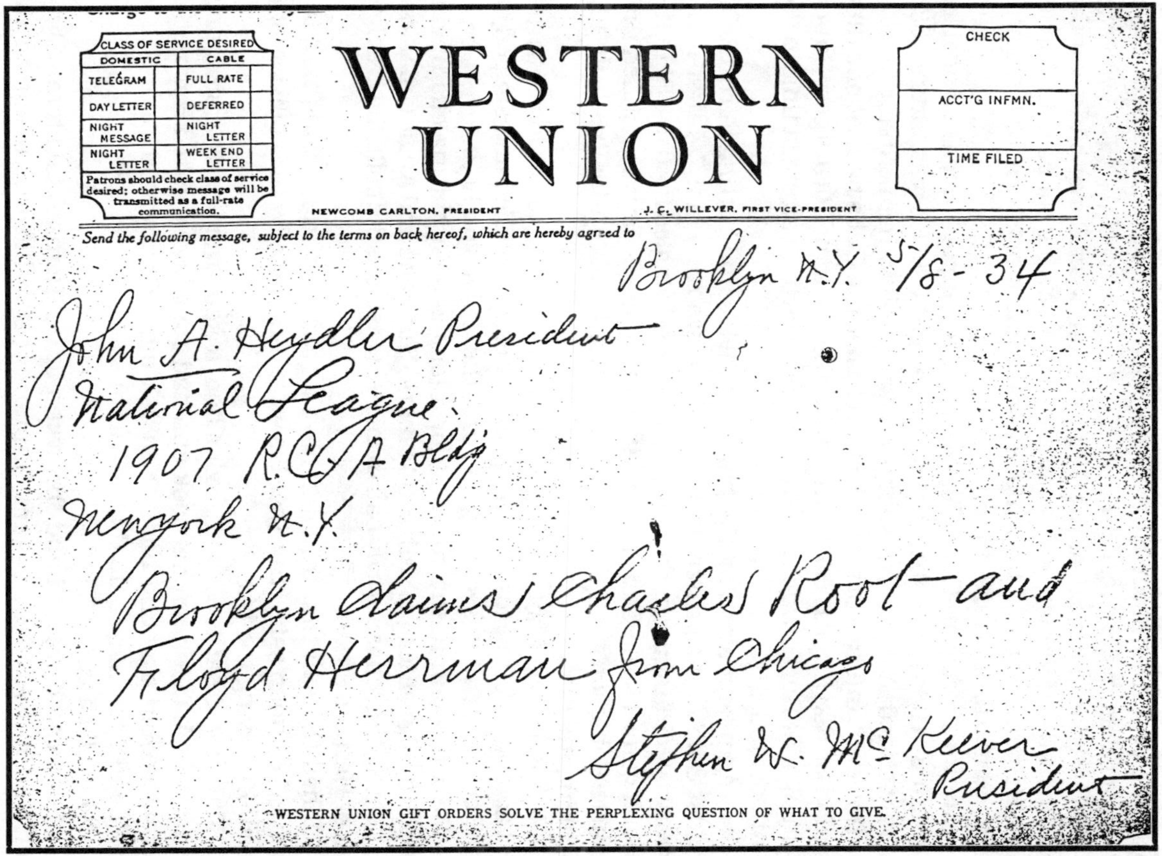

BROOKLYN PRESIDENT Stephen McKeever claimed Babe Herman and Charlie Root when Chicago offered them on waivers, but the Cubs withdrew the waivers and kept both players.

Telegram courtesy of Herb Ross

Babe missed the final two games of the series because of a strained shoulder.

Watching Herman methodically bang out hit after hit against the club each time they met, the Dodgers again decided they would like Babe back in Brooklyn. Babe's old nemesis Frank York had gone out for lunch one day in 1932 and hadn't come back. As many had predicted, the club that he had molded failed to draw at the gate and it was apparent things were going to get nothing but worse. Everyone waited for him to return but he never did. In a typical "It could only happen in Brooklyn," story, York, the president of the club, disappeared and never returned. Steve McKeever was made president.

As early as the start of the 1933 season, Max Carey had seen the error in trading Herman and wanted to get Babe's big bat back in Ebbets Field. He perhaps could have made a trade had it not been for Herman's three-home run barrage June.

Carey's successor, Casey Stengel, also attempted to make a deal for Herman in 1934 but Babe's bat again caught fire. He was hitting .334 as July ended and the Cubs felt they were still in the pennant hunt.

However, injuries destroyed what chance the Cubs had. At one time or another Kiki Cuyler, Bill Herman, Charlie Grimm, Bill Jurges, Chuck Klein, Woody English, Joe Bush and Gabby Hartnett all spent time in the local hospital.

Herman kept slashing the ball to all fields and batting in runs. On August 8 he singled three times, good for two runs in a 7-4 first-game victory over Pittsburgh, then tripled twice and singled for five RBI in the second game as the Cubs swept. After the game Babe was notified that Wilbert Robinson had died in Atlanta after falling in his bathtub and breaking his hip.

Herman stayed hot, hitting two homers off Paul Dean in St. Louis, and adding a double for good measure, then he doubled and singled off brother Dizzy in the second game and the Cubs won both.

He was again in the running for a long-sought batting championship, leading the league with a .344 mark. But Babe and Augie Galan ran into each other chasing a fly ball in mid-August and the collision cracked two of Herman's ribs.

"I had thought that if I could have a good road trip, I could lead the league," Herman said. "But the ribs were torn loose by the collision and I couldn't swing the bat.

Manager Charlie Grimm, who had taken over for the slumping Hurst, who had injured his back and had gone home, asked Hartnett if Herman could play first base. "You ask him," Gabby said.

"I can't ask him to do that," Grimm said.

"O.K., I'll ask."

"I can catch the ball and throw it a little," Herman told him, "But I won't hit a lick." Despite that Grimm put him into the lineup in the middle of September and, true to his prediction, Babe could hardly swing the bat.

Rookie Phil Caveretta was with the team at that time, but Commissioner Landis ordered the Cubs not to play him against the contenders—leaving only Herman available.

He had only five hits in the month of Sep-

Babe belts one during spring training on Catalina Island in 1934. The catcher is Paul Richards.

tember before Grimm reluctantly moved him out of the lineup again. During that period he had only nine hits in 58 trips to the plate, a .155 average. He slipped to .314 and it became apparent that he would be of little use to the Cubs for some time.

Slowly the Chicago team slid out of the pennant chase and Herman's average slipped from a high of .343 to .304 as the year mercifully closed.

The "Bring Herman back to Brooklyn" coalition was still strong, but Chicago was looking for a left-handed pitcher and the Dodgers could not match the offer made by Pittsburgh.

Dodger writers speculated that a Hack Wilson, plus other players, for Babe Herman trade was in the works to get both popular players back with their former clubs.

The Cubs were planning to use Herman at first base in 1935. "Buy a couple first baseman's gloves and break them in over the winter," Grimm told him.

However, the Pirates were looking for an outfielder and the Cubs wanted a left-hander pitcher. Pie Traynor, Pittsburgh manager, turned down Chicago's offer of outfielder Kiki Cuyler. Then on November 22 Chicago traded Herman, Guy Bush and Jim Weaver to Pittsburgh for Larry French and Freddie Lindstrom.

William Walker had finally gotten his way.

Pirate officials immediately spoke of trading Paul Waner to get a right-handed hitter in the lineup to play alongside Lloyd Waner and Herman.

Chapter 12

The Pirates opened training in 1935 in San Bernardino, California, but heavy rain forced practice indoors at the city auditorium where the Orange Exposition was held.

Pittsburgh was picked to finish fourth in the N.L. behind St. Louis, New York and Chicago.

Herman was scheduled to play left field, a new position for him. He said, "I'll play left and there won't be any complaints after I get started. It won't be any harder than playing right field or some other position."

Gus Suhr was the Pirates first baseman, Pep Young was at second, Arky Vaughan at short and manager Pie Traynor at third, although injuries limited his playing time and Tommy Thevenow filled the spot.

Paul and Lloyd Waner were in the outfield, along with right-handed Woody Jensen. Tom Padden and Earl Grace shared the catching.

Cy Blanton was the top winner on the club but Bill Swift, Jim Weaver and Guy Bush would all win in double figures. Red Lucas did well as a spot starter and Waite Hoyt worked 39 games in relief.

Babe stepped on a stone and suffered a deep bruise on his heel that limited him to pinch-hitting duties during spring training. After seven games he was 2-for-2 with three RBI in that role, then played his first game against the White Sox on March 18 and slammed two homers, good for three runs batted in. The Sox right fielder didn't even turn around as the second homer sailed far over the right field fence.

Volney Walsh of the Pittsburgh Press said, "Babe is a better fielder than most people will admit. He can throw and he is now learning to throw from the strange position of left field. He can run the bases and Traynor predicts he will startle Pittsburgh fans by his feats on the lines. In order to get Herman's punch in the line up, Traynor is willing to sacrifice a bit of fielding skill.

"Freddie Lindstrom was a good outfielder, but the Pirates got nowhere with him in left. And there is a good chance Babe will outhit his predecessor. Babe and everyone else is hoping his foot will heal completely soon."

David Fleming, president of the Pacific Coast League, banned exhibition play between major league teams and Los Angeles-area PCL clubs. He said ragged play and the fact that league regular season attendance suffered because of the games was the cause of the ban. The ruling closed Wrigley Field to the Cubs, White Sox and Pirates and forbid them to play within 10 miles of the park.

Herman shared billing with rookie sensation Cookie Lavagetto on the 23rd when both of them crashed bases loaded home runs. After 12 games, Herman was hitting .442 and had 17 RBI.

April 4 he made a circus catch off Al Simmons with the bases loaded and two out in the fifth. "Babe, by the way, came up with a catch that knocked the customers out of their seats, proving he can play left field," Walsh wrote.

"The bases were loaded and Al Simmons smacked a hard drive to left center. Babe stabbed the ball with one hand and robbed him of an extra base hit on the dead run. Much has been made of Herman's fielding deficiencies, but Traynor is entirely satisfied with him. Herman has done surprisingly well against the White Sox in left field, especially since his sore foot has healed.

"The Babe has always been considered an awkward outfielder, but against the Sox in the last 11 games he looks like Tris Speaker. Compared to the Chicago outfield he is as graceful as a swan. So far, Herman has been able to back-peddle and haul down long drives and has held every ball that was touched by his glove. In other words, when he reaches a drive, there's nothing to it.

"On ground balls, Herman isn't as good and occasionally gives you the jitters. But he has managed to gallop over to the foul line several times and make one-handed pickups just when you figure the ball was going past him for an extra-base hit. He has a good arm and is fast enough to cover the big left field in Pittsburgh. At any rate, Traynor is happy with Babe at his new position and he'll be there opening day."

Pittsburgh traveled east with the White Sox as exhibition game partners and Herman boomed a ball over the 403-foot center field wall in Fort Worth, then cracked a 425-foot shot in Little Rock off Ted Lyons, becoming only the fourth player to ever hit a ball over that section of the fence.

The new Pittsburgh theme was "It all depends on Babe." Papers noted that between Herman hitting safely and not was the difference between victory and defeat.

The Pirates opened the season at Cincinnati April 16 and Babe knocked in a run in the 12-6 win. He got another RBI the next day but the Reds won. Later, playing first base, he fumbled a bunt that led to a seven-run Giant inning.

On the 25th he doubled twice in a loss and added three doubles in St. Louis on the 27th. His first two bagger keyed a five run third and his second opened up a three run fourth inning as the Pirates won 8-5.

But when April ended it found him with only a .242 average and four RBI, despite the fact he was leading the N.L. with seven doubles.

He singled in three trips when the club moved into Brooklyn, but he pulled a tendon in his leg and was hobbled most of the month of May, appearing only as a pinch-hitter except for a rare start against Carl Hubbell of the Giants. He slugged a single and a double good for a pair of runs in an 11-4 win, but went back to the bench and appeared in only two more games that month.

He watched from the bench as an ageing Babe Ruth, closing his career with the Boston Braves, slammed his final three major league home runs and batted in six runs against the Pirates on May 25th.

Ruth banged his first homer off Red Lucas in the opening inning, the ball just clearing the screen and dropping into the right field seats. In the third he smashed one off Guy Bush that settled into the upper right field seats and in the fifth he punched a single to left to bat in another run. Ruth then galloped to third on a single and made it with a great slide. In the seventh he stunned the crowd and the Pirates with his final blast.

With Bush still on the mound the count went to 3-0, then Ruth swung and missed. The next pitch was a changeup curve and Ruth smashed it completely over the right field stands, becoming the first man to ever hit the ball out of the park.

Pittsburgh fans and players alike watched in stunned silence as the ball disappeared over the roof of the second deck. Then the screaming crowd gave him a standing ovation and Ruth circled the bases, ran directly into the dugout and disappeared into the clubhouse.

Almost from the start, it was apparent that Pittsburgh didn't really want Babe. He picked him up from Chicago with a second deal in mind, probably with Brooklyn

Casey Stengel called Pittsburgh and asked Traynor what he wanted for Herman. Traynor said "You can have him for $12,000 and Danny Taylor."

Stengel, still strapped by a financially troubled board of directors, admitted, "I can't come up with that kind of money. How about Taylor and $9,000?"

"Sorry, then we can't make a deal," Traynor said and the Pirates kept Herman. But just two weeks later Babe was sold to Cincinnati at the waiver price of $7,500. Pie was apparently fearful that if he swapped Herman back to the Dodgers and he started hitting again, it would make him look very bad.

Traynor announced that he had offered Herman to Brooklyn at the waiver price, but that the Dodgers had refused. General manager Bob Quinn replied, "He was never offered to us, but what of it?" That flippancy brought a flood of angry calls that again ignited the Brooklyn switchboard.

Babe was inserted as a pinch-hitter for Traynor against the Phillies on June 4 and scored a runner from third with a long fly. The Pittsburgh press called it a "Fine gesture," by manager Traynor, assuming that it was Herman's swan song and that he would soon be retiring from the game, either voluntarily or by invitation.

On June 21 Babe was sold to Cincinnati. The Reds were mired in the second division with a 22-33 record.

Herman wasted little time getting into a Cincinnati uniform. He cracked out a pair of hits the next afternoon in Brooklyn but the Reds lost a 17-4 contest. His presence in the lineup picked up the Reds and the fans responded.

But the Cincinnati team that Herman joined was not the club he left in 1932. Sidney Weil, after selling Herman to Chicago to keep the franchise on a paying basis, was hard-hit by the stock market crash and other bad investments that overwhelmed him. His debts continued to mount and he left the club after the 1934 season in the hands of the Central Trust Company, which was holding his stock. It is estimated that he lost $600,000 during his four-year struggle to move the Reds into contention.

In November, the bank announced that they had signed a new general manager. His name was Larry MacPhail.

MacPhail earned a law degree and enlisted in World War I the day after war was declared. He saw action on the front and was gassed. After the armistice, New Years Eve, 1918, he led a plot to kidnap the Kaiser. It was a crackpot idea, but it saw the group actually reach the Kaiser's drawing room after disarming a guard. They fled without taking their prisoner, although MacPhail snatched the Kaiser's ash tray as a souvenir on the way out.

After the war he managed a glass factory, sold cars, refereed sporting events and finally discovered baseball, purchasing an option on the St. Louis Cardinals farm club in Columbus. The club had finished in the league second division for fifteen straight seasons but MacPhail put the club back into contention and supervised a new stadium. But he battled the parent Cardinals club over the acquisition of one of his players and when the season ended he was fired.

He took over the Reds in late 1933 and immediately asked for options on the entire Cincinnati roster so he could get a feel for which of his players were desired by the other major league teams.

He made a number of trades and purchases to revitalize the team. He also recognized the need for a farm system. Needing more money to complete his plans he convinced Powel Crosley to purchase the club.

Cincinnati had started the 1934 season with Ivy Shiver, a former football star, in the outfield and MacPhail told the press he would "out-Ruth Ruth and out-Gehrig Gehrig." He did neither, finishing with a .230 average and a ticket to St. Paul.

Lincoln Blakely was initially intended to play in the Reds' minor league system but got a surprise start in Cincinnati. After a couple good games at the plate, he took the advice of a Cincinnati newsstand operator and went on strike to get his minor league contract upgraded to the major league level. He was sent to Toronto and never appeared again in the major leagues.

Harlin Pool, a rookie from Sacramento, was raining hits all over the park but played horrendously in the outfield. Lee Allen noted, "All the stories that were told about Babe Herman's fielding could have been applied with more justice to Harlan Pool."

Despite the deals, attendance still sagged and MacPhail suggested added lights to the park, now named Crosley Field. The proposal was met with derision from the old guard. Clark Griffith said, "There is no chance of night baseball ever becoming popular in the bigger cities. People there are educated to see the best there is and will stand for only the best. High-class baseball cannot be played at night under artificial light. Furthermore, the benefits derived from attending the game are largely due to fresh air and sunshine. Night air and electric lights are a poor substitute." However, the league, recognizing that the franchise was in financial trouble, allowed them to play seven games.

The first game was scheduled for May 23 but had to be postponed 24-hours because of rain. Then Franklin D. Roosevelt, seated in the White House, threw a switch that lit the 532 lights on the field on May 24, 1935. Philadelphia was the opponent that night and the two second-division clubs drew a stunning 20,422 fans, more than 10 times the number they would have had for an afternoon game.

Just thirteen years later all but one major league park would have lights and enjoy the same financial benefits.

Playing baseball under artificial lights began in 1883 at Fort Wayne, Indiana. The M.E. College nine battled a professional team from Quincey, with the pros winning 19-11. The Jenney Electric Light Company put 17 lights of 4,000 candle power each.

The Fort Wayne Gazette noted, "Baseball is the American national game but it was reserved for the city of Fort Wayne to be the first in the world to play it at night and by the rays of artificial sun. The degree of illumination was such that the game was well played, although an alarming number of strikes were called by Umpire Morrissey." Reports say a huge crowd of nearly 2,000 attended the game.

But it took the great depression to allow night baseball to be given a tentative trial by the traditionalists in the major leagues.

Minor League night baseball had been flourishing since 1930.

Daytime baseball could only be attended by those who were unemployed. It stood to reason that they would have little disposable income to support it.

Night games, however, enabled those with jobs to watch the contests. The move saved minor league baseball during this difficult time, and in turn also probably saved major league baseball.

Larry MacPhail knew all about this and had sold Crosley on the idea of lights on Crosley, nee Redland, Field.

When Herman was traded to Cincinnati in 1935, Bob O'Farrell was the manager, but he would be replaced by Charlie Dressen on July 28th with the club mired deep in the standings with a 31-60 record.

Babe's old pal, Jim Bottomly, was at first base for the Reds, Alex Kampouris at second, Billy Myers at short and Lew Riggs at third. In the outfield Val Goodman and Sammy Byrd flanked Herman, with Cuyler joining the club later. Lombardi was still the catcher.

Paul Derringer would win 22 for the club but none of the other starters were in double figures. The forgettable cast included Gene Schott, Al Hollinsworth, Benny Frey, Tony Freitas and Si Johnson in the starting rotation. Don Brennan was the relief man.

The Reds were scheduled to have opened the 1935 season at Pittsburgh. But Cincinnati, the home of professional baseball, had opened the season in their own park since 1877 and MacPhail burned up the telephone lines righting that wrong. The club was given permission to open the season at home a day earlier than the rest of the league; however, Pittsburgh spoiled things with a 12-6 victory.

But the team was obviously better than previous years and seemed even money to avoid the league cellar. At the end of May the club was 16-16 but then they started to slide under the .500 mark. Chick Hafey deserted the team, leaving a note that he was ill and was going home.

MacPhail then reached out and plucked Herman off the Pittsburgh roster to replace Hafey, and he could only have dreamed of how that deal would help the Cincinnati team.

Babe made his presence felt immediately. Late in June the Reds swept the Cardinals for the first time since 1927 as Herman banged a double, triple and two singles. Early in July, the Cubs tired of trying to trade holdout Kiki Cuyler and released him. He quickly signed with the Reds.

Cincinnati split with Chicago, swept the Pirates and moved onto the road. Their attendance spiked to 255,304 after 35 home games, just 50,000 off their entire 1934 total.

The Reds returned to Cincinnati to host the Dodgers and Herman's bat was never hotter, making Brooklyn's failed attempt to obtain Babe from Pittsburgh an even more bitter pill for Dodger fans and management.

In the opener he smacked the first night game homer in league history, appropriately enough off Brooklyn's Ray Benge to key a 15-2 rout. He singled home a run in a 5-4 win then doubled twice and singled as the Reds won the third game of the series 5-2.

When Cincinnati completed the five-game sweep with 9-4 and 4-2 wins, Brooklyn manager Casey Stengel told reporters that half the team would be gone next year and the club rebuilt along the lines of Cincinnati.

Babe smashed a homer, two doubles and a single good for four RBI in the final double-header against the Dodgers to run his record for the series to 10 hits in 20 trips; four doubles, two homers and nine RBI.

The Reds and Giants split a four-game set with Babe banging out nine hits in 16 trips and boosting his season's average to .312.

Late in the month, Edgar Brands of The Sporting News, wrote the first correct story of the "Three Men on Third" saga, as Herman spoke out for the first time to correct the account of the incident.

Writing of Herman's trade to Cincinnati, Tom Meany noted, "Everyone in the National League thought that when Herman was purchased by the Reds it was for their Toledo club. His salary was too much for the Reds to pay and outfielder—or anyone. And when they acquired Cuyler, too, it looked as if Herman's days were numbered.

"Babe knew that if he could last until August 6th he would be a 10-year man—thus he could not be sent to the minors without his consent. He joined the club June 22nd and hit .363 through July 17th, and during that period the Reds won 17 of 24 games. Taking over for injured Jim Bottomly at first, he is still a bit weak on ground balls but on the whole he's doing a good job."

On July 31st the World Champion Cardinals played a night game in Cincinnati. Interest in night baseball had spread throughout the area and an announced 30,450 fans crowded into Crosley Field, whose capacity was about 22,000, boosting the after-dark attendance to 109,000 for six games. It would swell to 130,000 for the full seven games, over 40 percent of their entire attendance total of the previous season.

With out-of-town fans gobbling up many of the reserved seats in advance, the general-admission crowd found no room available. The reserved seats were roped off, waiting for the special chartered trains bringing fans to the event to arrive. But when the trains were late, a rush for the vacant seats caused mass confusion. And when the proper ticket holders did arrive, many found their seats occupied, intensifying the carnival atmosphere.

The Reds' Tony Fritas and Cardinal Paul Dean were locked in a pitching duel but the battle paled in comparison to the battle for seats in the grandstands. Finally the crowd overflowed the stadium and as the game progressed, fans were seated everywhere, including just a few feet outside the foul lines.

No one will ever know the exact number of people who paid to get into the park that evening. And many did not pay to get in, just brushing through the turnstiles on their way to the stands.

Commissioner K. M. Landis was in attendance and even he had to stand on tiptoe to see any of the action on the field. MacPhail, seeing such delightful chaos, simply threw up his hands and left the park in the hands of secretary Frances Levy, who was finally unable to handle the crush of fans demanding their money back. She had to lock herself into the office and make refunds through a sliding panel in the door, reminding many of speak-easy days.

Then late in the game one of the most unusual occurrences in major league baseball history took place and, as usual, Babe Herman was directly involved. A young lady by the name of Kitty Burke emerged from the crowd standing on the field and said, "Give me the bat, Babe." Babe, waiting in the on-deck circle, asked, "What for?"

"Well," she said, "I want to hit." Babe handed her the bat and with a smile said, "Go ahead." She took the bat and strode to the plate.

Cardinal pitcher Paul Dean was stunned and didn't move for a time from the mound. Finally, when it became apparent that the umpires were not going to stop the young woman, he tossed the ball in underhand. She swung the heavy bat and rolled it toward first, then dashed down the line, wobbling in her high-heeled shoes. The first baseman fielded it and dove toward her as if to tackle her. She jumped over his hands and ran on to first.

That seemed to satisfy her and as the crowd applauded, Babe picked up his bat and the game continued, won by the Reds in the 10th inning. It would seem only proper that the first and only woman to bat in a major league game would 'pinch hit' for Babe Herman.

She later called Babe and asked if he could get her a Cincinnati uniform. Babe told her that he couldn't do that, but she should call the club. "MacPhail is probably silly enough to give you one," he said.

Babe called it correctly. MacPhail supplied her with an official Reds uniform and she got a 26-week singing engagement outside Cincinnati from the publicity she had received from the game.

Herman finished the month of August with a rush. He slugged two homers, two doubles and three singles good for eight RBI as the Reds took three of four from Philadelphia and he boomed a homer in the ninth to beat Brooklyn 5-4 in front of a slim crowd of only 500 Dodger rooters.

In Brooklyn on September 8 the National League, represented by Bill Klem, presented life-time passes to Herman, George Kelly, Jim Bottomly and Kiki Cuyler as ten-year men. At the same time Babe Ruth, then a Dodger coach, was given a lifetime pass to the National League. Oddly, no such offer had been made to Ruth by the American League.

In the following double header Cincinnati made 10 errors, none by Herman, and the Dodgers took both games.

The Reds won four of five from Boston and three of five with the

Phillies to assure themselves their best won-lost record since 1928.

Traveling to St. Louis for their final road games, the Reds had lost eight straight to the Cardinals before Herman slugged a double and two homers, batting in four runs, in a 9-7 victory.

Babe had seen action in 17 games at first base and the Reds were pleased with his play, reporting they were considering him for that position in 1936.

After hitting .235 in Pittsburgh, Herman had blistered the ball for a .335 mark in Cincinnati, boosting his average to .316 for the year.

Cincinnati was last with a 22-33 record when Herman arrived from the Pirates. They finished the season in sixth place with a 68-85 mark.

Herman had caught fire, just as Traynor had feared, but for the Cincinnati club, not Brooklyn.

MacPhail announced plans to take the Reds to train in Puerto Rico in 1936. Given a choice, only 11 of the players opted to fly, the rest were content to take a boat, and one rookie telegraphed, "If it is all the same to you, I'll drive."

Raises were tendered to 32 players on the 40-man roster. There was little doubt who MacPhail was talking about when he said, "One outfielder wants as much as Ott."

Herman, Ernie Lombardi, Lee Grissom, Tommy Theveneau and Ival Goodman didn't sign immediately. Herman worked out in Pasadena with the White Sox, infuriating MacPhail immensely.

Diz Dean was working out with the Red Sox while fighting a contractual battle with the Cardinals, holding a daily press conference to air his views. Commissioner Landis, weary of the daily reports, ruled that players could not work out with clubs other than their own.

Sox manager Jimmy Dykes showed Babe the telegram he had received from Landis, announcing the new rule. "That's O.K.," Herman told him. "This is a public park and as a private citizen I can certainly use the park myself."

So Babe would work out early, play pepper with the White Sox players before the games, then stay around afterward as Ted Lyons, Merv Shea or Jimmy Dykes himself, would stick around to pitch batting practice and field while Herman hit.

The manager and coaches were on their own time and, as a taxpayer, Babe was simply using the public park. After the workout, they would all play golf.

The Reds were looking for a replacement for first baseman Jim Bottomly. They acquired young Johnny Mize from the Cardinals but he required a knee operation and his price tag was $55,000 so they returned him to St. Louis on the recommendation of the Reds' team doctor.

It is not recorded, but the Cincinnati doctor was probably out of work as far as the club was concerned when Mize became a star after the operation.

George McQuinn was also tried and found wanting by the Reds, only to go to the American League for an 11-year run with the Browns, Athletics and Yankees.

Before the season started, MacPhail swapped Jim Bottomly to the St. Louis Browns for second baseman Johnny Burnett. Later in the season he purchased pitcher Bill Hallahan from St. Louis and traded Si Johnson for the Cardinals Bill Walker.

Les Scarsella was the Reds first baseman, Kampouris, Myers and Riggs were still at second, short and third, and Cuyler, Herman and Goodman were in the outfield

Lombardi caught a pitching staff of Derringer, Schott, Frey, Hollingsworth, Peaches Davis and Hallahan. Brennan again provided the bulk of the relief work.

In early April Herman flew to Florence, South Carolina, to meet with MacPhail and sign his contract. The general manager wanted to give Herman an additional $500 per payday for "hustling." Herman quickly agreed. Manager Charlie Dressen was to make the final determination.

Babe played in his first exhibition game on April 9, then banged out a double and three singles in the N.L. opener on April 14 against the Pirates and a red-faced Pie Traynor.

He hit in his first six games, opening with an 11-for-28 mark (.611), but the Reds went only 3-3. The club was second most of April but dropped into third as the month ended. MacPhail started to burn about the club's 7-7 record and on May 3rd he suspended 22-game winner Paul Derringer for "failing to slide at the plate," although many felt it was something other than his baserunning that caused the suspension.

After going 4-6 in the first 10 games of May, and slipping to fifth, MacPhail took the entire club to Atlantic City for a "vacation." The break seemed to do wonders for the team and they moved back into third place late in the month. Herman, sidelined by a Charlie horse, slammed a ninth inning pinch hit homer against the Cardinals but the two run shot wasn't enough.

Babe played little through the early part of June. The club displayed new uniforms of Palm Beach cloth with red pants for their night game schedule. Herman played first base, then after a homer and a single against Brooklyn he aggravated the leg again and was back to only pinch-hitting.

Ernie Lombardi split a finger and Ival Goodman tore a shoulder ligament as the club dipped to sixth place in the final week of June. But the club drew a record 33,469 hosting the Cubs in a night game on June 29 and with the win Cincinnati moved into fourth place.

In the middle of July the Brooklyn club drew only 7,477 in a night game and the next day MacPhail called the afternoon game because of "heat," although most knew the low attendance figure the previous night was the real cause. A double header was scheduled in August to make the game up.

The club stumbled through a July homestand, then moving into New York real trouble broke out. Derringer, reinstated by MacPhail, was locked in a battle with Hal Schumacher. The game was in the ninth with the score tied 4-4 when Dressen came out to ask if he wanted to pitch to Ott with a runner on.

"I don't have much trouble with him," Derringer said. "I'd rather pitch to him than Hank Leiber." Dressen said "O.K., but tell Les Scarsella (the first baseman) to play behind the runner." Derringer stretched, then turned to throw to first but with the first baseman playing back, there was no one to throw the ball to and a balk was called.

Dressen was back on the mound in a flash and was furious. "Put Ott on base" he shouted and left.

Then Leiber banged a shot to left field, the ball hit in a pool of water and scooted instead of bouncing. Babe charged the ball and made a stab at it, catching the ball in the webbing of his glove. He looked up, saw the runner only 20-feet from the plate and didn't attempt a throw to the plate. He tucked it into his pocket and trotted into the clubhouse.

Between games of the doubleheader Dressen screamed at Derringer, fining him $100 for the balk. Then he turned to Herman and shouted,

"What's the matter with you, Herman?"

"Nothing," Babe replied.

"Why didn't you throw home?"

"I couldn't have got him at the plate with a rifle."

"Oh, yea? That will cost you $100, too," Dressen fumed.

Herman was used only as a pinch hitter for the next 13 games, with Cincinnati losing eight of them. Dressen told Herman that the $500 hustle bonus was also off.

He started Babe in St. Louis and one of the coaches said, "Have a good series and Dressen will forget about that hustle thing and you'll get your money." Herman complied, slamming a pair of homers and a single in the first game and had three RBI. He doubled home a run in the first game of the double header the next day, then banged three doubles in the second game as the Reds swept.

He had a double and a single in the first game at Pittsburgh and a run-scoring single in the second game. He knocked in nine runs in five games and Cincinnati won three of them.

Returning home to Cincinnati, Babe was in the manager's office when MacPhail called Dressen. Charlie reported that all three of the players with hustle bonuses had played well—Don Brennan, Babe Herman and Kiki Cuyler. "O.K.," MacPhail said, "give them their money."

After hanging up, he called right back and shouted, "Don't give any of those (expletives) anything." He gave no reason for his change of mind.

Herman was furious and couldn't get the incident out of his mind. He waited for Dressen to return to the hotel, then told him, "I can't continue going through this sort of baloney. I'm going to talk to Landis," and he stalked out of the hotel.

When MacPhail heard that Herman had left the club, he told the Associated Press a different story. "I hope he has gone back to California. And if he has, he'll never come back. He just saves us about $100 a day by leaving. I kept him from going to the minors last year before he became a ten-year man. I'm willing to admit he played good ball for us last year, but this year he hasn't hustled. We paid him the $250 bonus four times, and then we stopped.

"We paid him $19,000 this year and under that contract he was just about the second highest paid outfielder in the National League, and he wasn't even able to make the team," he said.

The volatile MacPhail disliked players leaving him and if they were going to leave, he preferred to initiate the separation. In 1941, after an altercation with Dixie Walker, he told the press, "If the St. Louis club will promise to play Walker every day, I will give him to the Cardinals for nothing. I will pay his transportation." Obviously Dixie stayed and helped the Dodgers win a pair of N.L. pennants.

Herman drove to Chicago and met with Landis in his office. "Why didn't you wait for the club to come to Chicago? Aren't they going to be here in a couple days?" Landis asked. Herman said that perhaps he should have waited, "But the whole thing bothered me so much I decided to come and talk to you."

MacPhail was scheduled to go to Puerto Rico, but Landis called him and told him to come to Chicago. After hearing both sides of the story, Landis turned to Dressen and asked him what happened.

"Oh, Babe told the story right," Dressen admitted.

"But I'd like to hear it from you," Landis said and Dressen recounted the entire story just as Herman had told the commissioner earlier.

Landis then turned to Herman and said, "You go back to the club and play for this little guy (Dressen), and you let me know every nickel owed you that you don't get. Is that all right with you?"

"No," Herman said. "I'm not going back and play for that guy (MacPhail) and have him second-guess me all year long."

"You won't have to say 'Hello' or anything else," Landis said.

Herman finally agreed to return and had little trouble the rest of the season.

He was bothered by an injured leg through August and September. He played four straight games against St. Louis and Chicago the final month, winning three of them with extra base hits but the leg sidelined him again and he started only once more that year, slugging a three-run homer against Roy Parmlee of the Cardinals on that occasion.

MacPhail resigned as general manager of the Reds to look for greener pastures and Warren Giles replaced him. The club had drawn nearly 480,000 and made over $100,000, the best financial season since 1926. MacPhail would later rejuvenate the Brooklyn franchise and then move on to the New York Yankees, winning pennants with each club.

Herman finished the season with a .279 average, his lowest since 1928, and despite only 106 hits, knocked in 71 runs with 25 doubles and 13 homers. And despite coming to the plate only 380 times, he lacked just three RBI of leading the club in that department.

Chapter 13

New Cincinnati GM Warren Giles told reporters in the spring of 1937 that he felt Herman was washed up. When asked about it, Babe replied, "Why don't they trade me then? I know I can get a good job in the minors if the Reds or some other big league club doesn't want me."

Herman called Giles about his contract and he told him he couldn't expect the same money he'd received in 1936. "Dressen said you couldn't play regularly because of your legs," he said.

Herman said, "I've heard that before. My legs are all right and I want to be a regular until my legs break down. Last year they didn't bother me at all."

"But I asked for waivers on you and no one claimed you," Giles told him.

"Of course not," Babe said, "with a $19,000 salary."

"Well, if you're not worth $7,500 (the waiver price) to the other clubs, you're only worth $5,000 to me," Giles barked, using unusual logic. "But Dressen wants you in the outfield next year."

"I never realized it was possible for any ball player to fall so rapidly in one's estimation as I have in yours," Babe said resignedly, "Listen, Warren, just forget about me."

Herman was obviously not actually 'worthless,' or he would have been released. A few days later Herman was sold to Detroit for an undisclosed amount. Giles notifying Babe by phone. The next day, Mickey Cochrane called from Detroit and asked if he was ready to play. Herman was suffering from a slight muscle pull and told him "It won't take long."

"Take your time, but when you're ready, let me know," Cochrane said. Babe could have flown to Detroit, in which case Mickey said he would have started immediately in the opener April 20th. He took the train and arrived the second day of the season. Babe took extra batting practice and got into his first American League game on May 3rd, pinch-hitting against the White Sox, banging a line drive at the first baseman.

"I've got a guy that can drill that ball now," Cochrane told newsmen.

After five pinch-hitting appearances, Babe started against the St. Louis Browns on May 16 in left field. He doubled, stole two bases, demonstrating his legs were just fine, then singled in the winning run in the sixth inning to break a 4-4 tie. He played left field again the next game and doubled in a run.

A few days later Cochrane was seriously beaned by Bump Hadley in a game in New York and was out for the remainder of the season. For a few days it was feared he would die. Even after he passed the crisis, it was obvious that he would not be able to play again or soon even manage the Tigers from the dugout. Coach Del Baker took over the club.

Babe talked to Baker and said, "I'm in good shape and I'm hitting. I can help you now if you'll play me."

"I can't play you, Babe, until I get the order from Mickey Cochrane or Mr. Briggs, the owner." Baker told him. "I've been ordered to stay with the same lineup Mickey used." Cochrane was in the hospital with a 'no visitors' order and Briggs was on vacation in Italy. Babe and Hank Greenberg spent their time pitching batting practice to each other.

Babe did nothing but pinch-hit the rest of May. He singled in two runs in the ninth in New York to tie the game 4-4 but the Tigers lost in 13 innings. He also led off the ninth with a single in Cleveland that eventually tied the game, and on June 3rd he doubled against the Washington Senators. He played through June 6th.

Outfielder Marv Owens and catcher Red Hayworth were hit by pitches and suffered broken bones. Cliff Bolton, a left-hand hitter, was picked up from Washington to fill in for Hayworth behind the plate.

The Tigers decided to keep Pete Fox, Goose Goslin, Jo-Jo White and Gee Walker in the outfield, using White as a defensive replacement. Goslin would only play 79 games and hit .238. White played in 94 games and hit .246. However, Herman, who was hitting an even .300, was released.

Babe immediately got an offer from Al Sothorn at Milwaukee but before accepting it, he called on his old friend Fred Haney at Toledo in the American Association and shaking hands said, "Hello, Fred, need anybody to play left field?"

"We certainly do, Babe, who is it?" Haney replied.

"Me," said Herman.

"Get into uniform, you've got a contract," was all Haney said, setting a new record (30 seconds) for hiring Babe Herman.

Haney told Wish Egan the next afternoon, "I saw Babe earlier today and he told me he had a good job with a sporting goods store. I never saw a fellow with so many jobs before. He had four jobs outside baseball an hour after the Tigers gave him his release. He didn't take any of them."

Babe played his first game in late June. After a pair of hitless games he got his timing back and was hitting .354 after 12 games and the Mud Hens were in the thick of the American Association pennant race.

Herman hit in 28 of 29 games from July 8 through August 12 with only an unsuccessful pinch-hitting trip keeping him from a long consecutive game streak. In the 29-games Herman cracked out 53 hits in 121 time at bat for a .438 average and moved into a tie with Enos Slaughter for the league leadership at .377. During that period Toledo moved into second place only two games behind Minneapolis.

On August 16th Toledo played an exhibition game against Cincinnati and banged out a satisfying 16 hits in a 9-5 win over the National Leaguers.

Babe and Hank Greenberg

The pennant race went down to the wire, with Toledo holding first place briefly on August 29th after Babe slugged a two-run homer in a 7-5 victory at Kansas City.

In the final 10 games Herman collected 17 hits. He banged out a double, triple and homer in the next-to last game of the season, then doubled and tripled in the finale but Columbus, managed by Burt Shotton and led by Walter Alston at first base, edged them by a single game for the league title.

On the final day of the season the club had a day in his honor, coordinated by Jackie Farrell and Jack Horan. Newspapers thought it was his final season as an active player, but Babe told them he felt he had 'one more year' of good baseball in his system.

Milwaukee topped Toledo 4-2 in the playoffs. Herman hit two homers in the second game of the series, the final shot coming in the last of the tenth with two on to win 6-5.

Babe demonstrated he had not lost his remarkable hitting touch, finishing the season with a .348 average. Playing in only 85 games he had collected 117 hits, including 37 doubles, 12 homers and a remarkable 79 runs batted in. He had made only a single error in the outfield and had recorded a .993 fielding average.

Babe signed with Jersey City in the International League in 1938. Given a trial during spring training while the Jersey City club played major league competition, Herman hit a neat .421. Jersey City manager Stoney Jackson told Bill Terry he wanted him. Babe asked for a $10,000 salary and the Giants organization added a $10,000 bonus. Later Herman's former teammate Hank DeBerry took over as manager of the club.

Opening game in Jersey City drew 32,652 and the game went 3-3 into the top of the 10th when Toronto scored twice. In the last of the tenth inning with two out, Herman clubbed a long double into the corner with the bases loaded to plate three runners and win 6-5.

Babe started fast and was hitting .380 after 29 games, He missed his first game of the season on June 29th. Herman connected on what was believed to be the longest ball ever hit in Municipal Stadium in Syracuse when his drive was caught against the 450-foot marker in dead center field.

Before a game in Jersey City, Herman was surprised to receive a call from Larry MacPhail, now general manager of the Brooklyn club. As if there had never been any trouble between them, MacPhail said, "Babe, there's a pitcher in your league that we want to get. Bill Terry wants to buy him for $50,000 but I can steal him if you think he can do us any good. I trust your judgement."

Herman replied, "He's pitching against us tonight, Larry, but I don't think he can help you. We banged him around pretty good last time we met him. I'll watch him and let your know." Babe called the next day and told MacPhail, "I wouldn't buy him for any amount." Herman was right. A major league club later bought him but he never won a game for them.

A couple of weeks later MacPhail called again. "There is a player in Newark I can buy for $45,000. What do you think?" Babe said, "He's a pretty good player, you ought to take him. Why don't you put Tom Sheehan on him for 3-4 days and look for one thing. He and the shortstop ran into each other last night. He injured a knee and was limping when he got up. Check the knee out."

The next call came from Sheehan, who said, "Thanks for the tip, Babe. I'm not going to recommend him because of that bad knee."

Larry MacPhail, who had battled Herman so hard while Babe was in

Babe, while in Jersey City, posed with Baltimore Manager Rogers Hornsby and Ernest Lawrence Thayer, author of "Casey at the Bat."

Cincinnati, came to trust Herman's judgement on players. When Herman was holding out in the spring of 1939, the Hollywood general manager told MacPhail, "I'm going to have trouble signing Herman."

"Let him go then" MacPhail said. "I've got a job for him any time he wants one."

The Rochester Red Wings were trying out a shortstop with a strong arm, but the youngster hit only .118 and Sammy Baugh left baseball to try his hand at football.

As the season wound down, the club had a day for Herman at Roosevelt Stadium as the Giants closed out the season against Baltimore. Jackie Farrell, Jack Horan and a flock of other friends of The Babe combined to make the day a memorable one.

George Schreier wrote, "Herman is one of the few players under the new regime to live up to his far-famed reputation. Unlike dozens of other during 1937, the Babe had not fallen by the wayside under fire. Industrious and always conscientious, respected and liked by all and sundry, the man well deserves the honors which will be bestowed upon him."

Despite Herman's hitting, the Giants quickly dropped through the league standings and finished seventh. Babe hit .324, and in 145 games he had 171 hits, 40 doubles, 18 homers and 93 RBI, all club highs.

Babe was in contention for the 'Most Valuable Player' award in the league until slowed by a pulled muscle late in the season. Many thought he would return to the International League and a local paper wrote, "Unless he finds a managerial position that he'd like to land, he will return to Jersey City."

Chapter 14

In 1939 events were brewing back in California that would change Herman's destiny. Bob Cobb, president of the Brown Derby chain of restaurants, purchased the Hollywood Stars in the Pacific Coast League.

A new park was being built for the club near the famous Farmers Market on what was then the western outskirts of Los Angeles.

The original Hollywood club had moved to San Diego in 1936. The 1938 club was the transplanted San Francisco Missions. When they moved south to Los Angeles they were denied the use of Wrigley Field for their home games, then at the last moment they were allowed to use it, but only for the 1938 season.

Thus a new stadium was built, next to Gilmore Stadium, which was an oval park designed for football and auto racing. Gilmore field was constructed just east of the Stadium and would be ready for the 1939 season.

Cobb, married to actress Gail Patrick, didn't have sufficient funds to purchase the entire club in 1939, so he announced that blocks of stock would be sold to some of the brightest stars in Hollywood and the initial list of stockholders included, along with Miss Patrick, Gary Cooper, George Raft, Robert Taylor, Cecil B. DeMille, Barbara Stanwick, Bing Crosby and William Powell.

Later Babe purchased some stock in the club himself, an act that was contrary to baseball law, but he had it registered under the name of a relative.

Cobb purchased Herman from the Jersey City club, along with a number of other players, and true to his tradition, Babe held out for a better contract offer. The Stars purchased long-time minor leaguer Spencer Harris to play first and told Babe to try to make a deal for himself somewhere else.

But both sides were posturing and Herman, as usual in excellent shape, signed a $10,000 contract the day before the 1939 Pacific Coast League season opened.

Babe would play in Hollywood for six seasons, 1939 through 1944. Over the final years he played sparingly but was an extremely successful pinch-hitter. He recorded averages that ranged from .307 to .354, actually 'leading' the Pacific Coast League in hitting on several occasions but falling short of the necessary times at bat to be considered the official batting champion.

After the 1939 flag-raising ceremonies, Mayor Fletcher Bouron zipped a fast ball past the ear of the 'hitter' Joe E. Brown and almost knocked the glove off Sheriff Gene Biscailuz who was catching. Brown singled to right field on the next pitch and the season was officially open.

Also true to his tradition of being able to hit any time and any where, without any formal spring training, Babe smacked the first pitch thrown to him by Los Angeles Angels pitcher Fay Thomas for a home run with a pair of runners on base.

Herman added two more singles to his total and the Stars beat their traditional rivals 10-9, Babe's heroics making him an instant favorite of the Hollywood crowd.

Gilmore Field wasn't ready for the season opener, so the club played in Gilmore Stadium. There were no dugouts, just benches, and the right field wall was only 270 feet from home plate. Ground rules allowed only a double for a shot over the short fence. The outfield ran into the race track and was banked for the cars, making fielding a real adventure. In the first seven game series there were 15 homers hit by the Stars and the visiting Portland Beavers.

One of Babe's homers cleared the pressbox and the east straightaway, an estimated 450-foot shot.

Gilman Field opened officially on May 2 to the greatest pomp and circumstance ever witnessed in a PCL contest. The evening before the park had been opened for inspection, with free beer, peanuts, popcorn and hot dogs for all.

Before a packed house opening day, Miss Patrick threw out the first ball to catcher Joe E. Brown as Jane Withers batted. Brown ran for his life when Patrick wound up for the first pitch. Other stars at the opener included Jack Benny, Al Jolson, Bing Crosby, Martha Raye and Rudy Vallee.

Nine tiny cars drove onto the field, hidden behind white placards with large stars on them. They aligned themselves around the infield and outfield and the nine Hollywood starters jumped out from behind them.

The finish was almost right out of a Hollywood script as the home team loaded the bases in the last of the ninth, trailing 5-6, but the final hitter flew out to end the game.

Babe hit for cycle for the fifth time in his career on May 5th against Seattle, batting in three runs in a 6-4, 12-inning victory over Seattle. Attendance boomed, peaking at 400 percent above the 1938 mark in the second-month of the season. Herman was eighth in the league with a .359 average and had knocked in 37 runs in the first 37 games.

'Star-fever' was rampant in Hollywood and Miss Patrick turned down three movie offers so she could follow the team on the road. Film stars were on hand at every home game and,

Babe in Hollywood ... 1939

coupled with an exciting team on the field, fans streamed into Gilmore. The club drew 265,000 fans into the 12,000-capacity park during the season.

On June 4, Babe slugged a home run over the 420-foot center field wall at Seals Stadium in San Francisco, the first shot over that barrier in four years.

But on July 1st, Ray Prim of the Angels broke Herman's wrist with an inside pitch and Babe was finished for the season. In a half season, Herman had collected 111 hits, 36 doubles, 13 homers and 71 RBI, posting a .317 average.

He spent the rest of the season conducting the Hollywood baseball school for players in the city. He worked with 165 players during the final months of the summer and most of the youngsters were scouted, interviewed and chosen by Herman.

Seven of his graduates were signed for other Star farm clubs and fifteen more were expected to sign when the regular spring training period opened.

Babe and Glenn Wright with starlets

In 1939 the Stars finished sixth and had high hopes for the 1940 season, arranging for a working agreement with the Detroit team at the Winter Meetings. However the Tiger system was cleaned out when Commissioner Landis freed 91 Detroit players for a number of irregularities in their playing contracts.

At the Hollywood opener, Gracie Allen, presidential candidate of the 'Surprise Party,' threw out the first ball and the usual compliment of stars were in attendance.

Herman started slowly, widening his stance during spring training at Santa Barbara. When the season started he was in a deep slump and was used mostly as a pinch-hitter during the first month.

But his bat awoke in May and he boomed a single, two doubles and a triple good for four RBI to help beat San Francisco 11-9. His average slowly climbed as the season progressed but the club finished in the league basement.

On June 26 he celebrated his 36th birthday with three hits as Hollywood beat Oakland 7-3. He had hit in six of his last nine times at bat, with three doubles and six RBI.

Babe had purchased an 18-acre ranch just 11 miles from his home in Glendale with the idea of developing it into an orange grove. Instead he turned it into a turkey ranch after talking to Cobb, owner of a chain of restaurants and Stars' stockholder George Young, head of a large string of markets. Herman introduced the broad-breast turkey, very desirable because of the additional white meat, to Southern California.

A pulled leg muscle slowed him in August and again he was cast in pinch-hit roles. He ended the season with a .307 average but included were 45 doubles and he had 93 RBI. He led the club with nine home runs.

During the season he had banged out his 3,000th professional hit, but the event went unnoticed.

Babe was used sparingly in 1941, but on April 24 the rival Los Angeles club invaded Gilmore Stadium and when the visitors scored four times in the top of the ninth inning, the score was tied 6-6.

Hollywood loaded the bases and third-base coach Babe Herman went to the bat rack and selected his favorite club. With two strikes on him he slugged a long shot over the right field wall for four runs and the game. Although it was early in the season, it was the second time he had won a game with a pinch-hit homer.

During the month of May, Herman had 57 hits in 47 games, along with eight home runs, and recorded a .396 average. He was selected as the Southern California athlete of the month by sports editors in the area. A gold medal was presented by the Helms Athletic Foundation as the club celebrated "Babe Herman Night" on June 26, which incidentally was not only his 38th birthday but alos Ladies Night.

Herman hit .354 and 'led' the Pacific Coast League, however the official title went to Johnny Moore of Los Angeles who hit .331. Babe had played in 110 games and had 272 official times at bat. He collected 16 doubles, 11 homers and 63 RBI.

After the 1941 season Herman was the technical consultant in "Pride of the Yankees," a movie on Lou Gehrig's life. Gary Cooper played the part of Gehrig, but was unfamiliar with baseball. His father had been a diplomatic official in England and Cooper grew up playing cricket.

Cooper was also right-handed, so the movie was shot with jersey numbers sewed on backward and the film was then reversed so that the number would read correctly and Cooper would look left-handed.

Babe did the hitting for Cooper (as Gehrig) and Babe Ruth in the long shots, making him, in a manner of speaking and including his movie roles, the only player in the history of baseball to 'pinch-hit' for Cobb, Speaker, Ruth and Gehrig.

During batting practice for the movie shots in Wrigley Field in Los Angeles, Herman slugged a long drive onto the center field scaffold that held the cameras. The distance to the bleachers was 345 feet and the ball landed in the scaffolding, which was 50 feet high.

When asked later in life to compare Ruth and Cobb, Herman said, "They were both just about perfect, except Babe never threw to the wrong

On the set of 'Pride of the Yankees,' Babe posed with Babe Dahlgren, Babe Ruth and director Sam Wood.

base."

While filming in Hollywood, Charlie Root came onto the movie set and Herman asked him if he had ever met Babe Ruth. Root had been the Chicago pitcher that served up the supposed "Called Shot" by Ruth during the 1932 World Series.

"No, I've never met him," Root said, so Herman took him over to the Bambino.

Root looked Ruth directly in the eye and said, "You never pointed out to center field before you hit that homer off of me."

Ruth just smiled and said, "Hell, kid, I know that. But didn't it make a great story?"

The studio wanted Babe to double for Gary Cooper in "For Whom the Bell Tolls." Babe told them if he could have the stand-in and the double job, he would quit playing for the Hollywood Stars.

But the union said, "No, he's got to do one or the other," and Herman stayed on the diamond.

Herman had previously worked in the movie "Slide Kelly, Slide" in 1926, doubling for Tris Speaker in center field. As the light started to fail he moved to left field to film a catch and finally moved to right field to complete the scene by throwing to the plate. Even Speaker himself would have had trouble covering ground like that.

He also 'played' Cardinal first baseman Jim Bottomly in the World Series scenes. "Irish" and Bob Musial and Tony Lazzeri were also in the baseball movie.

In December, at the Minor League meetings in Jacksonville, Florida, Herman and Edward Farrell, Los Angeles businessman, attempted to buy the Portland Beavers in the Pacific Coast League. Bill Sweeney, former Portland and Hollywood manager, accompanied them to the meeting to make the bid. However the deal fell through when Pearl Harbor was bombed and war was declared.

There were doubts that the season would even be allowed to start due to the war, but on January 14, 1942, president Roosevelt gave approval for the continuation of organized baseball in his famous 'green light' letter to commissioner Landis.

Since there was a fear that California would be invaded by the Japanese, the army allowed crowds that would not exceed the 1941 average (3,423) at Hollywood night games. Later in August the army cancelled its permission for night baseball. The edict continued in force through the 1943 season.

A player shortage made it difficult to field a competitive team. Charlie Root was added to the pitching staff and was made manager in 1943.

John Lardner wrote an apocryphal story about Herman's abilities during the 1942 season Lardner wrote in an article headlined,

He's Heard of Herman:'

"Floyd Caves (Babe) Herman was once called, by no less an expert than Rogers Hornsby, 'The perfect free swinger.' Later in his career he constructed part of his legend—as one of the fiercest sluggers in the game.

"He swung his big bat like a cane, and he could drive the ball through a brick wall. This was the reputation that followed him down to the end of his playing days. All by itself, the legend of Herman the hitter broke up one of the last games he played in Hollywood in 1942.

"The Babe was 39 by then, too old and plump to be risking his brains in the field. Maybe he was too old to be swinging a bat, as well. But a boy named Soriano didn't know that. Like every man and child on the Babe's native West Coast, what Soriano knew was that Herman ate pitchers alive.

"The youngster, pitching for Seattle, had whiffed 10 Hollywood batsmen as the game went into the 10th inning tied. In the home half, Hollywood filled the bases with two out.

" 'You in shape to pinch-hit, Babe? He's still fast,' the manager

said.

" 'I won't need to hit him,' said Herman, reaching for a bat. I'll paralyze him.'

"He slouched to the plate. He scowled at the pitcher and held his bat like a butcher's cleaver over a side of beef. He never swung it. Five pitches went by—three balls, two strikes. Then the Babe pounded the plate, gnashed his teeth, and drew back the club as though to tear a hole in the fence.

"The weight of his fame came home full force to Soriano now—and the last pitch showed it. It hit the ground a full yard in front of Herman's feet for ball four. A run came in, and the game was over.

" 'There's a well-read kid,' said the Babe, throwing his bat away for almost the last time in his life. 'He's heard of Herman.' "

Babe, now 39, played only 85 games but had 48 hits, 42 RBI and hit .322

Only 15 men were under contract as the 1943 season started.

The Hollywood club again held a "Babe Herman Night" on his 40th birthday, June 26, 1943. One of the special gifts was presented by actor

Gene Paulette who gave Babe with a turkey he had borrowed from Herman's turkey farm earlier in the day.

Babe set some sort of record by banging three pinch homers in succession during the season and during a series with the rival Angles, Babe won three games with two homers and a single.

Despite a Charley horse that plagued him most of the season, Herman, at age 40, hit .354, again 'leading' the Pacific Coast League. He was in 81 games, connecting for 52 hits. He played 19 games in the outfield and was used extensively as a pinch-hitter.

Early in the 1944 season the Hollywood club released coach Glenn Wright. A few days later a story appeared in the paper that he was rehired.

What the story didn't say was that after his original release, a player approached Victor Collins, club vice president, and said, "It's too bad about Wright leaving. He's a fine fellow and he needs the job. If it doesn't make any difference to you, would you give Wright back his job and release me?

"I've been around baseball a good long time and baseball has been good to me. I'm pretty well fixed right now and could quit and get along just fine."

Collins was so impressed that he rehired Wright, and refused to consider firing the good Samaritan who, of course, was Babe Herman.

The Los Angeles paper finished the story "Just a clown, a screwball and a dumbell, huh?"

Babe played 13 games at first base but was used mostly as a pinch-hitter during the season. For the first time in his baseball career he did not hit a home run.

Six times he hit for John Dickshot, the league-leading hitter. "What do I have to do to stay in the game?" Dickshot asked as he returned to the bench after being replaced by the 41-year-old Herman.

Then he answered his own question by saying, "Why am I complaining, he gets a hit each time he comes in for me?"

Babe finished the season with a booming .346 average, collecting 37 hits in 107 at bats. He had 23 RBI.

George Davis, Sports Editor of the Los Angeles Evening Herald and Express, wrote, "Ladies and gentlemen of the baseball jury, let us plead the case of Mr. Floyd "Babe" Herman, the eminent turkey rancher and family man of Glendale.

"To baseball fans the length and breadth of the land, he needs no introduction. His successes are legion. Some people have called him dumb. But they should have added 'like a fox.'

"With the exception of Babe Ruth and Ty Cobb and possibly one or two others, Herman has more to show today for his baseball earning than any other big leaguer past or present. Just to keep the record straight, he had no outside counsel in making his varied investments as did Ruth and Cobb.

"Diamond fans will never have to pass the hat for Babe Herman and his grand family. When it comes to baseball, his thinking is equally solid—no short circuits. Throughout his long and varied diamond experience, little has escaped his keen observation. For Babe Herman is—and always has been— a solid student of the game.

Babe switches 'uniforms' with old friend Gene Autry.

"Now he is nearing the end of his brilliant playing career, he's definitely deserving of a chance to manage a club in his chosen profession.

"Where, may we ask, would there be a better place for him to start than Hollywood? What better time than right now?

"The stars are looking for a manager, so we understand, or haven't you heard?" he concluded.

If Herman was offered the job, he didn't accept it.

He retired, seemingly for good, following the 1944 season and concentrated on his turkey ranch in the foothills of the Verdugo Mountains
At the time he felt he had put on a baseball uniform for the final time
He was wrong.

Chapter 15

Despite the feeling that Herman was trying to avoid spring training and squeeze out a fatter contract, the Hollywood front office found out Babe had finally hung up his spikes in 1945 to spend full time at his turkey ranch. But one morning in late June he received a call from Branch Rickey in Brooklyn, asking him to return the call.

The remarkable Dodgers, a seventh-place club in 1944, were leading the National League and manager Leo Durocher was asking for a left-handed pinch-hitter.

"Babe," Rickey said, "I've been looking for a pinch hitter for weeks. A club that is in first place in July forces my consideration, no matter what I may have thought in April. I want a man who can come up to the plate and drive in a run instead of striking out. Can you still hit, Babe?"

"Yes I can, Mr. Rickey," Herman said. "But I haven't been playing at all this year and I can't run a lick."

"You won't have to run much," Rickey told him. "Just hit the ball. We will pay you $7,500."

He was interested but checked with Ann and the children and they all decided it would be good to return to Brooklyn to see their old friends again. Herman called him back said he was agreeable, but that he belonged to the Hollywood club.

The Stars wouldn't give him his release and Brooklyn had to negotiate a deal for his contract but no figures were announced. Catcher Red Hayworth was released to make room for Babe on the roster.

Babe worked out briefly with the Los Angeles Angels in Wrigley Field while his family packed, and manager Bill Sweeney said, "Herman is a natural hitter. He'll be able to hit even if he has to be brought out to the plate in a wheel chair. He hit the ball well here and even hit some over the fence."

Before he left California, Babe sold his stock in the Hollywood club.

Tom Meaney welcomed him back to New York in his column, writing "It is an accepted axiom of literature that truth is stranger than fiction. The hitch is, of course, that fiction pays better, which may explain the many tall tales flooding the press of the nation about Floyd Caves Herman, now 42, who is back with the Dodgers some 13 years after he originally was traded away from Brooklyn."

"It isn't my intention to rap anybody in the racket, but from some of the stories which have appeared about Herman it is obvious the boys have him mixed up with somebody else—maybe Ring Lardner's "You Know Me, Al," or possibly Superman.

"Herman is paying the penalty for having become a legend. Guys who never saw the Babe play are now sitting down at typewriters explaining very meticulously how he came to parlay a triple into a triple play. I don't believe Herman ever hit into a triple play in his life, and I know that in the distorted incident which resulted in a traffic jam at third base, there was one out when Babe hit the ball, which would make a triple play impossible, unless they were playing four out that day.

"The sad part about the Herman myth is that nobody has to invent any stories about Babe. He did all right on his own."

On his arrival in Brooklyn on July 5, manager Leo Durocher told him that he would have two weeks to work out before he would use him. Babe was issued jersey No. 4 but later switched to No. 3 It was the first time he had worn a Brooklyn jersey with a number on it.

Bill Boylan, a Brooklyn milkman in the 1930's who would hurry through his route so he could get back to Ebbets Field and pitch batting practice, was now in charge of the press bar in Ebbets Field. When he found Herman had returned, he put his apron on the bar and came down to pitch batting practice again to Babe. He hit for hours on July 6th and 7th and his hands had to be taped to cover the blisters.

Then on July 8th, against the Cardinals, Durocher looked down the Dodger bench. Curt Davis said, "I think he is looking at you."

"I just got here," Babe said.

"Can you hit this guy?" Durocher asked.

"Yea, I can hit him," Babe said and got his bat out of the rack. The crowd spotted him as he came out of the dugout and his reception was so loud it drowned out the public address announcement.

"I had brought only two of my bats along and on the first pitch I broke one fouling off an inside pitch," Babe said. "I went back to the rack and got my other bat and slugged the ball off the screen in right field, scoring Luis Olmo from third base.

"I rounded first base and Durocher shouted 'go,' then changed his mind and yelled, 'get back.' I put on the brakes but slipped and fell because my spikes were worn down so short. I had to dive and crawl back to the base. You couldn't buy new baseball shoes during those war years, and I had sent my others out to get new spikes on them.

"Well, you can imagine what the papers wrote the next day about my falling down when I tried to stop. Some said I tripped over the bag and one had headlines that said, 'Same Old Herman.'"

Despite the RBI the Dodgers lost a 6-4 decision to the Cardinals and fell out of first place for the first time in 25 days. Babe unsuccessfully pinch-hit in the second game of the double header, another 6-4 Dodger loss, and The Sporting News noted, "Herman lost .500 points in the second game."

Babe played in an exhibition game the next day against the Washington Senators. He singled in the ninth and Olmo doubled. When Frenchy Bordagary grounded out, Herman was thrown out at the plate and the relay to first got Bordagary who had rounded the bag, slipped and fell.

Babe singled again in his next pinch-hitting roll, then started for Dixie Walker in right field on July 15th in Pittsburgh. He missed the first pitch, a low-inside curve, then hit the next ball into the seats off Ken Gables. It was his first major league home run since 1936 and at the time it made him the oldest Dodger in the history of the club to hit a homer.

Two days later he walked with the bases loaded to force in the tying run against the Pirates, but he was hitless in his next four appearances. Then he singled home a pair of runs against Boston in a nine-run fourth inning.

During the game Tommy Holmes of the Braves doubled into the right field corner and Dodger catcher Mike Sandlock, jumped out of the bullpen, fielded the ball and threw it to second. The umpires either didn't see the play or didn't want to do anything about it.

The game was also unique because a three-piece band, calling themselves "The Brooklyn Mudcats," serenaded the Dodgers and their opponents.

In the second game of two against Boston on July 29th, Herman smashed a double off the right field wall in Ebbets Field, sparking a nine-run rally that helped bury the Braves 15-2. His hit drew more cheers than any of the other sixteen the Dodgers recorded in the victory. Augie Galan belted a shot into Bedford Avenue to drive in his eighth run of the double header, and Goody Rosen had six hits in seven trips during the afternoon.

On August 9th the Dodgers and Cincinnati were tied in the last of the 12th when Herman was sent in to hit for young Ralph Branca. Facing Howie Fox, he slashed a single off third baseman Kermit Wall's leg to score Bordagary from second with the winning run and send the Ebbets Field crowd into hysterics. The hit knocked in the winning run in Branca's first major league complete game.

Babe, with his hands bandaged from hours of batting practice, in final major league season, 1945.

After the game, one of the reporters asked Babe when he started playing in the Major Leagues. "In 1926," he told him.

"Did you realize, Ralph Branca was born that year?" the writer asked.

Three days later he got his fifth pinch-hit in 12 trips when he singled for Ed Basinski against the Cardinals. The following day Branch Rickey, Walter O'Malley and John Smith bought controlling stock in the Dodgers for $750,000 from the Ebbets heirs, ending 55 years of Ebbets baseball influence in Brooklyn.

It was a long, dry spell (11 appearances) before Babe got his next hit. He got a chance to play in the outfield two games in succession against the Pirates and singled in each, collecting an RBI in the first, and scoring the winning run in the second.

The Dodgers moved into St. Louis and Durocher was furious when he found a twi-night double-header had been scheduled the evening before the team was to travel to Chicago. After the Dodgers had won both games, two losses from which the Cardinals could never recover, the Brooklyn club left St. Louis by rail late at night to play the Cubs in an afternoon game the following day.

Their ten-car chartered day coach struck a gasoline tanker at 6:30 a.m. outside Manhatten, Illinois. The tanker split open and the train was enveloped in a sheet of flames that charred the paint and cracked the windows in the car the players were riding in. None of the players were hurt, but the truck driver and two trainmen were killed. And by the time the club finally pulled into Chicago, it was a shaken Dodger team that took the field.

The 3,363rd and final hit of a remarkable 25-year career came at Cincinnati on September 9th. He singled in the eighth inning for Vic Lombardi but the Dodgers lost a 6-4 decision.

His last major league appearance was on September 16th. The following day he was hit on the knee in batting practice. It was obvious that the deep bruise would keep him out of the rest of the season so the Dodgers released him and he returned to California.

Herman, at the age of 42, had collected nine hits and nine RBI in 34 times at bat for a .265 average. He had three hits in five trips while playing in the outfield. When the club split third-place money, they voted Herman a half-share of the $700 allotment.

For six years, beginning in 1946, Herman tracked down talent for the Pittsburgh Pirates. He coached for the Pirates in 1951 until July 4 when he was reassigned as a scout. He scouted for the Yankees from 1952 through 1954, for the Phillies 1955-59, very briefly for the Mets in 1961, for the Yankees again 1961-63 and for the Giants in 1964.

Late in 1957, Babe was hired to manage the Bakersfield Bears of the Class 'C' California League during the final month of the season. Herman was a Philadelphia scout at the time.

The team had a reputation as 'good hit, no field,' and after scoring four times in the ninth inning to win their in Herman's debut, Babe noted, "The guys hit four homers, two of them in the ninth to win. We sure can't blame that on my masterminding. Joe Gannon, the Bears' president, and I have been good friends for a long time. I agreed to take over the club when he asked me to but I'm not planning to return next year."

The Bears finished the season with a 64-75 record and in sixth place. Johnny Callison led the Bears at the plate with a .340 average. He would later play with the Cubs, White Sox, Phillies and Yankees.

Babe signed pitcher Vernon Law as well as Bill Koski, Al Grunwald, Dale Coogan and Jimmy Mangan. All five were on the Pittsburgh roster before they were 21. He also signed Bob Chesnes, Bill Werle, Wally

Westlake, Ed Fitz Gerald and Dino Restelli.

He signed Chuck Essegian for the Phillies and later, as a scout for the Mets, signed Paul Blair.

Babe scouted Jim Maloney, liked him and called Roy Hamey in Pittsburgh. "We can get him for $50,000," Herman told Hamey. Before he could get approval the right-hander signed with Cincinnati, where he won 134 games. Andy Carey signed with the Yankees for $50,000 while Herman was trying to get approval to sign him with Pittsburgh.

In 1947 Hamey called Babe and said that he had just sent $50,000 and Billy Cox and Preacher Roe to the Dodgers for Dixie Walker, Hal Gregg and Stan Rojek.

Babe told him, "Forget Walker. I've got a kid out here who is great. Offer Brooklyn $50,000 for him." Branch Rickey turned down cash offer from Pittsburgh and Herman told the youngster, Duke Snider, "If you wouldn't have had such a great Little World Series, we'd have had you."

In 1953, Frank Finch of the Los Angeles Times, asked Herman how he sized up a prospect. "First of all," Babe told him, "the kid has to catch your eye. He has to have that certain something...a touch of class, maybe. It's like choosing a necktie or an automobile—you pick out a certain one from the bunch because you like it.

"After you've found a kid like that, you start picking him apart. How's his arm? Can he run? Any power? Desire, hustle, mental attitude, they're equally important. Well, if you think his faults can be corrected you go along with him. But if he doesn't have at least some of these fundamentals that I've named, you might just as well forget about him.

"I did some pitching as a kid and I've batted against the best, so I guess I know a little something about how to pitch. A kid should learn to spot his fastball first, then his curve. There'll be plenty of time to go into a change of pace. A kid doesn't need a change to win, just so long as he's got a good fastball.

"A good hitter has to be born, but I think you can improve his hitting. Without coordination you're worthless, but if you've got it you can be helped. Most kids can hit the fastball, but they have to learn to hit the curve. They must learn how to pick the ball up for long liners and homers. I hit more home runs on curves than I did on fastballs, because I always could pull the breaking stuff better."

Babe noted that nobody helped him with hitting tips as he was battling his way up the minor league ladder. "You're all right, just keep swinging," was the total instruction he received.

Asked to rate the greatest hitters, Herman replied:

"Babe Ruth and Rogers Hornsby. I'm talking about power hitters, now. I've heard balls whistle over my head in right field that Rogers hit—and he was a right-hander. Put Lou Gehrig in there third. And I'd have to rate Ted Williams up there with Ruth and Gehrig as one of the greatest—and by that I mean guys that really rared into the ball and tore the cover off of it.

"Ty Cobb and Paul Waner were great hitters, too, but of a different type. Cobb fit his hitting to his style. He was a 'legger.' He was content to hit the ball on the ground and beat it out. He was satisfied to hit for an average, yet he could lace them out there when he wanted too.

"Waner hit the ball sharper—got more wood on it— than any batter I ever saw. Williams and Joe DiMaggio were great, and Stan Musial, too."

"The game is better now," Herman said. "Baseball has improved just as track, football, golf and basketball. The equipment is better, for one thing. Kids have the advantage of expert instruction today. When I played, nobody wanted you to make good because it might mean their job. Now you see the veterans going out of their way to help the rookies.

"And the pitching—it's much tougher now. When I played they didn't change up as often as they do now; they'd overpower you. Maybe the old timers had better curves and the general run of pitchers were faster, but they didn't have the assortment of stuff that they throw at you now.

"And playing fields have improved 100 percent since I went up in 1926. Outfields are smoother now than the infields in the old days. Now you see big league outfielders change ground balls and play 'em like shortstops, one-handed. Couldn't do it in my day. Too risky."

When asked about being hit on the head with a fly, Babe said, "I just wish some of those newspaper guys had to play that sun field at Ebbets. I had been playing first base most of the time for eight years when Robbie sent me to right field to make room for Del Bissonette at first. Bissonette had a sore arm and couldn't throw, but Robbie wanted both of us in the lineup for our power.

"It was really rough out there at first. I never quit on a ball in my life. If I lost 'em, I'd still try to grab for that black spot in the sky. Sure I made me look awkward and I dropped some balls, but I never quit trying."

Late in 1950 Branch Rickey left Brooklyn and later became general manager at Pittsburgh. He assigned Babe to scout the West Coast. He served as a Pirate scout, then he coached for Roy Hamey at Pittsburgh and was also the club hitting instructor. He also scouted for the Yankees and then became a scout for Philadelphia. He was associated briefly with the Mets. On his second tour of duty with the Yankees, Hamey became sick and New York released Babe. Horace Stoneham hired him for the San Francisco Giants in 1964. Babe had a trip to Japan scheduled and Stoneham told him to go right along and enjoy himself, paying Herman the entire time.

In 1964 he retired.

But the following year he got a call from a White Sox scout asking if he would coach San Luis Potosi as well as the Mexico City Reds and Guadalajara. Three Mexican doctors paid for the instructions and for three years he coached the young Mexican players, particularly the hitters.

He was assigned to go to the Mexico City farm club and cut six players off the roster. After watching the players, he cut six regulars, inserted six rookies in the lineup and the club won the pennant for the

Willard Mullin joked about Babe's scouting assignment

first time in years.

He worked with Aurelio Rodriguez and Ellie Hendricks, helping each of them a great deal. Hendricks would ask for Herman each spring as the training season opened.

Babe then settled down at his home in Glendale. He left baseball for the final time, save for periodic appearances at old timers games.

His son Don was an orchid grower and while helping him, Babe became interested himself. He would later become the president of the Orchid Society of Southern California, developing a prize-winning orchid called Rajah's Ruby with the varietal name of 'Babe's Baby,' named by Babe's wife Ann because her husband babied it so much.

Babe and friend Casey Stengel

In 1981 he was honored by the New York Chapter of the Baseball Writers of America with the Casey Stengel "You Could Look it Up Award" on the 50th anniversary of his record .393 batting average. The ceremonies were held at the Sharaton Centre in New York.

Maury Allen, writing in the BBWA 'Scorebook,' the program for the ceremonies, said, "We honor him tonight for a non-winning 1930 .393 season and for carrying a franchise on his broad shoulders for half a dozen glorious Brooklyn years.

"He honors us with his still-constant dedication to the game of baseball, his ever-present good humor and his living link to the sweet legends of Ebbets Field.

"The Yankees had their Babe but Brooklyn's Babe helped Dodger fans hold their heads high a half century ago. Take two and hit another liner to right, Babe."

Although he considered himself retired, he was a daily golfer, a longtime member of the Kiwanis Club of Glendale, a member of the Helms Hall of Fame, Stanislaus County Hall of Fame and the Glendale High School Hall of Fame, chairman of the Glendale High School's 75th anniversary and president of the Glendale Old Settlers organization. He also served as program chairman of the Orchid Society of Southern California.

He was honored by the Glendale Chamber of Commerce with their Humanitarian Award for his lifetime of service in the community.

The Verdugo Little League field was renamed the 'Babe Herman Field' in his honor. Former Dodgers Wes Parker and Al Downing were on hand for the ceremonies. He received a plaque for his long career with the Dodgers and a special Dodger jacket with his number (#3) on the back.

The annual Babe Herman Baseball Tournament, featuring sixteen local high school teams, has been played in Glendale since 1963.

Babe was one of the first four members selected to the 'Dodger Fans Hall of Fame,' a fans' organization that honors former Dodger players. He was selected along with Jackie Robinson, Sandy Koufax and Zach Wheat in 1980.

Chapter 16

Babe Herman was invited back to Brooklyn to be inducted into the Brooklyn Baseball Hall of Fame just a few years before he died. He was surrounded by cheering Brooklyn fans who made him realize that he would never be forgotten.

After the ceremonies, Babe visited the site where Ebbets Field once stood. Braced against a bitter cold wind, Herman stood at the corner of Bedford Avenue and Sullivan Place again and tried to visualize the field.

"Finally I saw the surrounding buildings that hadn't changed and it all came back to me," Babe said. "I got a sick feeling in the pit of my stomach.

"I spent the heyday of my career in that old park and now it was gone."

But still hovering about the old site, now the New Ebbets Field apartments, are memories of the intimate old ballpark where Dazzy Vance fired his fastball through the tattered sleeve of his sweatshirt; where Zach Wheat banged out nearly 3,000 hits; where Wilbert Robinson argued strategy after games with red-faced fans; where Babe learned to catch flys in the blinding sun; where Van Lingo Mungo hurled his fastball and cursed his fate; where Leo Durocher screamed at the umpires and kicked dirt on their shoes and where Higbe and Whit, PeeWee and Pete, Jackie and Duke, Campy and Newk, Preach and Carl and Pod thrilled an adoring city and nation.

And where the memory of three Brooklyn Robins perching on third base at the same time continues to delight new listeners every year.

Some stories are just too good to die.

When Babe left baseball for the final time, he had been in uniform for 48 years. He was proud of the fact that he had hit safely his final six times during old-timer's affairs. Shortly before he died, at age 84, he said, "I think I could still hit if my legs would hold me up."

The last time he came to bat in an Oldtimers' Game he hit for Cookie Lavagetto after the former Dodger infielder pulled a leg muscle. Babe had not batted for years but when Lavagetto was being attended to in the clubhouse, they sent him up to the plate.

He pulled a ball into the hole between the outfielders and when Babe reached first the coach said, "Take second." Babe pulled up and said, "You run for me. I wouldn't run to second for Eisenhower."

Stu Nahan interviews two of the most popular players in Brooklyn baseball history, Dixie Walker and Babe Herman at an Oldtimers' Game in L.A.

He was an excellent golfer, shooting a 67 at age 66, and continued to play into his 80's. He was always a shrewd investor, and initiated by his father-in-law S. A. Merriken, had a number of lucrative real estate properties in Glendale.

Babe's health started to fail in 1984 and a series of strokes deprived him and the hundreds of fans who still asked in person and by mail for his stylish autograph. He watched with interest for the Veteran's Committee Hall of Fame announcement each spring and tried to not look concerned each time he was passed over.

He was asked by the Dodgers to throw out the first ball at the season opener in 1986. He went into his den and picked up a baseball. It slipped from his big hand and he shook his head. His wife Ann called the Dodgers to politely decline the offer.

His legs failed him, some 50 years after the Cincinnati front office expected they would, and he was confined to a hospital bed in his home. But his mind was sharp, and although his voice was impaired by the strokes, he enjoyed talking about baseball almost to the end.

Babe died from pneumonia in Glendale Hospital on November 27, 1987 at the age of 84. Newspaper accounts of his death predictably trotted out stories of being a member of the 'Daffy Dodgers,' that he had

Two the Dodgers' greatest left-handed hitters, Babe Herman and Duke Snider, pose for a photo before an Old Timers' game in Dodger Stadium.

been hit on the head by fly balls and that he had tripled into a triple play.

Services were held December 1st at the Little Church of the Flowers at Forest Lawn in Glendale. Jerold Milner and former Dodger Wes Parker delivered the eulogy. The packed church included many Glendale political and business leaders as well as Peter O'Malley, owner, and Fred Claire, executive vice president, of the Los Angeles Dodgers.

Babe was survived by his wife Ann, who had celebrated their 64th wedding anniversary with him earlier in the year before he returned to the hospital for the final time; by two sons, Robert and Don, and by a daughter, Dorothy (Mrs. Richard McWhirter); five grandchildren and five great-grandchildren. A son, Jack, and a grandson, Douglas, preceded him in death.

Robert Herman had been associated with Rudolph Bing of the Metropolitan Opera as assistant manager and recently retired as General Manager of the Miami Opera Company. Don recently retired as a teacher and is an ex-president of the Orchid Society of Southern California. He now travels internationally as an orchid lecturer and orchid contest judge.

Chapter 17

Babe picked an all-time National League opponent's team, saying "There are a lot of good ones, but it's not hard to pick a team." He chose Dazzy Vance and Dizzy Dean as right-hand pitchers and Carl Hubbell as the left-hander. The toughest choice came at the catching position. "Al Lopez was the best receiver I ever saw but Gabby Hartnett was a better hitter." He selected Bill Terry at first; Rogers Hornsby over Frank Frisch at second; Pie Traynor at third ('I could never beat a bunt out on him. He got me after I had 11 in a row and I think I tried 15 times but never made it on him.'); Glenn Wright at short, Chick Hafey, Paul Waner and Hack Wilson in the outfield.

Babe also selected an all-time Brooklyn team, including Al Lopez and Roy Campanella catching, Gil Hodges over Steve Garvey at first base, Jackie Robinson at second, PeeWee Reese at short, Jim Gilliam over Bill Cox at third, Zach Wheat, Duke Snider and Babe Herman in the outfield. His pitching staff includes Nap Rucker, Dazzy Vance, Burleigh Grimes, Don Drysdale, Sandy Koufax, Johnny Podres and Carl Erskine.

Roger Kahn, author of "The Boys of Summer," selected an all-time Dodger team. Included was Babe Herman in left field. The team: PeeWee Reese, ss; Jackie Robinson, 2b; Duke Snider, cf; Roy Campanella, c; Babe Herman, lf; Steve Garvey, 1b; Carl Furillo, rf; Billy Cox, 3b; Sandy Koufax, p; Don Drysdale, p; Clem Labine, p; Ron Perranoski, p.

Frank Graham, who covered the Dodgers for many years for the New York Journal-American, selected his all-star team in 1949. It included: Jake Daubert, 1b; Eddie Stanky, 2b; James Johnston, 3b;

PeeWee Reese, ss; Zach Wheat, lf; Dixie Walker, cf; Babe Herman, rf; Otto Miller, c; Nap Rucker, Jeff Pfeffer, Dazzy Vance and Whitlow Wyatt, p.

Bouquets

"Babe Herman was probably the greatest ball player the Dodgers have ever had."—Walter O'Malley.

Babe Herman has been enshrined, not in Cooperstown, where he and his lethal bat surely belong, but in the more enduring corridors of folklore."—Donald Honig.

"People think Herman was a stupid clown when he was at the heights of his career. I know differently because I played with him and also managed him. Let me tell you Herman was a good outfielder. He could hit and throw. He was nobody's fool. Sure, once in a while he had a bad day. But with any other club except Brooklyn during the Wilbert Robinson regime, the fly balls he missed would have gone unnoticed. He wasn't one-tenth as clumsy as he was made out to be. And he could hit the ball with the best of them."—Charlie Dressen.

"Mellower, less critical judgement, suggests the Babe was more sinned against than sinning, but it must be admitted that he had a positive genius for getting himself caught in the switches. He was a left-hander to whom left-handed things happened."—Bill Corum.

"The real 'Peoples Choice' in Brooklyn was Babe Herman and not Dixie Walker."—Bill McCullough.

"I don't remember one game in which he was skulled while fielding a ball. I saw him drop a few and throw to the wrong base but never get skulled. He had as good a throwing arm as Mel Ott, Pep Young or any of the top throwers. I wonder how many can remember when Babe threw out Wally Berger at the plate in the ninth inning to save a dramatic ball game? It was the greatest throw I ever saw. I don't care what they say about Herman but, in my estimation, the Babe was the greatest and most colorful player Brooklyn has had since Zach Wheat. What player did the Dodgers ever have who hit .393 for them since the Babe left? The Babe did it. He hit more home runs in any one season than any other Dodger to that time. Now thoughtless ones call him a clown. I'd like to have a club roster packed with slugging, throwing, running, colorful, competitive clowns like that.—Jimmy Powers, New York Daily News.

"Herman was the stylist of them all. Babe swung a bat with more ease and grace than any man I ever saw. You could fool him on a pitch and at the last second he'd reach out with one hand and knock it over, or against the fence."—Hall of Famer Al Lopez, rating Rogers Hornsby, Bill Terry, Lefty O'Doul, Chuck Klein and Herman.

"Herman is a bad man to pitch to. I'll say that Paul Waner isn't in his class. You can pitch to Waner. You can't pitch to Herman. You can fool him on a ball, but he'll hit it so hard he knock an infielder down with it. He's the hardest hitter in the league."—Guy Bush.

"Herman is bad medicine for a pitcher. In my last game against Brooklyn, I fooled him three times on a ball and every time he hit that ball safe. He's so tall and rangy and can reach so far that he can hit anything, high, low, inside or off side. There's no real rule for pitching to fellows like that. Just mix them up and trust to luck."—Hall of Famer Grover Cleveland Alexander.

"Herman is a slugger and you could say that the best dope for sluggers is slow curves. I try to give Herman plenty of slow stuff, but it doesn't always work. He can hit anything."—Hall of Famer Jesse Haines.

"Herman is a great natural hitter. He hits the ball so hard that it develops queen's English and takes freak hops. But that's part of his system and he is entitled to the results."—Hall of Famer Eppa Rixey.

"Perhaps a more accurate appraisal of Brooklyn's original 'Peepul's Cherce," would go like this: great ball player...devoted and dutiful family man...successful businessman."—Frank Finch, Los Angeles Times.

"Herman is the greatest free swinging hitter in the National League. Only Al Simmons can rival him in any league. He is a reckless base runner, but always aggressive, always threatening. He has surprising speed of foot, is a most deceiving runner and has developed an effective slide."—F.C. Lane, Baseball Magazine, 1930.

"Tape measure clouts? The Babe invented them and yes, I saw Ruth often enough and Mantle and the other titans, but one clout by Herman, I do swear, if hit in Yankee Stadium might have been the first and ever to clear the roof. When it left Ebbets Field it went out over the gleaming gold ball atop the center-field flag pole and was lost in a low-hanging cloud. For that one Abe Stark shoulda give Our Babe his whole damn store!"—Norb Kearns.

Dodger baseball was represented through seven decades when Steve Yeager, Van Lingo Mungo, Roy Campanella, Duke Snider, Babe Herman, Tommy Davis and Wes Parker were chosen to throw out the firdst ball before a NLCS contest.

The numbers

During Herman's six years in a Brooklyn uniform, excluding his brief appearance in 1945, the team was mediocre at best, recording a winning percentage of only .488.

As a measure of Herman's worth, the Dodgers played at a .535 clip in games when Herman collected one hit or more, but when Babe was hitless, the club had only a .313 percentage.

The six year Brooklyn record:

	W-L Herman hitless	W-L Herman 1+ hits	Overall Team W-L
1926	13-24 .351	46-51 .474	71-82 .464
1927	10-29 .256	52-49 .515	65-88 .425
1928	5-18 .217	67-57 .540	77-76 .503
1929	3-21 .125	63-60 .512	70-83 .458
1930	13-16 .448	73-51 .589	86-68 .558
1931	16-24 .400	62-48 .564	79-73 .520
Totals	60-132	363-316	448-470
Percentage	.313	.535	.488

Babe among league leaders

Herman ranked among the National League top ten hitters on 45 different occasions during his eleven full years, although he only led the league on one occasion when he slammed 19 triples for Cincinnati in 1932.

He set a major league record in 1932, handling 392 chances in right field, more than any other player in the history of the game. The record stood until 1971 when Del Unser of Washington handled 394 to set an American League and major league mark. Herman's mark is still a National League record.

Nine of the 11 years he was in the top 10 in slugging percentage. He was second in the loop twice in batting average, once in triples and twice in stolen bases. Third place finishes came in slugging percentage (twice), doubles (twice) and hits.

In 1930, his peak season, Herman finished in the top five in the league in average, slugging, hits, doubles, homers, stolen bases and runs batted in.

The top 10 chart

Year	average	slugging	hits	2b	3b	HR	sb	RBI
1926	.319 (9th)	.500 (5th)	158	35 (4*)	11	11	8	81
1927	.272	.481	112	26	9	14 (8*)	4	73
1928	.340 (5th)	.514 (8th)	165	37 (7)	6	12	1	91
1929	.381 (2nd)	.612 (7th)	217 (6)	42 (7*)	13 (5)	21 (10*)	21(4*)	113 (11)
1930	.393 (2nd)	.678 (3rd)	241 (3)	48 (3)	11	35 (5)	18 (2*)	130 (4)
1931	.313	.525 (6th)	191 (7)	43 (3*)	16 (2)	18 (4*)	17 (2)	97 (5)
1932	.326 (8th)	.541 (5th)	199 (9*)	38 (9)	19 (1)	16 (10*)	7	87 (9)
1933	.292	.502 (3rd)	147	36 (6)	12 (3*)	16 (5*)	6	93 (6)
1934	.304	.488 (8th)	138	34 (10)	5	14	6	84
1935	.316	.486 (9th)	136	31	6	10	5	65
1936	.279	.458	106	25	2	13	4	71
1937	.300	.450	6	3	0	0	2	3
1945	.265	.382	9	1	0	1	0	9
Total	.324	.532	1818	399	110	181	94	997

*=indicates tie.

Floyd Caves "Babe" Herman

Born June 26, 1903 at Buffalo, New York
Died November 27, 1987 at Glendale, California
Threw and batted lefthanded
Married Anna Merriken, November 9, 1923

Hit three home runs July 20, 1933; hit for cycle three times, May 18, 1931, July 24, 1931 and September 30, 1933; hit first home run ever made by major league player under the lights at Cincinnati against Brooklyn, July 10, 1935; led National League in triples, 1932. Scout, Pittsburgh Piraates, 1946-50; coach, Pittsburgh Pirates, 1951; coach, Seattle, 1952; 1953-54; scout, Phillies 1955-59; scout, New York Mets, 1961; scout, Yankees, 1962-63, scout, San Francisco Giants, 1964.

year—team	g	ab	r	h	2b	3b	hr	rbi	ba
1921—Edmonton	107	409	53	135	24	*18	7	--	.330
1922—Reading	9	31	3	8	0	0	0	--	.258
1922—Omaha	92	310	55	129	34	7	9	--	.416
1923—At./Mem.	145	551	69	187	36	10	13	100	.339
1924—SaAntonio	21	86	13	30	6	0	2	21	.349
1924—Little Rock	69	239	32	76	14	3	4	40	.318
1925—Seattle	167	651	115	206	52	13	15	131	.316
1926—Brooklyn	137	496	65	158	35	11	11	81	.313
1927—Brooklyn	130	412	65	112	26	9	14	73	.272
1928—Brooklyn	134	486	64	165	37	6	12	91	.340
1929—Brooklyn	146	569	105	217	42	13	21	113	.381
1930—Brooklyn	153	614	143	241	48	11	35	130	.393
1931—Brooklyn	151	610	93	191	43	16	18	97	.313
1932—Cincinnati	148	577	87	188	38	*19	16	87	.326
1933—Chicago	137	508	77	147	35	12	16	93	.289
1934—Chicago	125	467	65	142	34	5	14	84	.304
1935—Pittsburgh	26	81	8	19	1	0	7	10	.235
1935—Cincinnati	92	349	44	117	23	5	10	58	.335
*1935—Total	118	430	52	136	31	6	10	65	.316
1936—Cincinnati	119	380	59	106	25	2	13	71	.279
1937—Detroit	17	20	2	6	3	0	0	3	.300
1937—Toledo	85	336	76	117	37	4	12	79	.348
1938—Jersey City	145	527	89	171	40	5	18	93	.324
1939—Hollywood	90	350	69	111	36	5	13	71	.317
1940—Hollywood	148	469	62	144	45	7	9	80	.307
1941—Hollywood	110	272	41	94	16	1	11	63	.346
1942—Hollywood	85	149	18	48	5	0	5	42	.322
1943—Hollywood	81	147	15	52	8	1	4	22	.354
1944—Hollywood	78	107	8	37	8	1	0	23	.346
1945—Brooklyn	37	34	6	9	1	0	1	9	.265
Nat.l League total	1535	5583	880	1812	396	110	181	994	.325
Am. League tot.	17	20	2	6	3	0	0	3	.300
Major League total	1552	5603	882	1818	399	110	181	997	.324
Professional total	2984	10,237	1,600	3,363	760	185	303	•1,762	.329

•incomplete

Herman ranks high in full season comparisons

The final total behind a player's name often does not show his relative worth to his team. Many players have short but brilliant careers in Dodger Blue and their raw numbers do not compare with those who have played many more games. The figures show how valuable Babe Herman was to his Brooklyn team.

The 162-game totals shows a player's average season record. Individual totals (runs, hits, doubles, ect.) are divided by total games played, then multiplied by a 162-game schedule, even though before expansion, seasons were composed of 140 or 154 games.

The following figures are taken from batters who have played at least 500 games. Brooklyn or Los Angeles leaders are included if they are not on the original 15-man list.

Hits

1 Willie Keeler	241.86	
2 Fielder Jones	201.46	
3 Babe Herman	**199.40**	
4 Zack Wheat	195.63	
5 Johnny Frederick	191.99	
6 Mike Griffin	191.57	
7 Dixie Walker	187.23	
8 Jake Daubert	185.24	
9 *Steve Garvey	184.61	
10 Jimmy Johnston	184.27	
11 Mike Marshall	182.48	
12 Jimmy Sheckard	181.92	
13 Steve Sax	180.86	
14 Tommy Davis	179.96	
15 Jackie Robinson	177.94	

9 Pete Reiser 105.19
10 Jimmy Sheckard 105.02
11 Dolph Camilli 104.27
12 Candy LaChance 103.54
13 Bill Shindle 103.11
14 *Davey Lopes 101.87
15 Duke Snider 101.01
*=LA leader

*=LA leader

Run

1 Mike Griffin 144.75
2 Willie Keeler 134.52
3 Fielder Jones 126.69
4 Tom Daly 116.54
5 Oyster Burns 114.70
6 Jackie Robinson 111.01
7 Dave Foutz 108.29
8 Eddie Stanky 108.10

Doubles

1. **Babe Herman** **42.32**
2. Johnny Frederick 40.25
3. Augie Galan 37.72
4. Billy Herman 37.51
5. Dixie Walker 36.78
6. Pete Reiser 35.50
7. Babe Phelps 35.41
8. Joe Medwick 35.16
9. Tony Cuccinello 35.15
10. Mike Griffin 34.50
11. Zack Wheat 32.37
12. Oyster Burns 32.30
13. Jackie Robinson 32.00
14. Del Bissonette 31.91
15. *Steve Garvey 31.24
*=LA leader

BROOKLYN'S BABE—PAGE 239

Triples
1. Oyster Burns   16.78
2. Candy LaChance   15.12
3. Harry Lumley   14.65
4. Willie Keeler   14.60
5. Jimmy Sheckard   14.52
6. Del Bissonette   13.64
7. Hy Myers   13.48
8. Tommy Corcoran   13.13
9. Whitey Alperman   12.96
10. Dave Foutz   12.84
11. Babe Herman   12.04
12. Casey Stengel   11.98
13. Zack Wheat   11.93
14. John Hummel   11.66
15. Jake Daubert   11.62
24. *Willie Davis   9.13
  *=LA leader

HR
1 Duke Snider   32.77
2 Roy Campanella   32.27
3 Frank Howard   31.93
4 Gil Hodges   29.15
5 Reggie Smith   28.99
6 *Dolph Camilli   26.84
7 Pedro Guerrero   26.74
8 Jack Fournier   25.60
9 Ron Cey   24.94
10 Mike Marshall   23.92
11 Joe Ferguson   20.89
12 Dusty Baker   20.88
13 Babe Herman   20.43
14 Steve Garvey   19.79
15 Rick Monday   18.33
  *=LA leader

RBI
1 Oyster Burns   124.36
2 Jack Fournier   123.61
3 Roy Campanella   114.13
4 Dolph Camilli   110.45
5 Candy LaChance   110.23
6 Babe Herman   108.36
7 Duke Snider   107.07
8 Dave Foutz   106.83
9 Del Bissonette   106.64
10 Gil Hodges   101.27
11 *Frank Howard   99.17
12 Bill Shindle   97.36
13 Dixie Walker   97.31
14 Carl Furillo   94.90
15 Steve Garvey   93.05
  *=LA leader

SB
1 Davey Lopes   56.10
2 Maurie Wills   49.83
3 Mariano Duncan   43.09
4 Steve Sax   43.06
5 *Jimmy Sheckard   38.92
6 Willie Keeler   36.64
7 Bill Dahlen   35.73
8 Joe Kelley   32.48
9 George Cutshaw   31.83
10 Bill Maloney   30.57
11 Willie Davis   27.80
12 Jake Daubert   24.97
13 Harry Lumley   24.41
14 Jackie Robinson   23.09
15 Fielder Jones   22.59
  *=Brooklyn leader

Author's Note

A great many authors much more talented than I had asked Babe for permission to do a story on his life, but each time he politely declined. He feared that the book might be embellished with bogus bedroom scenes in an effort to sell more copies. He turned down a proposed movie of his life for the same reason. He said wanted the book to cover his baseball life only, and I have attempted to the best of my ability to follow his wishes.

I wrote a feature story about Babe Herman in my second (1979) Dodgers Blue Book, using all the crazy tales that have been written and rewritten over the many years since he fought his way though the minor league maze and arrived in that Camelot-by-the-Hudson called Brooklyn. I mailed to to him and asked for his comments. Quickly came a note that said, "It was a pretty good story, but if you want the real facts, call me." Obviously, he didn't want to get in the way if I were just going to do a rehash of the 'Three Men on Third' extravaganza or if I wanted to write that it was Babe that dropped the grapefruit out of the airplane that Wilbert Robinson caught with his chest and, drenched with juice, thought he had been killed. The culprit was, of course, Casey Stengel.

A call to his Glendale home not only gave me the real facts, but started a friendship that lasted until he died in 1987. Over the years I continued to ask if I could do a proper book on his remarkable life, and finally, late in 1985 he agreed.

I spent a great number of hours with 'Brooklyn's Babe,' much of them in his home and at Dodger Stadium where he enjoyed watching the game he played so well. It quickly became apparent that the many stories written about him over the years were fabrications.

However, depite the enjoyable hours shared with Babe, my task would have been much more difficult without the help of Babe's family, of whom he thought so much. When Babe's legs went bad on him toward the end, he leaned on his wife Ann and the sight of his six-foot, four-inch frame being steadied by his four-foot, ten-inch wife will remain with me forever. And as he leaned on her physically, so he also leaned on her through his career and after, for support in many other ways. I was also privileged to visit at length with his son, Don, and his daughter, Dorothy, as well as her husband Richard McWhirter. Regretfully, my visits to the Herman home never coincided with visits from Miami's Bob Herman, Babe and Ann's oldest son.

During one of the fascinating evenings spent with Babe in his dining room, when the legs of the once fleet outfielder would not carry him steadily any more, he remarked, "This is a hell of a way to go." But then the old fire blazed again in his eyes and he added, "I think I could still hit, if my legs would hold me up."

Listening to the old Brooklyn outfielder, I was reminded of Roger Kahn's splended, "The Boys of Summer," writing of how time had dealt harshly with some of them: "But one does not come away from visits with them, from long nights remembering the past and considering the present, full of sorrow. In the end, quite the other way, one is renewed. Yes, it is fiercely difficult for the athlete to grow old, but to age with dignity and with courage cuts close to what it is to be a man."

Using that parameter, if no other, Floyd Caves 'Babe' Herman was, above all, a man.

Tot Holmes
July 1985-March, 1990